THE NATIONAL ARMY MUSEUM BOOK OF

THE CRIMEAN WAR

THE NATIONAL ARMY MUSEUM BOOK OF

THE CRIMEAN WAR

THE UNTOLD STORIES

Alastair Massie

SIDGWICK & JACKSON

in association with

The National Army Museum

First published 2004 by Sidgwick & Jackson
an imprint of Pan Macmillan Ltd
Pan Macmillan, 20 New Wharf Road, London N1 9RR
Basingstoke and Oxford
Associated companies throughout the world
www.panmacmillan.com

ISBN 0 283 07355 1

1 3 5 7 9 8 6 4 2

A CIP catalogue record for this book is available from
the British Library.

Typeset by Intype Libra Ltd
Printed and bound in Great Britain by
Mackays of Chatham plc, Chatham, Kent

WILLIAM MASSIE
1916–1989

Acknowledgements

In the preparation of this book for publication I have been greatly assisted by Ingrid Connell and Nicholas Blake, my chief points of contact at the publishers. I am similarly grateful to William Armstrong, also of Sidgwick & Jackson, for his encouraging comments on the book's first draft. Support was also derived from the many friends and colleagues with whom I worked in the preparation of the National Army Museum's special exhibition *A Most Desperate Undertaking: The British Army in the Crimea, 1854–56*, which opened in October 2003. My chief lieutenants on that occasion were Miss Emma Armstrong, Miss Sara Jones and Mrs Gill Brewer. My attention was drawn to sources for this book which I might otherwise have missed by Dr Peter Boyden; I also learned much from the research undertaken by Dr Alan J. Guy and Mr Michael Ball into the Russian and French armies respectively.

Contents

Maps

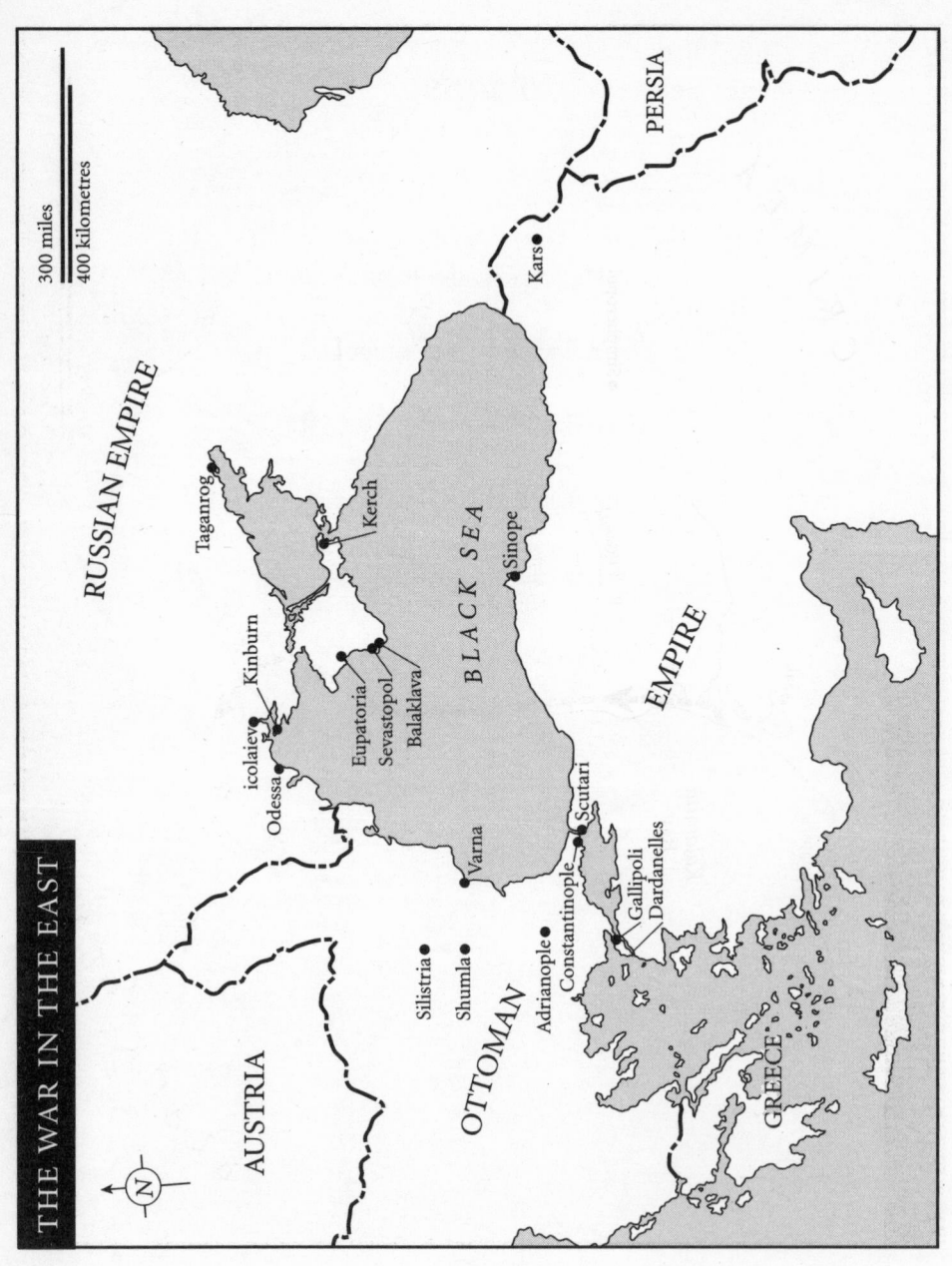

THE WAR IN THE EAST

N

300 miles
400 kilometres

RUSSIAN EMPIRE

AUSTRIA

Taganrog

Kerch

Kinburn

icolaiev

Odessa

Eupatoria
Sevastopol
Balaklava

BLACK SEA

Sinope

OTTOMAN

Silistria

Shumla

Varna

Adrianople

Constantinople

Scutari

Gallipoli
Dardanelles

EMPIRE

PERSIA

Kars

GREECE

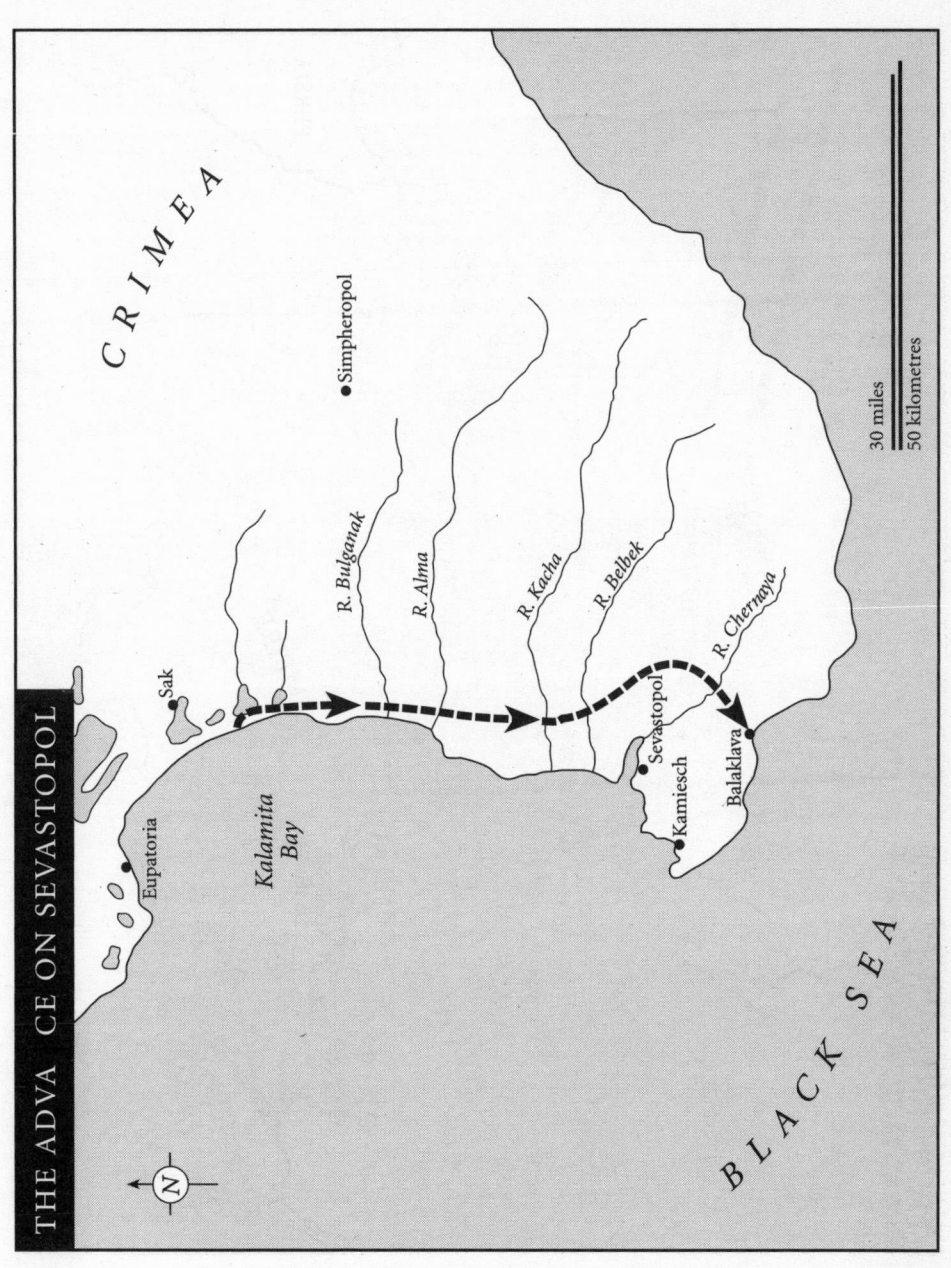

THE ADVACE ON SEVASTOPOL

C R I M E A

•Simpheropol

R. Bulganak

R. Alma

R. Kacha

R. Belbek

R. Chernaya

•Sak

Eupatoria

Kalamita Bay

Sevastopol

Kamiesch

Balaklava

B L A C K   S E A

N

30 miles

50 kilometres

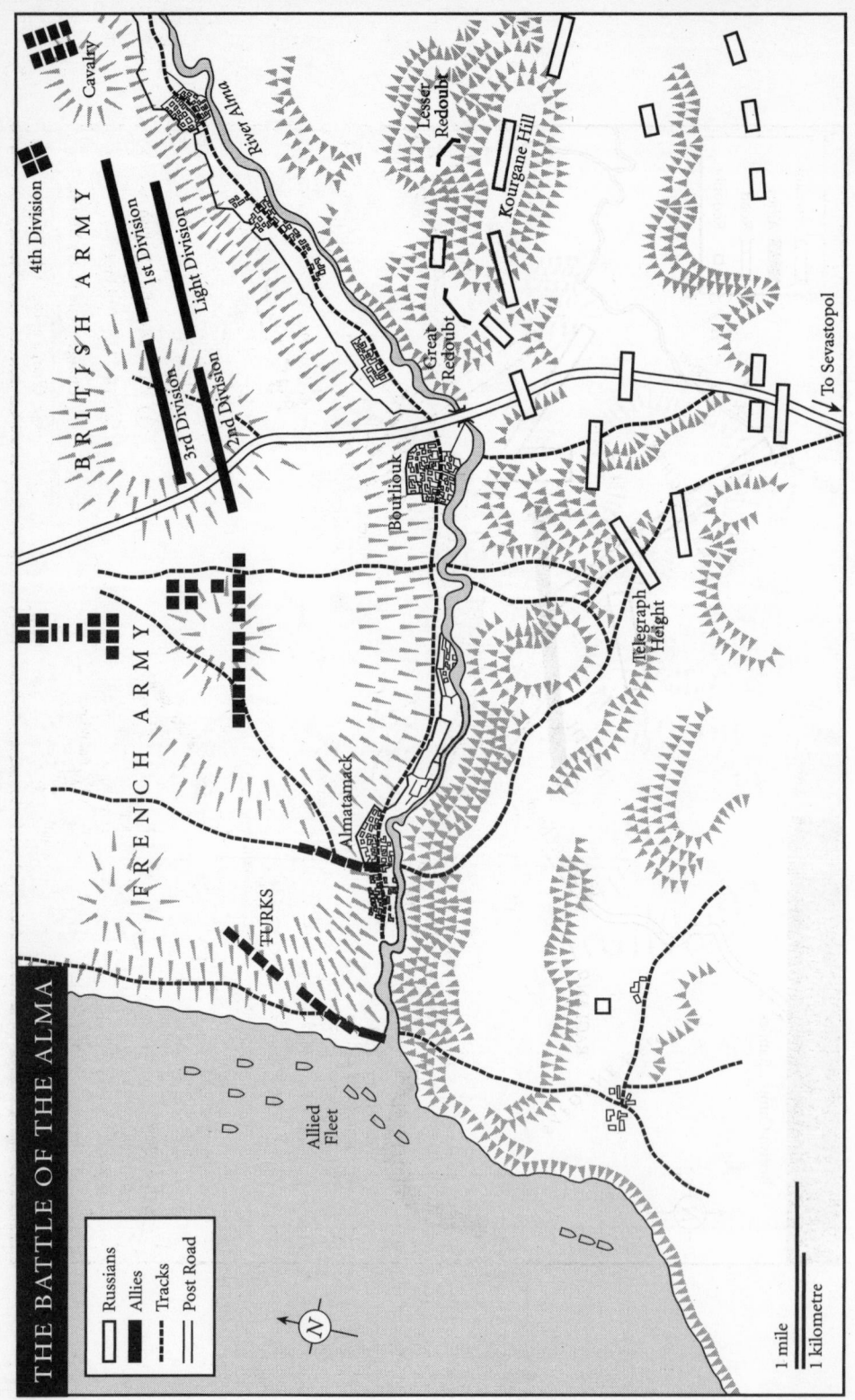

THE BATTLE OF THE ALMA

Russians
Allies
Tracks
Post Road

N

Allied Fleet

BRITISH ARMY

4th Division
1st Division
Light Division
3rd Division
2nd Division

Cavalry

River Alma

Bourliouk

Lesser Redoubt
Kourgane Hill
Great Redoubt

To Sevastopol

Telegraph Height

FRENCH ARMY

TURKS

Almatamack

1 mile
1 kilometre

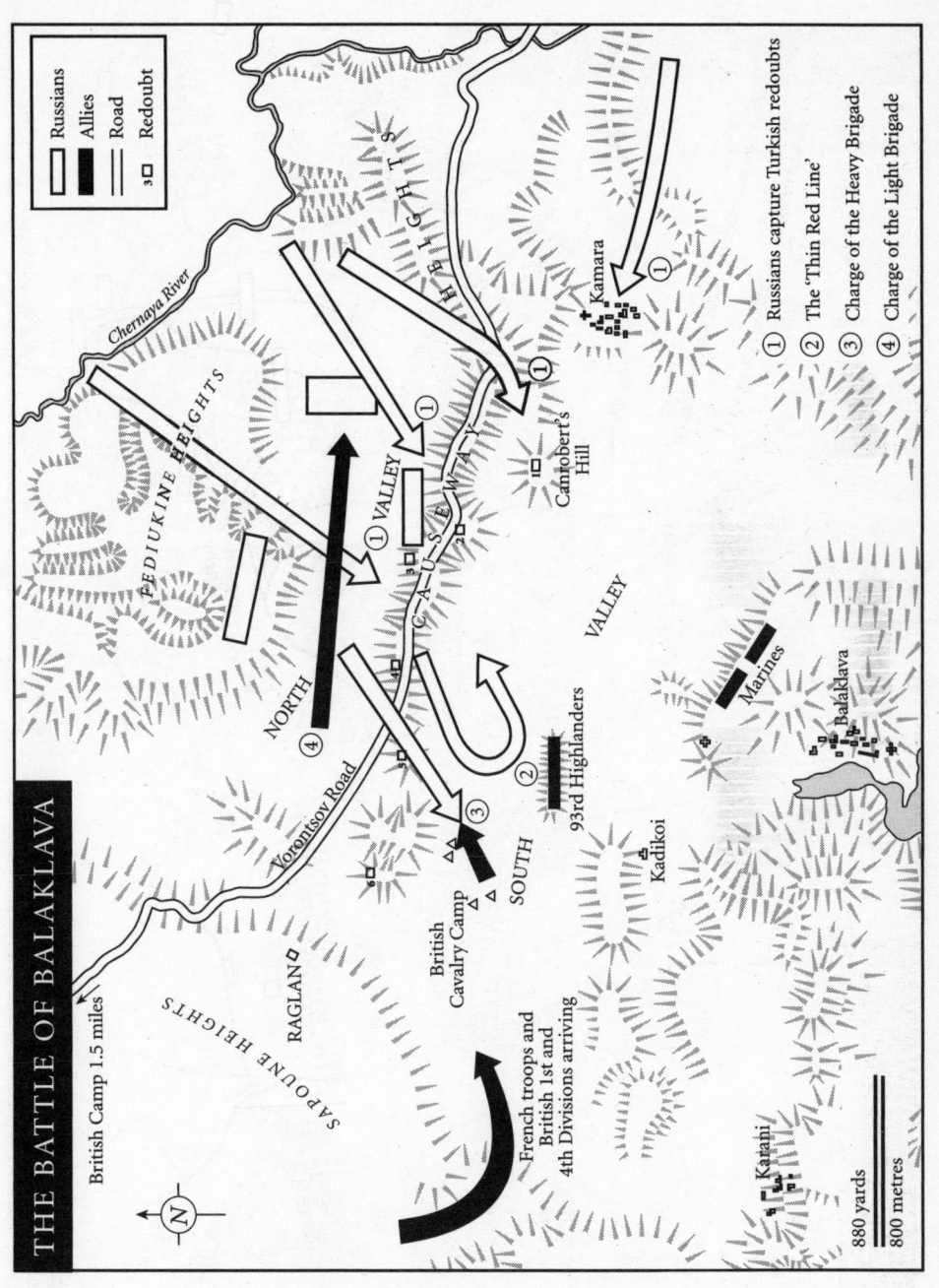

THE BATTLE OF BALAKLAVA

Russians
Allies
Road
Redoubt

British Camp 1.5 miles

Chernaya River

PEDIUKINE HEIGHTS

HEIGHTS

NORTH VALLEY

CAUSEWAY

Kamara

Canrobert's Hill

SOUTH VALLEY

Voronisov Road

British Cavalry Camp

93rd Highlanders

Kadikoi

Marines

Balaklava

RAGLAN

SAPOUNE HEIGHTS

French troops and British 1st and 4th Divisions arriving

Kamari

N

880 yards
800 metres

(1) Russians capture Turkish redoubts
(2) The 'Thin Red Line'
(3) Charge of the Heavy Brigade
(4) Charge of the Light Brigade

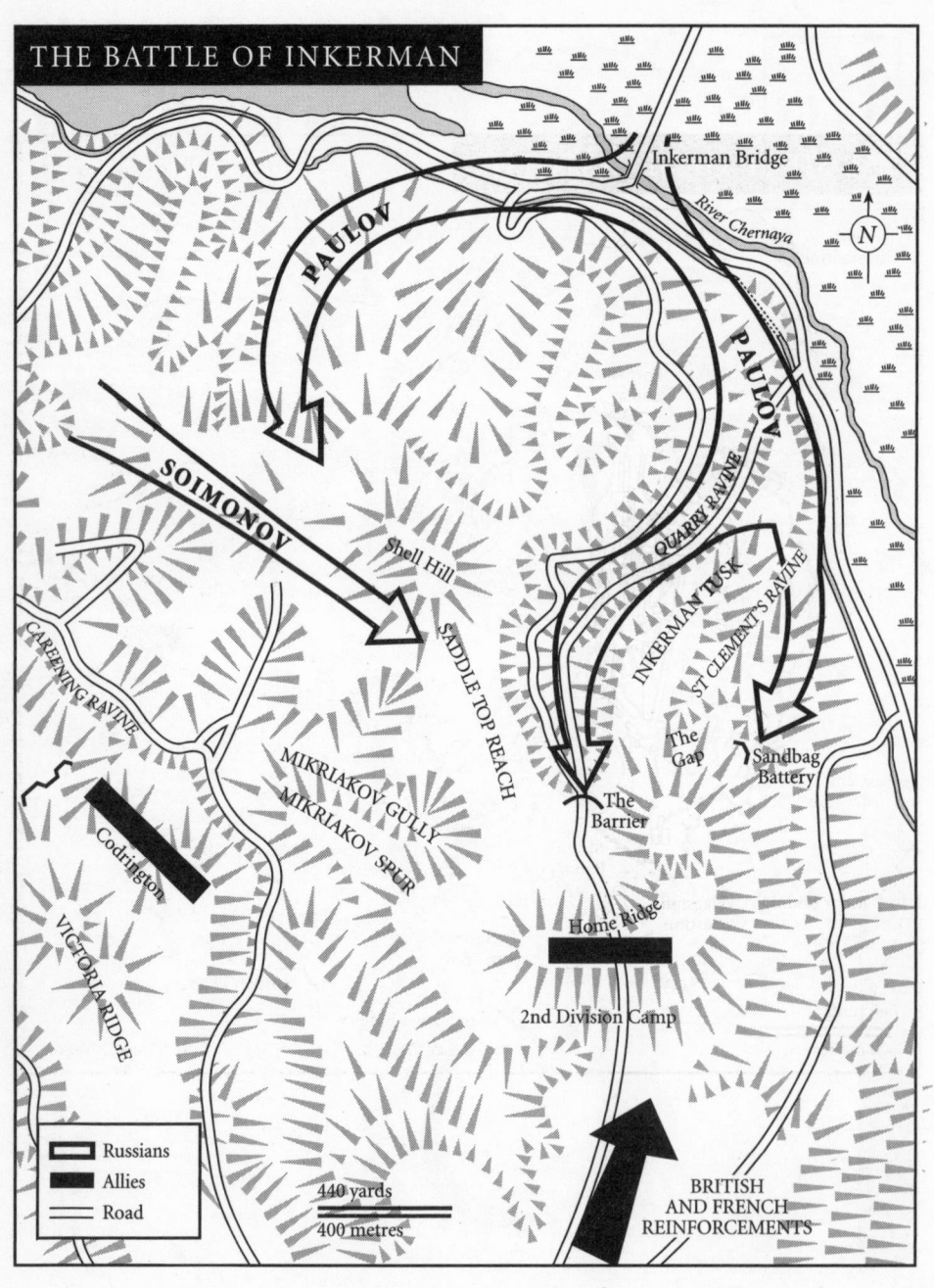

THE BATTLE OF INKERMAN

Inkerman Bridge

River Chernaya

N

PAULOV

PAULOV

SOIMONOV

Shell Hill

QUARRY RAVINE

SADDLE TOP REACH

CAREENING RAVINE

INKERMAN TUSK

ST CLEMENT'S RAVINE

The Gap

Sandbag Battery

MIKRIAKOV GULLY

MIKRIAKOV SPUR

The Barrier

Codrington

VICTORIA RIDGE

Home Ridge

2nd Division Camp

Russians
Allies
Road

440 yards
400 metres

BRITISH
AND FRENCH
REINFORCEMENTS

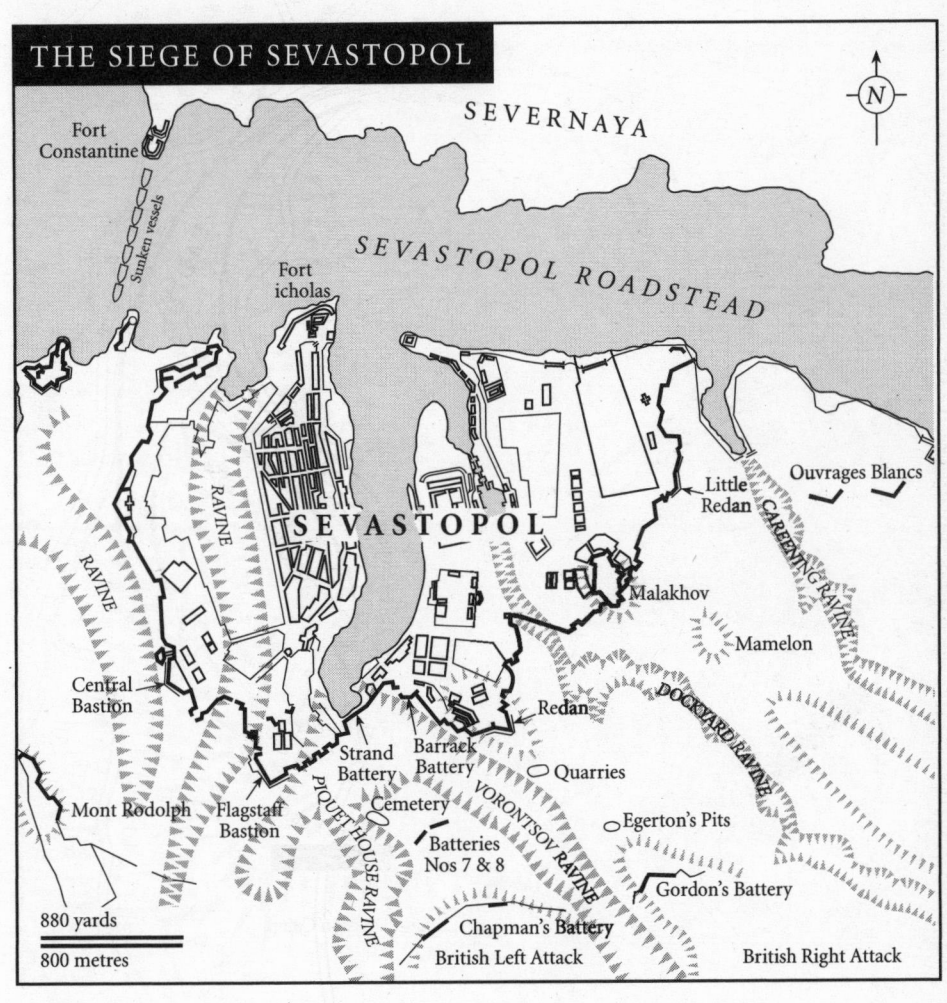

THE SIEGE OF SEVASTOPOL

Fort
Constantine

Sunken vessels

SEVERNAYA

SEVASTOPOL ROADSTEAD

Fort
icholas

SEVASTOPOL

RAVINE

RAVINE

Ouvrages Blancs

Little
Redan

CAREENING RAVINE

Malakhov

Mamelon

Central
Bastion

DOCKYARD RAVINE

Redan

Strand
Battery

Barrack
Battery

Quarries

Mont Rodolph

Flagstaff
Bastion

PIQUETHOUSE RAVINE

Cemetery

VORONTSOV RAVINE

Egerton's Pits

Batteries
Nos 7 & 8

Gordon's Battery

880 yards

800 metres

Chapman's Battery
British Left Attack

British Right Attack

Preface

On 28 March 1854, Great Britain declared war on Russia; its involvement in what became known as the Crimean War, although ultimately successful, proved traumatic. Now, a hundred and fifty years later, to commemorate a conflict which provided a severe jolt to the military and political establishments of early Victorian Britain, there appears this, the latest addition to the series of National Army Museum books published by Sidgwick & Jackson.

It was in 2001 that the Museum's then Director, the late Mr Ian G. Robertson, asked me to write the present book. I had already been tasked to curate the Museum's forthcoming Crimean War exhibition – which eventually opened in 2003 – and he no doubt thought that if I undertook both projects, one would benefit the other. Needless to say, I accepted his kind invitation with alacrity. Although by training a historian of the eighteenth century, curators at the National Army Museum have to be generalists and I considered the Crimean War a plum assignment. Casting back my mind, I suppose my first acquaintance with the Crimean War was when as a schoolboy I went to see Tony Richardson's 1968 film *The Charge of the Light Brigade* at the Ilkley Essoldo. Little could I have imagined that thirty-five years later I would be delivering a lecture on Balaklava with the aid of the sizeable topographical model constructed by Woodfall Films to assist its filming of the same climactic battle. My interest at the time was certainly fired sufficiently to read Christopher Hibbert's *The Destruction of Lord Raglan* and William Howard Russell's *Despatches from the Crimea*, and to take R. L. V. Ffrench-Blake's short history of the war on a visit to the Crimea in 1973, although in those Cold War days the Sevastopol naval base was closed to foreigners and I got no nearer the historic seat of battle than Yalta.

Another reason why I was so eager to write this book was because, after ten years of working at the Museum, I was aware of the extent to which its holdings of Crimean War documents were among the best in the world. They included, for instance, the Raglan papers, transferred to the National Army Museum from the Royal United Service Institution in the 1960s. A vast collection, it had been used by Alexander Kinglake and Christopher Hibbert to write magisterial histories of the Crimean War in the form of an amplified biography of the British commander-in-chief, Lord Raglan. However, so voluminous are the contents of the Raglan papers that they could be used to write a variety of books, each one drawing upon new material. Like others, I found useful the battle reports submitted to Raglan by his divisional commanders and other subordinate officers, but I also found particularly helpful Raglan's correspondence with General Sir George Brown. Readers of Fanny Duberly's *Journal kept during the Russian War* need no longer wonder why Lord Erroll was detained in camp on 4 June 1854, so depriving Mrs Duberly the opportunity of meeting his wife; Brown's letters make it clear that Erroll was under arrest for insulting his commanding officer. This is just one of the many untold stories revealed in the course of this book.

Compared to the Raglan archive, General Codrington's Light Division papers and his official correspondence as General Commanding-in-Chief of the Army of the East have been little used by historians. In part this is because of the tendency of some of the best historians of the Crimean War to treat the subject in the manner of a biographical study of Lord Raglan. But Raglan's death in June 1855 means the second attack on the Redan the following September tends to become a footnote, and until now no one has used the quite exceptional series of reports in the Codrington papers which was submitted to the high command – some by quite junior officers, their superiors having fallen casualty – in the wake of the doomed assault.

Indeed, one of the reasons the present book can claim to tell the untold stories is because half its contents deal with events in the Crimea which occurred after 5 November 1854. The many gruelling months of the Siege of Sevastopol have often been eclipsed in histories of the Crimean War by the flashy drama of the few weeks in the autumn which saw the battles of the Alma, Balaklava and Inkerman follow one another in quick succession. Yet it stands to reason that the vast majority of letters and diary entries to come down to us from the Crimean War will deal with the many months of hard slog rather than the few weeks of breathless excitement. This is when the true nature of the war emerged, and it is its character during the ten months that elapsed between the

Battle of Inkerman and the fall of Sevastopol in September 1855 which the bulk of the material I consulted describes. I have attempted to reflect this. In so doing I amassed such a quantity of testimony that to impose sense upon it I found it simplest to arrange the material in chronological order and see what themes emerged. While at no point did writing this book become an exercise of placing material in the straitjacket of preconceived notions, it was truly in these chapters that I came closest to letting the soldiers' concerns speak for themselves. To concentrate on the heroism of the long-service regulars who fought and won at the Alma and Inkerman and neglect the story of how their replacements – frightened raw recruits in many instances – were slaughtered at the Redan would be to present an unbalanced and distorted picture of the war.

I realized when compiling the index that the entry for 'British army, demoralization of' bulked disconcertingly large. Soldiers, it is true, love to grumble but it is indisputable that during the winter of 1854–55 they had justification. And for the first time their letters of complaint had an effect. An efficient postal service with mail delivered by steamship, allied to the use of the electric telegraph by print journalists such as Russell, meant that the public at home heard of the privations of the army almost at the same time as they occurred. The clamour became such that it precipitated the downfall of the government. Only in later wars did the authorities respond to the advent of improved communications by the imposition of censorship; and it is this, of course, which makes soldiers' letters from the Crimea (compared to those written by their twentieth-century counterparts) so interesting: they could be totally uninhibited. Moreover, the onset of regular (and relatively cheap) postal communication meant that for the first time it was worthwhile writing home on a regular basis; consequently, some of the Museum's collections of officers' letters – including the Kingscote, Mundy and Earle correspondences – number well in excess of a hundred items. In contrast, letters written by other ranks are much thinner on the ground and most collections number just one or two items. For this a lack of literacy was largely responsible; only after the 1870 Elementary Education Act had exerted its influence would the correspondence of other ranks – for example during the Boer War – become substantial. There are of course exceptions: the Cruse correspondence is both extensive and well written; so too is that of Hospital Sergeant Newman. The highly literate letters of Private Hood show the benefits of a Scottish education, and those of Private Pine demonstrate why he was eligible to be appointed a clerk. Yet to a significant extent the surviving testimony of private soldiers or junior non-commissioned officers consists of memoirs written after the event, whether it be immediately afterwards, as in the case of John Fisher, or nearly sixty years later as with Daniel Bourke; the common factor is that the writer had greater leisure time and conditions were more conducive. Private Charles Henry Smith of the 7th Regiment of Foot (Royal Fusiliers), whose memoirs were donated to the Museum after the main text of this book was written, wrote his memoirs in 1860; they are worth quoting here because they show a documentary source at its best, dealing with personal experiences rather than trying to provide a summary of events to which the writer was not party. Also, the role of the Royal Fusiliers at the Battle of the Alma deserves greater prominence than I could previously give it. Smith begins by praising the Russian artillery:

> I must acknowledge that the Enemy had plan[n]ed every thing out to the best advantage, for they even had Poles put out on the Plain for the different ranges of their guns, so that when our men came up to these Poles, they knew what Range to take to be able to drop a shot in our Ranks, which they could do with great skill.

Eventually, the Russian fire became only too accurate:

> A Cannon shot came and struck my comarade soldier in the brest which caused instant death, and at the same time, the said soldier was C H Smith's front rank man, but the Ball struck him, and with one bound it fell upon Brevet Major the Honorable W Hare* ... This Cannon shot s[truc]k the Majors Horse in the fetlock and broke the bone in several Piceses [pieces], from thence bounding, and falling in the Columns of Guards, and unfortunately it fell on one of the mens head it causing an instant death and the Soldiers Bearskin was seen flying in the air, the ball loosing its stren[g]th when lighted on the ground. The Officer above mentioned, as soon as he found that his Horse was wounded, he dismounted from his Horse, drew a Revolver and shot the Horse on the spot to put the poor animal out

---

* Smith appears to have confused the Honourable C. L. Hare with the Honourable W. Monk. The former died as the result of wounds received at the Alma; the latter was killed outright.

of his Missery. The next scene that Smith whitnessed, was a young man of the 95th Regiment lying on a heap of stones which I saw myself with his thigh shattered into many Picesses, this reppresenting a most fearful sight, perticulary at the begining of the . . . Action.

Major Hare's good fortune was not to last, however:

As soon as they reac[h]ed the Enemys first line of skirmishers, . . . one of the skirmishers made a very despret Plunge at the Major with his firelock and Bayonet and caught the Major in his Chest. This gallant Officer seeing that he was in danger of his life, made a fearfull Plunge at his Enemy with His Sword and met His Enemy in the lower Part of his Bowels, and they both fell together on the ground quite lifeless.

Other collections donated to the Museum after the writing of the main text was complete include a prisoner-of-war letter of Private Richard Palframan of the 8th Hussars describing his capture during the Charge of the Light Brigade. It provides an admirable contrast to the prisoner-of-war letters of Cornet George Clowes of the same regiment. The second is the diary of Captain Jackson Wray of the 88th Connaught Rangers, whose references to Colonel George Mundy, interestingly enough, suggest that to his juniors at least he was an amusing companion; it was his superiors who considered him a 'humbug'.

The sadness that some material arrived too late for inclusion in this book is tempered by the knowledge that many other sources of letters and journals already in the Museum had to be omitted because they lacked the immediacy to make exciting reading (which is not, however, to deny their other merits). But this still means that the choicest parts of dozens of collections of letters – as well as of many journals and diaries – are published here for the first time. When the first publication nowadays of a single series of Crimean War letters, or of a diary, quite justifiably attracts attention, it suggests that the appearance of this book should be considered an event.

A small proportion of the ostensibly new material on show might appear familiar to the Crimean War expert, and it is true that some of the more literary minded officers, such as George Bell and Nathaniel Steevens, subsequently worked their journals or letters up into books. Here, nonetheless, one can read for the first time the raw material of their later publications – the unvarnished truth. The final manuscript version of Anthony Sterling's *The Highland Brigade in the Crimea* is also held in the Museum's archives, and although this reads as subsequently published, the Museum's possession of the manuscript was thought to warrant its selective quotation. Sterling's jaundiced view of the way in which the war was conducted is well known, but he reinforced the message by inscribing in the front of his manuscript the following legend: 'A marvellous tale of jackasses and women who sadly mismanaged our soldiers . . . wrote out on the spot by a mournful eyewitness of all their great folly'.

Among other items whose inclusion in this book might possibly be questioned are the Annesley journal and the Lawrence letters. In the case of the former, in 1897 Hugh Annesley, having earlier made his Crimean journal available to Kinglake, presented a typed and bound copy to his second wife. Eighty years later this found its way to the Museum's archives. Similarly, the letters to his wife of Arthur Lawrence, so valuable for the Battle of the Alma and the initial occupation of Balaklava, were transcribed by Sir William Cope while compiling his history of the Rifle Brigade (published in 1877). Cope's notebooks containing them are also now held by the Museum.

There are two other collections the importance of which require highlighting. One is the Wetherall papers, which as far as I am aware no historian other than Professor Hew Strachan has used before. This is surprising: George Wetherall was the British army's Adjutant-General and his correspondents in the Crimea wrote him frank letters deploring the condition of their units and of the troops generally. The observations made by the likes of Estcourt and Lacy Yea are of often quite startling candour.

The second collection contains transcripts of the letters written by General Sir William Codrington to his wife. The Museum's archive holds a large number of Crimean War documents – modern transcripts and photocopies – which, principally for copyright reasons, were not included in this book. The Codrington letters were the one exception. Transcribed in 1932 and checked for accuracy by his son, General Sir Alfred Codrington, the loan of the 2,042 pages of transcripts was subsequently converted into a gift to the Museum in 2002 through the generosity of Mr Richard Codrington. Because Sir William Codrington, with his meteoric ascent to supreme command, was in many respects the British 'Man of the Match' during the Crimean War, it would have been impossible to contemplate exclusion of his hitherto unpublished private correspondence from the present book, especially when its mass of detail helps shed light on so many different aspects of the conflict. The quote that follows provides a suitable example; it would not have sat easily in the main text, but it nevertheless serves to demonstrate the conviction of the British that, however low they sank during the winter of 1854–55, the French had gone further:

> A most horrid story Airey* told me to-day of the French having buried a man alive – and not by accident either. As the earth was being shovelled on the upper part of the body, he moved – but the fellows said 'ah! nous n'avons pas le temps' and they literally covered him up. Canrobert is said to be in a tremendous taking about this (well he may) and at the knowledge of it by others. I don't know how Airey got the information – but he told it to me: and that he, Airey saw them burying a horse *not dead*. Tried to borrow a pistol himself, could get none – appealed to a French officer to prevent this but ah! ma foi voyez vous, – pauvre animal – il ne peut pas vivre, or some such expression – and went his way! Funny things these.

At a distance of a hundred and fifty years, some of the words written by soldiers in the Crimea might sound quaint to modern ears. Others might find Victorian sentimentality cloying, or, in the case of Nathaniel Steevens' description of the death of the young and diminutive Captain Lemprière (and Colonel Egerton's response to it), positively outré. However, a notebook that has recently came to light – again since the main text was written – during sorting of the Museum's Middlesex Regiment archive reveals that Steevens' description of events was faithful. The notebook, containing drawings by Lemprière and letters of reaction to his death, also includes a letter written by Captain Edward Chawner, present during the attack on the rifle pits on the night of 19/20 April 1855:

> We made a dash out & possessed ourselves with less difficulty than we imagined of the two pits; bayonetting five men in the work & making one officer & 8 men prisoners. We then agreeably to instructions extended ourselves in skirmishing order in front of the pits.

---

* Lieutenant-Colonel J. T. Airey of the Light Division's staff.

Poor Lempriere was shot whilst putting his men out. The ball entered his hip & passing upwards lodged in his chest & killed him instantaneously. Our gallant Colonel took him up in his arms & carried him under cover, crying out, 'Make way there for God's sake, I must save my poor little boy'. He was put on a stretcher & carried up to camp, & the Colonel on returning to us said he was sure it was a mortal wound. Poor fellow! It turned me quite sick to think of it, he was such a favorite with us all, & our poor Colonel loved him as if he had been his own son.

The pathos is then ratcheted up further by the death, in the moment of victory, of Colonel Egerton:

Almost at the end of the row, I was standing close to the Colonel looking over the parapet, when I felt as I thought a blow on the head, & was knocked down. I heard the men say, 'Good God, there is Capt Chawner & the Colonel down'. I jumped up saying 'I am not hurt my men!' & looking down saw our noble Colonel stretched on the ground quite dead, in his fall he had fallen against me, & knocked me down. I took a glance at him & could see it was all over with him. The ball had entered his mouth carried away four teeth & went out at the back of his head. I had him taken up to camp & sat down & could have cried.

Although photography was in its infancy during the Crimean War, the book's illustrations feature a surprising number of men who are quoted in the text. Sometimes the individuals in group photographs are identified by the publisher's original caption; on other occasions it requires the letters of the officers themselves to identify the sitters. In some cases, the illustrations and the text marry up in a serendipitous fashion: Henry Alderson's letters and his watercolours, for instance, were received by the Museum twenty-five years apart and from unrelated sources.

In conclusion to this preface, it only remains to point out that individuals mentioned in passing in the text are, in 98 per cent of cases, identified by their full name and rank in the index. To avoid the possibility of confusion, officers are given their substantive ranks throughout, eschewing the use of local (i.e. temporary) ranks.

1

EASTWARD BOUND

At the outbreak of the Crimean War in 1854, Great Britain, relative to the rest of the world, was approaching the zenith of its power. The advantages of early industrialization, allied to commercial reach and financial strength, made the nation the wealthiest in Europe. The self-confidence of the early Victorians received fitting expression in the Great Exhibition of 1851, when Britain's industrial ingenuity was demonstrated to the peoples of the earth. The country also possessed political stability. In 1848 much of Europe had been convulsed by revolution. Britain was one of the few countries to escape. To its self-satisfied social elite, this was proof of the benefits of parliamentary government. Never did the expression 'the government which governs least governs best' seem more appropriate. In Britain, it was the heyday of laissez-faire political economy. Adam Smith's 'invisible hand' was given free rein to create wealth in the economy without interference from government. Indeed, ever since the end of the Napoleonic Wars forty years before, government budgets had been relentlessly slashed. Taxation had fallen accordingly.

The retreat of government might have been good for the economy, but it was not conducive to the maintenance of the state apparatus for mobilizing resources in the event of war. Since 1815 the army had suffered particularly badly. To many of Britain's political classes, the military was a deadweight. It created no wealth and so, on a utilitarian basis, lacked justification. Estimates were cut to the bone. The army budget fell from £43 million in 1815 to £8 million in 1836. Its personnel declined to a total of 109,000. The garrisoning requirements of India and the colonies meant that there were rarely more than 50,000 troops left in the British Isles. There were other consequences of economy. The army's Commander-in-Chief, the Duke of Wellington, became so suspicious of politicians' motives that he refused to countenance the subject of army reform, believing that it would serve as an excuse to cut budgets further. Army administration in particular ossified: the War

Office, Commander-in-Chief, Board of Ordnance and Treasury all possessed responsibilities which cut across one another.

Yet whatever the theories of the political economists, in the end
politicians had to operate in the real world, and periodic invasion alarms
prompted by French sabre-rattling across the Channel led to an increase
in military budgets throughout the 1840s. By 1854 Britain had an army
of 153,000 men, of whom one-third were available to provide homeland
security: the remainder were abroad garrisoning the Empire. Other
change was in the air. In September 1852 the Duke of Wellington had
died. His successor as Commander-in-Chief, Lord Hardinge, was by
comparison considered a reformer. Even this might not have led to
much, however, until circumstances suddenly forced Hardinge's hand.
In December 1851 a coup d'état occurred in France which installed in
power a dictator, Louis Napoleon. Later to declare himself the Emperor
Napoleon III, he was a Bonaparte and a nephew of the great Napoleon,
ruler of France forty years before. The suspicion rapidly arose that he
wished to undo the effects of his uncle's defeat at Waterloo. Threatening
noises had supposedly been made towards Belgium. Once again in Britain
there was an invasion alarm. Hardinge was painfully aware that to repel
a French invasion the army, ordinarily dispersed around the country,
would need to concentrate rapidly; yet it was completely unused to
conducting operations on a brigade, let alone a divisional, basis. Hence
the innovation between June and August of 1853 of holding a summer
camp of exercise at Chobham in Surrey. Generals were given the opportunity to experience large-scale manoeuvres. The men learned to live
under canvas. Land was purchased at Aldershot to build a permanent
camp. To better equip the army for field service, the artillery received
more field guns. The Enfield rifled musket, a handier and smaller-calibre
successor to the Minié, itself only adopted in 1851, was approved for
production. A School of Musketry was established at Hythe. These were
all measures intended to improve the army's state of readiness for home
defence, yet, as it would transpire, it was also the kind of preparation
that the expeditionary force which would depart Britain's shores the
following year desperately needed.

The Crimean War, which would be Britain's first European war since
1815, had its origins in the celebrated Eastern Question: what was to
be done with Turkey, 'the sick man of Europe'? The independence of
the Ottoman Empire, as Turkey was usually styled, had been under threat

ever since the Greek War of Liberation (1821–30) when a Russian army advanced nearly as far as Constantinople. In 1840 Britain, which wished to maintain Turkey as a bulwark against Russian expansion into the eastern Mediterranean,* took action to prevent an insurgent Mehemet Ali, Pasha of Egypt, destabilizing the Ottoman Empire further. Thereafter, Russia and France jockeyed for predominance at Constantinople; this was the situation in the east which Napoleon III inherited. Accordingly, rather than threaten Britain, it was eastwards that he turned in order to further his ambition of overthrowing the Vienna settlement of 1815 (which, he considered, disadvantaged France). By championing the rights of the Latin monks over the rival Orthodox monks to protect the Holy Places in Palestine, Napoleon not only propitiated Roman Catholic opinion in France, but he challenged the prestige of Tsar Nicholas I of Russia, the protector of the Orthodox monks and guardian of the status quo in Europe. Throughout 1852 the Turkish authorities in Palestine were buffeted by claim and counter-claim made by each side until, following a show of naval power by the French, the keys to the Church of the Nativity in Bethlehem were handed to the Latin monks in December. Tsar Nicholas was outraged: aside from the religious rebuff, it conceded to Napoleon III diplomatic pre-eminence at Constantinople, something which he considered to have been his ever since the Treaty of Unkiar Skelessi in 1833. Troops were moved to the Turkish border. In February 1853 a browbeating mission under the undiplomatic Prince Menshikov was despatched to Constantinople to claim for the Tsar a protectorate over all the Orthodox subjects of the Ottoman Empire. Until this point the British Government had been vaguely sympathetic to the Russian position. The Prime Minister, Lord Aberdeen, had been prepared not to take seriously Tsar Nicholas's musings to the British Ambassador about Turkey being 'a sick man', carrying with it the implication that arrangements should be made for the Turkish Empire's partition; after all, he had spoken the same language on a visit to England in 1844. But the claim for a protectorate threatened Turkish independence too explicitly. The possibility was conjured of the Russians gaining control of Constantinople and securing access to the Mediterranean for their Black Sea Fleet. In the Cabinet, Lord Palmerston, the Home Secretary,

---

* The British were particularly anxious to prevent the Russians threatening the short overland route to India across the Suez Isthmus.

urged a forceful response. British suspicion of the Russians displaced that of the French. In June the British Mediterranean Fleet was ordered to Besika Bay outside the Dardanelles. The French fleet followed.

The Tsar knew that the British Cabinet was divided and he had great faith in the pacific intentions of Lord Aberdeen. He did not countermand the orders that he had given his forces following the failure of the Menshikov mission to occupy Turkey's Danubian Principalities, Moldavia and Wallachia. Palmerston wanted to send the fleet through the Straits but was overruled. Instead, Britain and France, in conjunction with Austria and Prussia, attempted to resolve the crisis by means of the Vienna Note, tendered by the Austrian Foreign Minister, Count Buol. By this the Turkish Sultan was to promise to protect the Christian religion in his domains in accordance with past treaties. Although the Turks bristled at the idea that the Russians and French should police the agreement, it eventually foundered because the Russian Chancellor, Nesselrode, suddenly reasserted his country's claim to a protectorate over Orthodox Christians within the Ottoman Empire. In response, Britain and France ordered their fleets through the Dardanelles. This encouraged the Turks who on 4 October presented an ultimatum to Russia demanding the withdrawal of its forces from the principalities within two weeks. It was a declaration of war.

Britain and France were horrified by the Turkish action. The British Ambassador at Constantinople, Lord Stratford de Redcliffe, led the efforts to secure a truce. Fighting however broke out along the Danube. When the Turks attempted to ship supplies across the Black Sea to the Caucasus front – where fighting had also begun – their flotilla was intercepted by the Russian fleet at Sinope on 30 November and destroyed. The war clamour in Britain, already loud, became deafening. Bullied in Cabinet by the bellicose Palmerston and Lord John Russell, Aberdeen agreed to send the fleet into the Black Sea in cooperation with the French; the Russians were told to confine their ships to harbour at the naval base of Sevastopol. A joint ultimatum to withdraw from the principalities was issued on 27 February 1854. No answer being forthcoming, on 28 March Britain and France declared war.

The 'drift' to war, to use a phrase coined at the time, caught the British army as much by surprise as anybody. On 8 February 1854 the Government had decided to send 10,000 troops to Malta. They would act as the nucleus of any future 'Army of the East'. Among the troops despatched were the Scots Fusilier Guards; they left London on 28 February. Lieutenant the Hon. Hugh Annesley described in his journal the farewell given them by Queen Victoria:

> When we got in front of Buckingham Palace the Regiment halted in line, the officers came to the front, the colours were lowered, and the whole presented arms. Her Majesty, the Prince, and the Royal children, appeared on the balcony and acknowledged the salute, then the Colonel turned to the men, waved his sword, and a thousand voices gave three hearty hurrahs for their Majesties, waving their bearskin caps in the air and by every gesture manifesting the most intense enthusiasm and loyalty. Her Majesty appeared much affected, and bowed and smiled most graciously on her gallant third Regiment of Guards.

Not for nothing were the Scots Fusilier Guards believed to be the Queen's favourite regiment.

The outbreak of war was greeted enthusiastically but for many different reasons. Those of a liberal disposition welcomed the opportunity to cross swords with Tsar Nicholas I, the despot of Europe: in 1848–49 his troops had helped the Austrians crush the nationalist revolt in Hungary. Some soldiers welcomed the outbreak of hostilities for professional reasons. 'Now for what I so often wished for, a European war, and deuced tired I will in all probability be of it before peace again arrives', wrote Captain James Kingsley of the 95th (The Derbyshire) Regiment. At a time when religious observance was still marked, the Eastern Question was interpreted by others in the light of biblical prophecy about the return of the Jews to Israel. Lieutenant Henry Spalding of HMS *London* was serving in the Black Sea when he wrote the following letter:

> I do not know my dear Helen what view you take in this war but I fancy I can see the happy result of it. Russia being a despotic government and the Emperors feeling most probably that unless people are kept in ignorance it could never remain so, have in past ages forbidden or at any rate have never encouraged the light of Christianity and I believe at this moment the use of the Bible is entirely forbidden in the whole of the Russian dominions. The result of our interference in his wicked ambition will be I feel the conversion (for such it will certainly be as Christians the poor people cannot be) of

all Russia. I have a strange feeling about this war and cannot help
thinking from its proximity to Jerusalem, from Faber's explanation
of prophecy in which he 17 years ago foretold the revival of the
French Emperorship* as also from the wonderful conversion which
if we can conquer must spread over nearly one quarter of the world,
I say from all this I have a very strong feeling that the Hand of God
is visible in this war more than in any other I have ever read of . . .
I only regret that we are leagued with infidels I mean the French &
Turks. The French are but perverted Christians after all & the Turk
knows no better.

Spalding's view of the enemy reflected the widespread belief that
Russia was an obscurantist state populated by down-trodden serfs. It was
certainly true that the 850,000–strong Russian army was a serf army:
although freedom was the notional reward for the conscripted serf at the
end of his twenty-five years' service, few lived to see it. The conviction
that military service was a death sentence – guaranteed by hard conditions and poor supply – accentuated in the Russian soldier the national
trait of fatalism, and gave him that quality of bovine stoicism which
would make him a doughty defender of Sevastopol but less effective on
the open field of battle. It did not help that the expense of equipping
such a large army left it vulnerable to crippling economies; there was
certainly no money to re-equip the ordinary rank and file with the rifled
musket, which meant that the Russian soldier, armed with an obsolete
percussion musket, was left to face British and French troops carrying
the vastly superior Minié.

Following the official outbreak of war, further British troops set sail
for the eastern Mediterranean. More than once horse transports would
suffer severely in the heavy seas. Cornet George Clowes of the 8th (The
King's Royal Irish) Regiment of Light Dragoons (Hussars) wrote to his
father on 5 May 1854, after leaving Plymouth:

In the evening the wind turned against us, and it gradually became
very rough. About 10 o'clock pm we were in the Bay of Biscay,
where there was a tremendous sea which got gradually worse, and at
midnight there was a precious scene, the ship rolling awfully. The

* George Stanley Faber, *The Revival of the French Emperorship, anticipated from the
Necessity of Prophecy* (1852).

Captain said he never saw a ship roll worse, or a nastier sea just there. Everybody was dreadfully sick in all directions; obliged to stop below with the horses, who could not keep their legs and were down on the ground in all directions in heaps, lashing out at each other, mad with fright and screaming like children. I never saw such a scene. Every man so ill they could hardly stand, and when one managed to get on deck for a bit of fresh air, one got washed about from side to side by the sea, which was dashing over the vessel in tremendous waves as if it delighted in our misery. Four horses we could not get on their legs again and so were lashed down to the deck, but all four died before morning. Luckily they were all troopers[' horses]. This sea continued till 10 o'clock the next morning, when we were all pretty well worn out, and then got calm. The wind was against us through all day, and we did not gain an inch. The next night it was calm luckily, for another night like the last and we should not have had a horse left. They were so beat with trying to keep their legs.

The eventual expansion of the so-called Army of the East to a total of 27,000 men upon its commitment to the Balkans posed problems. It had never been envisaged that in addition to its twin responsibilities of imperial and home defence, the army would have to supply a European expeditionary force as well. Of its 153,000 men, nearly two-thirds were already overseas; and among these were the army's most experienced troops. Depots were ransacked for soldiers. Drafts were made. The 63rd (The West Suffolk) Regiment was just one of many that had to recruit heavily before departure, beating the drum in Dublin. Lord Hardinge encountered similar difficulties in finding generals for the expeditionary force. The dearth of generals of sufficient youthful vigour meant that all the Army of the East's infantry brigades had to be given to colonels furnished with the brevet rank of brigadier-general. Among divisional commanders, half had not seen any active service – if they had seen any at all – since the Napoleonic Wars of their youth. Lord Raglan, the sixty-six-year-old overall commander, was no exception. The commander of the 4th Division, sixty-year-old Sir George Cathcart, who had just returned from the Cape, was given a dormant commission to succeed Raglan in the event of his incapacitation simply because he was the only general with recent experience of independent command. Such was the gravity of the situation that a commission on promotion met in February

1854 to bring forward younger officers. A large brevet promotion –
giving an officer enhanced rank in the army even if a regimental vacancy
was unavailable – followed in June to try and improve the pool of officers
for the Crimea.

In some quarters the prospect of promotion caused anxiety. Colonel
William John Codrington of the Coldstream Regiment of Foot Guards
had not been one of those ordered to join the Army of the East, but he
sailed with the Brigade of Guards anyway as a supernumerary major,
hoping for a permanent appointment. He feared that his promotion to
major-general, in common with other colonels appointed in 1846, would
render him ineligible for any regimental vacancy that might arise. He
wrote home to his wife from Malta on 11 April with other concerns as
well. Although within a year the British army would be equipped with
the new Enfield rifle, it was only just being issued with the Minié
approved for use in 1851. The muzzle-loading Minié fired an expanding
conical bullet which facilitated ease of loading and possessed four times
the range and accuracy of the old Pattern 42 smoothbore percussion
musket. Codrington continued:

> The arrangements about our arms do not seem at present to be very
> satisfactory. What with establishments at Woolwich and Hythe, and
> practice with Miniés and rifles of all sorts, upwards of two years
> must have been passed in trials and firings, &c. And yet we do not
> know positively (except by a trial today) how we should manage in
> the confusion of action with supplies of the different sorts. Today we
> had 3 companies, one from each Batt[alio]n to try the common
> round ball fired from the Minié rifle; it was so far a failure that in
> quick firing the men could not get the balls down, and all sorts of
> ramming and jamming was the consequence of only 15 rounds –
> one firelock burst (at muzzle luckily) and many more would have
> done so I think had we continued quick firing, for the men not being
> able several of them to get the balls down, would have fired off with
> it a few inches from the muzzle and probably burst to the danger of
> all. At present we have scarcely any Minié ammunition; I believe only
> 10 rounds per Minié – and we are liable to embark at any moment.

By the end of May the 1st Division, of which the Brigade of Guards
was part, had been fully issued with Miniés. This Lord Raglan confirmed
in a letter to the Secretary of State for War, the Duke of Newcastle, on

14 June: 'I have armed the Light, the 1st and the 2nd Divisions with Miniés, and I shall arm the 3rd as far as I am able, but to do so entirely, I require 1500 stand more than I have.' Although most of the 4th Division, which joined the Army of the East later, had to make do with Pattern 42 smoothbores until 1855, the 3rd Division received its full complement of Miniés. Captain Arthur Layard of the 38th (The 1st Staffordshire) Regiment was unimpressed with the way the transaction was managed, as he complained to his brother, the radical Member of Parliament Austen Henry Layard, in a letter of 2 July from Varna in Bulgaria:

Ld Raglan they say cannot make up his mind to do anything and is undecided in everything. He is not, I fear, the man for us out here. The authorities at home also go hand in hand with him in his vacillating course of action. I need only quote one instance out of many to show you their mode of proceeding. Before the 38th left England, nearly six weeks I think, they took away the few Minié rifles we had (250) for the purpose we were told, of giving them to the regiments who were going abroad on active service. In a week after they were taken, they were returned to us, and a short time after cases containing rifles for the whole regiment were sent down with orders not to open them until we reached Turkey. On our reaching Gallipoli they were ordered into store and we saw nothing more of them. After remaining at Gallipoli from the 17th May to the 23rd June we were ordered here, and in arriving off Scutari we received an order to take our rifles for the whole regiment, changing of course nearly the whole of our old ammunition. Having to get rid of 48,000 rounds, and receive the same quantity, and nearly 800 muskets to change, everything to be examined before going over and taking it, is not to be done in a few minutes, especially when there are numerous other duties to get through, such as taking on board camp equipage, stores etc etc. We arrived about midday and had imperative orders to start for Varna by three P.M. the same day, so you may imagine the scene of confusion on board. With the quantity of loose ammunition on deck I am astonished we had no accidents for everybody who liked had free access to the ship and her decks were crowded with the scum of Pera. One of the lot was observed to light his cigar and cooly to sit down upon an open case containing 20,000 rounds of ammunition. He was quickly kicked out of that position, only to go a little further forward and light another which I believe he smoked out in peace, as we were all too busy from the cabin boy upwards to look after him, the crew of the ship adding to the general confusion by taking on water and provisions and clearing the screw from a hawser which had got foul of it at Gallipoli whilst taking in tow the Transport with our baggage animals. It appears that Ld R had only made up his mind to give us the Minié just before leaving Scutari, so that we have now arms with no mark on them to distinguish regiment or company, which is always customary, and the country as well as the service will suffer, for none of us Captains can or will be responsible for arms we cannot identify. The first scrimmage we get into, there will be many a rifle lost that should not be, and also damage done.

The quality of the army's staff work did not impress Lieutenant-Colonel Anthony Sterling, brigade major of Sir Colin Campbell's Highland Brigade. When he wrote on 10 June, the 1st Division, of which the Highland Brigade was part, had shipped from Malta to Scutari, on the eastern or Asiatic shores of the Bosphorus across from the Turkish capital, Constantinople.

When I consider the composition of our Staff, the prospect looks dubious. In the Quarter-Master General's department there is only one officer who has ever served in that department before . . . How they are all to become in a moment expert at their work is a mystery . . . The Adjutant-General [James B. Bucknall Estcourt] is a very amiable man, a perfect gentleman and a good Christian, but as innocent of the meaning of discipline as a sucking baby. Someone must be responsible for the selection of the Staff; the ultimate responsibility of course must fall on the Commander-in-Chief, who however capable, as I believe him to be, cannot do every one's work and his own too.

The staff of France's own *Armée de l'Orient*, which had sailed to Turkey slightly before the British, contrived to create – superficially at least – a more favourable impression. Colonel George Bell of the 1st or Royal Regiment was, at the end of May, with the 3rd Division near Gallipoli, at the entrance to the Dardanelles.

We were under arms at 4 in the morning and away miles across the country to join with the rest of the army here in a grand field day for Marshal de St Arnaud. Prince Nap[oleon] & Gen[era]l Canrobert were also on the ground. They had a splendid Staff some 150 or 200 sabres flashing in the sun; it was something superior to any ensemble of cocked hats that I ever saw in our Country. The Marshal glanced firmly at every man & as I presented arms he said en passant down the line, 'How you do, Col. Bell'.

Marshal Jacques Leroy de Saint-Arnaud had received his command as a reward for supporting Louis Napoleon's seizure of power. A chequered if colourful military career had seen him spend time as a dancing instructor in England – which gave him his command of the language – and more recently kill a fellow general in a duel. His army, unlike the British, had extensive combat experience, having only recently concluded a twenty-year war in Algeria. At one point a third of the French army's 350,000 men had been deployed there. French military administration had also benefited from its North African experience: the superior mobility achieved by the French army did not come about at the expense of its logistic support. Of this all but the most blinkered of British observers was aware, just as they were increasingly aware of the extent to which the conquest of Algeria had introduced to the French army a number of exotic native troops. These ranged from the Berber Tirailleurs Indigènes, through the Zouaves (by 1854 mostly Metropolitan Frenchmen dressed as North Africans) to the Spahi cavalry which provided Saint-Arnaud's escort.

Captain Nigel Kingscote who, in common with most of Lord Raglan's other aides-de-camp, was one of his nephews, initially formed an ill opinion of Britain's other allies, the Turks. He wrote to his father from Constantinople on 29 April:

The little I have seen of the Turks makes me think they are very poor Allies and of this I am certain they are the greatest liars on the face of the earth. If they say they have 150,000 men you will find that on enquiry there are only 30,000. Everything in the same proportion, and from all I hear, I cannot make out why the Russians have not walked over them.

Famously, Lord Raglan, who had served on the Duke of Wellington's staff throughout the Peninsular War of 1808–14 and who lost an arm at Waterloo, would on occasion absent-mindedly refer to the French as the enemy, when of course he meant the Russians. For others too France was still the natural enemy. 'Fancy what a bore it is for us,' Nigel Kingscote wrote on 15 May,

> we are to have two Frenchmen attached to us and my Lord will have to feed them &c as Marshal St Arnaud has done the same to our two officers attached to him. What on earth the use of them can be I don't know and I heartily wish them at New York Town. I hate the French and all St Arnaud's staff, with one or two exceptions, are just like monkeys, girthed up as tight as they can be and sticking out above and below like balloons.

Saint-Arnaud himself gave grounds for offence by his very pretensions. He first claimed that the Turkish Sultan had vested in him command of his army. Raglan was disconcerted: 'Many reasons are opposed to the supreme command of the French and Turkish Armies being vested in the General in Chief of the former. It would, as I see it, materially weaken my position, and leave me much to his mercy,' he told the Duke of Newcastle. Even when it was shown that Saint-Arnaud's claim was untrue, he remained unabashed; his proposal that in the event of French and British troops acting together the senior officer should take command irrespective of nationality was viewed simply as a further attempt by him to establish control over the Allied armies (British officers would invariably be outranked by their French counterparts). 'I am satisfied that the more our Officers feel themselves independent of their Allies,' wrote Raglan, who was having none of it, 'the better will be the concert, the more ready the cooperation.'

In the middle of May, Raglan and Saint-Arnaud heard that the Russians were laying siege to Silistria, a town on the River Danube. They sailed to Bulgaria to confer with the Turkish commander Omar Pasha in his fortified camp at Shumla. Seeing Omar Pasha's battle-hardened men, even Nigel Kingscote's prejudices began to abate:

> We were very much surprised at the Turkish troops. They are strong built men and move very quickly, which we did not expect and I believe there is hardly such a thing as crime among them. There are 45,000 Infantry and 5,000 Cavalry and Artillery with more Cavalry in the neighbourhood. Omar Pasha is a fine looking fellow, unlike the Turks, dresses in a plain grey frock coat with Jack boots, and sits well on his horse with an English seat. He does everything himself

and must see it done or it is not done, the staff of every kind being the worst part of the Turkish Army.

Although both Raglan and Saint-Arnaud promised to support Omar Pasha with a division each, the Frenchman subsequently endeavoured to renege on the commitment; only Raglan's firmness prevented this. The Light Division under Lieutenant-General Sir George Brown had already left Scutari for the Bulgarian port of Varna. Throughout June and July the 1st, 2nd and 3rd Divisions would follow, as well as the first regiments of the Cavalry.

Questions, meanwhile, were being asked back in England about the well-being of the troops in Turkey. The Secretary of State for War wrote to Raglan concerning the necessity for the men to wear tight-fitting leather stocks inside their coatee collars and to remain clean-shaven. 'I am much obliged to you for your suggestions respecting the stocks and chins,' replied Raglan on 15 May. Upon the subject of stocks he was not going to insist; nevertheless

> I view your proposition for the introduction of beards in somewhat a different light, and it cannot be necessary to adopt it at present. I am somewhat old fashioned in my ideas, and I cling to the desire that an Englishman should look like an Englishman, notwithstanding that the French are endeavouring to make themselves appear as Africans, Turks, and Infidels.
>
> I have always remarked in the lower orders in England, that their first notion of cleanliness is shaving, and I dare say this feeling prevails in a great degree in our ranks, though some of our officers may envy the hairy men amongst our Allies . . .
>
> However, if when we come to march and are exposed to great heat and dirt, I remark that the sun makes inroads on the faces of the men, I will consider whether it be desirable to relax or not, but let us still appear as Englishmen.

In spite of Raglan's misgivings, by July the wearing of beards enjoyed official sanction.

The British soldier's appearance, in other respects, was looking increasingly old-fashioned. He still wore the coatee, when most armies of Continental Europe had adopted the looser-fitting tunic; and his headdress still consisted of the tall shako, known as the 'Albert' after the Prince Consort, who supposedly designed it. Writing from Scutari

in June, Colonel Bell criticized the practicality of both the soldier's
uniform and his equipment:

> A suit on his back & a change in his pack is all the men require but
> still he is loaded like a donkey – G[rea]t coat & blanket, tight broad
> well pipe-clayed belts that cling to his lungs like death, his arms &
> acc[outremen]ts, 60 rounds of Minie am[munitio]n, pack & contents.
> The stiff leather choaker we have abolished thanks to 'Punch' & the
> 'Times'. The reasoning of 40 years experience would not move
> the mil[itary] authorities to let the soldier go into the field until he
> was ½ strangled & unable to move under his load until public
> opinion & the Newspapers came in to relieve him. The next thing I
> want to pitch aside is the abominable Albert as it is called, whereon
> a man may fry his ration beef at mid-day in this climate, the top
> being patent leather to attract a 10 fold more portion of the sun's
> rays to madden his brain. In eastern climates the natives wear white
> to keep the head cool. I found it so boiling in Constant[inople]
> yesterday I got a white turban put round my forage cap which caught
> the eye of the Turks & with my blue coat & medals they did not
> know what to make of me.

At Silistria, meanwhile, as the end of May approached the Russian
siege intensified. The Turkish defenders had been joined by two British
volunteers, James Armar Butler, a half-pay captain in the Ceylon Rifles,
and Lieutenant Charles Nasmyth of the Bombay Artillery. They were
soon acting as advisers to the Turkish commander, Mustapha Pasha.
Writing in his journal on 29 May, after heavy Russian attacks on the
key outwork of Arab Tabia, Butler criticized the Turkish commander's
priorities.

> On going to the Stamboul gateway this morning we found Moussa
> [sic] Pasha sitting at the receipt of custom receiving the arms & other
> trophies taken from the Russian dead, registering them, & issuing
> rewards for each, shewing his Hebrew extraction in this employ-
> ment, which might have been conducted by an understrapper, &
> which he continued throughout the day instead of riding up to
> Arab Tabia, complimenting the troops there on their gallant behav-
> iour & pursuing the other duties incumbent on a general under the
> circumstances. It seems the affair of last night was a bloody one, the
> garrison of A[rab] T[abia] being taken by surprise in the first attack.

No alarm was given until the enemy was actually in the redoubt. The first to enter was a Russian Officer who cut down a Turkish Lieut: of Artillery but was immediately knocked over by a handspike & killed by the men about. A fierce hand to hand conflict ensued with the enemy who clambered up from the ditch & poured in through the embrasures & over the parapet. They were driven out back into the ditch when a terrific slaughter took place, our guns pouring grape & canister among them.

Butler then went up to Arab Tabia to see things for himself.

The Russian dead . . . were still unburied. A disgusting sight. Those who were in the ditch had all been stripped & were lying in various attitudes. Some headless trunks, others with throats half cut, arms extended in the air, or pointing upwards as they fell or were thrown back into the ditch. Those outside had their clothes still on as the Russian riflemen kept up a smart fire from their batteries to prevent their mutilation. The smell was already becoming very offensive. On returning to Silistra spoke to M[ustapha] P[asha] about it telling him that a fever would break out amongst the men there if measures were not adopted for their immediate interment. This had already been urged on him several times, but he received it with his usual indecisive & dilatory way.

In spite of the stubborn resistance of the Turkish garrison, it seemed Silistria must fall. Mustapha Pasha was killed. Butler was wounded and subsequently died. Then, on 22 June, with victory apparently within their grasp, the Russians withdrew. Austria had presented them with an ultimatum demanding their evacuation of the Danubian Principalities. Tsar Nicholas felt compelled to comply. Great was the surprise when the news reached Raglan's headquarters at Varna. A 200–strong patrol, drawn from the Light Brigade of Cavalry and commanded by Lord Cardigan, was sent to ascertain that the Russians had retreated. Cornet George Clowes of the 8th Hussars was not among them.

We were very much disappointed at being left behind. The next day though an order came to send one of our Captains (who has been up the country before in search of water), as far as he could go towards the Danube, and not to come back before he had seen the Russians, and found out where they were. And he was told to take a Subaltern with him. Then there was great excitement amongst the Subalterns who was to go, though it was supposed to be amongst the Lieutenants. To my astonishment however, I was ordered to go, so we started at 2 o'clock on Monday afternoon.

On the first day of the expedition Clowes covered twelve miles.

The next day we had a long march to a place called Tourk Tahilar; we left at half past five in the morning and did not get in till three in the afternoon, and a very hot day [it was]. I was much disappointed with the country. I saw nothing pretty about it, it is all the same, scattered with little oak trees and not a single stream of water in the country, nothing but wells and small fountains to water at. There is no water between here and the Danube anywhere along the country, and I do not know how we shall manage to march from here. We shall have to go in small detachments or we shall never be able to water the horses.

At Tourk Tahilar we got a very nasty farmyard to sleep in and packs of wild dogs making an awful row around us all night. I had a bag of biscuits for my pillow and was seriously disturbed in my slumbers by one hungry animal trying to run away with it. I had to collect a pile of stones, and whenever they awoke us to half kill one of the nearest. But they got too sharp at last and directly they saw me move were off like a shot. We left this place early the next morning determined to go to Silistra or as near as we could, and marched for 12 hours to Kainardjik, where we arrived pretty well beat, both men and horses. We found all the villages around burnt to the ground by those brutes, the Bashi Bazouks,* the inhabitants having deserted them since the Russians had been there. However Kainardjik itself was saved as a Turkish Colonel had been sent there to prevent them pillaging. However it was utterly deserted. We heard to our astonishment from this man that the last of the Russians had that day recrossed the Danube so we might walk into Silistra with a bold face. We started early the next morning for Silistra, it being only four hours journey from Tourk Tahilar, and got there about half past eleven in the morning. It was a curious scene when we got on the hills just above the town and saw the immense Russian camp on the other side of the river, about a mile off, and the little

---

* Auxiliary Turkish light cavalry.

poky town with one ditch round it that they had been unable to take. All outside the town was a nice mess. It had been all orchards and gardens, but now it was a mass of zigzag approaches, blown up field works, a few shot, and remains of shells, and here and there a dead Russian, which our Turkish escort immediately galloped off to see, and grinned over like dogs. When we got into the town we were crowded round by wondering Turks, who rejoiced in the idea of how astonished the Russians would be at us. We were marched off to Hasson Pasha, who was commanding there. He was the man who commanded at Oltenitza, and was made a Pasha for it. He was a jolly old bird. We had great fun with him, and splendid pipes and coffee. We found staying in the same house as him two English engineers,* who had been there as volunteers during the siege, and to whose exertions entirely they owe the saving of the town, and defeat of the Russians. They took the affair into their own hands, having the rank of Colonels given them, and would not allow the Turkish officers to give any orders but through them. Poor Captain Butler who was shot while looking through one of the loop holes was one of the party . . . They told us the Turks were very hard-working soldiers, but that the officers were no use at all, and never did anything. They said though that the Turks were great savages. They committed all sort of atrocities on the dead Russians and paraded about the streets with the heads of the Russians they killed strung on a stick over their shoulders.

For the British soldiers back in the vicinity of Varna, meanwhile, there had been some relief from the trying climate: white cap covers had at last been issued for their Albert shakos. Otherwise, life was monotonous, as Private Robert Hull of the 50th (The Queen's Own) Regiment complained in a letter to his wife of 12 July:

We have all got white hoods to wear to keep the sun from burning our eyes out which I can asure you it is very hot . . . Dear Wife I have very little news to send you for we might as well be out of the World for we can neighter here or se nothing but a jungle. We can se plenty of snakes by day and plenty of wolfs by night. We are beside a fresh water lake which we amuse our selves with Bathing [in] and there is now and then a man Drowned. We have had one two Days

---

* Another British volunteer, Lieutenant John Archibald Ballard, Bombay Engineers, had arrived in Silistria after Captain Butler's death.

together now. Wm Beale the Taylor was found Dead in the jungle a few Day[s] ago through Drinking Brandy in the French Camp so we buried him in the jungle with out a Coffin just sewed him up in his Blanket and put him in a hole. The Women is getting on about the same the[y] keep Fighting and Drinking as usehall [usual]. Their is getting a good many Children amongst us all ready.

As Hull intimated, some soldiers' wives had elected to travel on campaign with their husbands. Their lot was not an enviable one, as Captain Arthur Layard had written from Gallipoli to his brother, A. H. Layard, six weeks earlier:

On the troops being ordered for service in Turkey, a circular was sent to every regiment directing com[man]d[ing] officers to allow four women per company for each regiment. Many women availed themselves of the priviledge (if one) and came out tho' not near the number authorized. On their arrival here they were told that no covering or tent would be allowed them, so there were these unfortunate beings without a place to rest their heads th[r]ough the rain & snow, which fell on the arrival of the first batch of troops. The women are living in holes dug in the banks, they cannot go into the tents with the men, our bell tents are crowded now with sixteen men in them without any addition to their numbers. The weather now is luckily fine. I pity the women if it comes on to rain. The poor creatures were conveyed out by the authorities and then left to shift for themselves in a country w[h]ere everything is different to the rest, I may say, of Europe. And this is the age when so much humanity mongering is going on and when our convicts are fed and lodged far better than half the poor peasants and Secretarys at war spout about the ameliorated condition of the soldier and the boons conferred to their wives.

A few officers' ladies also chose to accompany their husbands to the east. Among them was Eliza Amelia, Lady Erroll, whose situation was brought to Lord Raglan's attention in an unfortunate fashion when her husband William Henry, Earl of Erroll, an officer of the 2nd Battalion Rifle Brigade, insulted his commanding officer, Lieutenant-Colonel Arthur Lawrence. Sir George Brown, commanding the Light Division, wrote to Raglan from Varna on 3 June asking his advice:

The fact is that Lord Erroll, when at all excited, becomes stark staring mad, & is unsafe to live with, for one never knows when he may take offence or when he may break out!

He has been a positive nuisance to the Regiment for years, & but for the constant vigilance of Lady Erroll who follows him everywhere, he must have been compelled to quit the scene long ago, notwithstanding the forbearance of his Commanding Officer, who out of regard for her & respect for his family, has treated him with great leniency throughout. If I saw any chance of reclaiming him, or if it were possible under any circumstances to place the slightest reliance in him, be assured I should not at this moment have troubled you with the disposal of his case, but believing him to be much too mad to continue any longer in the Army, if not too insane to be left at large, I am compelled to refer it to you in the hope should you not deem it expedient that he be brought to trial that you may be enabled to suggest some other mode of disposing of him.

Raglan replied on 7 June, writing from Scutari where he was still based. He agreed that Erroll was guilty of an 'outrageous act of misconduct & insubordination' but pointed out the difficulty in asking an officer to solicit retirement on the eve of action, suggesting instead that Erroll be asked to apologize in front of his fellow officers. A week later, Brown reported the outcome of this course of action.

I rode out to Camp yesterday morning in order to dispose of Lord Erroll's case & found, as I expected, that Colonel Lawrence was perfectly well disposed to come into your views & to meet your wishes by accepting any reasonable apology & concession that His Lordship might be induced to make to him.

I therefore assembled all the Officers of the Battalion near Airey's tent, & in presence of him & Buller read to them your letter, admonished Lord Erroll & then called upon him to express his regret for the breach of discipline he had committed & the gross insult he had offered to a brother officer.

This he at once did to the satisfaction of all parties & I was about to dismiss them when Lawrence with the utmost kindness of manner & without any hint from me stepped forward holding out & offering his hand to Lord Erroll which however His Lordship had the utmost bad taste & churlishness to reject!

Nothing could be more insulting than his whole manner & I

fancied that after all the trouble we had taken I should have failed in my mission. I however told Norcott & Sullivan to draw him aside & advise him when after a little hesitation he came forward & offered his hand to Lawrence apologizing for his rudeness. The matter therefore is patched up for the present, but I have less hope than ever from what I saw yesterday, that it will be possible to go on with him for I am now satisfied he is not only a madman but a ruffian!

It was presumably a relief to all concerned when a wound sustained by Erroll three months later at the Battle of the Alma forced his return home.

A martinet and a stickler for dress regulations, Sir George Brown was deeply unpopular with the men of his command. Writing from the camp near Devna on 21 July, Private Manasseh Dennison of the 7th Regiment of Foot (Royal Fusiliers) gave vent to his feelings:

> Our Division is commanded by Sir George Brown & he is a regular tyrant. He takes us out to a field day every morning. We fall in about half past 5, & sometimes it is 9 before we get our Packs off. Then the remainder of the day is taking up with carrying Water Wood etc. We have to forage for Wood & sometimes it takes us 3 hours to get one days allowance. The Water is a good mile off, & then it is as filthy as that we had to use at Chobham. It is as only yesterday that we were allowed or could procure either pepper or salt. We had nothing but Beef Tea in lieu of soup, & the Carrion, I cannot call it Beef, was as tough as leather. We are a great distance from any town & as we cannot go more than a mile from Camp we cannot get anything but what we are allowed by the Commissariat. Altogether we are in a miserable condition, & it makes us begin to fancy that we are treated worse than convicts, & if we murmur our reward is the infernal Cat, no other punishment but flogging is resorted to here, & it is carried on to an awful extent.

But some officers were not going to apologize for the ready resort to flogging. Captain William Cameron of the 3rd Battalion Grenadier Guards, writing home to his father from Varna on 19 June, was forthright:

> Say what you like, the common soldier, who is with all that is done for him, a great brute, is to be kept in good order by a good flogging better than any other way. If you heard the horrid, brutal,

blasphemous language and saw their habits as we do in camp, where we see and hear everything, you would say punish them as you do the brute and lay it on well. Harsh it may sound to the uninitiated, but as appealing to feelings is a farce nothing else does. We gave the utmost extent the other day to a man (50 lashes) and the hardened brute did not mind it a bit, but looked more ready to laugh. However they say the greatest blackguards are the best soldiers.

By June 1854, the Russians' raising of the siege of Silistria and subsequent retirement from the Danubian Principalities left the Allied expedition to Bulgaria lacking a purpose. Without the cooperation of Austria, neither Russia nor the Allies could act decisively in the Balkans; and although the threat of intervention in the war by Vienna had forced Russian withdrawal, the Austrians were otherwise determined to remain neutral, as they would inevitably bear the brunt of any fighting if they became involved. The British contemplated an amphibious warfare strategy instead. Ever since Sinope, the First Lord of the Admiralty, Sir James Graham, had urged the necessity of destroying the Russian naval base at Sevastopol. Although the ministers of Lord Aberdeen's coalition Government proved to be as divided on this issue as they had been on the question of war or peace, by the end of June 1854, after *The Times* had printed a fiery editorial, the tide was running strongly in favour of Sevastopol. On 27 June the Duke of Newcastle, the Secretary of State for War, brought the proposal for an invasion of the Crimea before the Cabinet. Most of the Cabinet fell asleep during the course of the meeting, but at its close the proposal was approved. Lord Raglan was given definite instructions to proceed to the Crimea.

Sevastopol was a naval objective. Ever since the Inspector General of Fortifications, Sir John Burgoyne, had submitted an unfavourable report in April, military opinion had been against the expedition. 'The Press in England is pushing us forward very violently! A strong Press and a weak Government are the worst Enemies any Army can have,' complained Brigadier Richard Airey on 22 July. There was moreover a crippling lack of intelligence. 'The task we are called upon to undertake, is of the most serious character, and the information we have upon the Crimea generally and upon Sevastopol, is as imperfect as it was when I left England', Raglan warned Newcastle. Where was the best place to land in the Crimea? What was the number of Russian troops? How were they disposed? No one knew.

While Raglan's sense of duty would not allow him to express his reservations to Newcastle any more strongly than that, he had concerns nonetheless about the state of the army's system of supply and transport.

> The Commissariat is in its infancy, and we are all disposed to throw a stone at it. Mr Filder is an able man, and labours from Morning to Night, but his department is weak in numbers, and deficient in Field experience, and he is surrounded with difficulties.

It did not help that supply and transport were controlled, not by the War Office, but by the Treasury. The situation was the worst of the many anomalies of Britain's unreformed military administration.

In the second half of July the British Army of the East came to face a new enemy – cholera. The disease had been brought from France by the French army, first to Gallipoli and then Bulgaria. Losses mounted. The troops shifted camp to try and escape the disease, but to no avail. On 22 August Sergeant George Cruse of the 1st (Royal) Regiment of Dragoons wrote to his wife from Camp Adrianople, near Varna: 'Not a day passes without my seeing several funerals in the different Camps around me. The Foot Guards are the nearest Regt to us, they generally bury three or four a day, and this morning they buried one of their Captains.' Cruse had a theory about susceptibility to cholera: 'I have remarked that those who suffer most are those who have abused their constitutions by excessive drinking.' In the camp at Aladyn, seventeen-year-old William Wharin, a trumpeter in the Royal Artillery, thought that he had discovered a way of mitigating the effect of the contagion.

> As we exercised our horses we were allowed freedom so that in galloping about it afforded pleasure to the men and kept their minds & bodies in action so that our losses were trifling compared to the other troops. We were out foraging one day and on returning to camp found that the infantry had moved away and only the sutlers' marquees were left. Stringent orders were issued that no one was to go near the site vacated, but it was not long before several of our men who were left in camp came rolling in with as much brandy as they could carry, both inside and out. The sutlers had fled

leaving their stock, or they may have become victims to the dread disease.

At the same time as the cholera epidemic broke, the army's Ambulance Corps arrived from England. Unable to find recruits in the ordinary way, its ranks were filled with unwilling army pensioners recalled to the colours. Observing them and their heavy ambulances, Major-General William Codrington was filled with foreboding:

I am afraid the pensioners will not do for the hard work which they [the ambulances] will entail upon them. I suspect instead of old pensioners, they will tax the energy of strong young men, if they are to be made available in the immediate neighbourhood of action. And I am afraid that what I heard said by one old fellow with medals, 'There was I living on the best of the land in comfort and I am come out here to be miserable', will be the feeling of very many of them independent of the ailments and diseases for which they were discharged making their appearance on them again.

When the Guards moved camp from Aladyn to nearer Varna, getting there proved an ordeal. General Codrington was once again disturbed by what he saw.

I have occupied myself during the day in various nothings – first at 7 o'clock I rode out to meet our Brigade of Guards marching across the flat shore of the bay of Varna, their 3d. day's march (the *whole* being only about 16 miles) to their new camp on the heights 2 miles from hence. Their march today was only about 6 miles – their knapsacks were carried – they were in their bearskins, red coats, arms and belts, and ammunition of course – and yet on arriving at the ground, and even on halting a mile short of it up hill near a fountain – about 1/2 or 1/3d. of each company looked to me weak and distressed. Not that they fell out much, but on halting, even with such a distance, they looked weak and leaning about, their caps hanging anywhere, a lassitude of movement and apparent weakness: the day was hot, not any breeze on the hill side and in a narrowish bush road up a steepish place of a mile and a half or so. And yet these same men, or a similar sort of former days, I have accompanied in a 25 miles march in marching order from the Tower [of London] to Windsor – nearly at the rate of 3 miles an hour in the forenoon! Such is the effect of climate!

Codrington, however, had good news a fortnight later. Richard Airey had been moved from command of his brigade of the Light Division to take over as the army's Quartermaster-General. The vacancy created was Codrington's; he would now have the opportunity of making the closer acquaintance of Sir George Brown, his divisional commander.

One man who had been feeling less cause for satisfaction for some time now was the commander of the Cavalry Division, the Earl of Lucan. He was infuriated that his subordinate and brother-in-law, Lord Cardigan, who reciprocated the cordial dislike which Lucan felt towards him, had hitherto been allowed by the indulgence of Lord Raglan to exercise a largely independent command over the Light Brigade of Cavalry. Lucan worked out his frustrations by compulsively drilling the Heavy Brigade, commanded by Brigadier James Scarlett. Unfortunately, this merely exposed the fact that Lucan, who had been retired from the army seventeen years before receiving his present appointment, was entirely unfamiliar with the latest drill. Major William Charles Forrest of the 4th (Royal Irish) Regiment of Dragoon Guards, writing to his wife on 27 August, was troubled:

> Lord Lucan is no doubt a clever sharp fellow, but he has been so long on the shelf that he has no idea of moving cavalry, does not even know the words of command & is very self willed about it, thinks himself right. He has had a lot of very indifferent Field days, which we only hope may have taught him and his staff something for certainly no one else has learnt anything. If he is shewn by the drill book that he is wrong, he says, 'Ah I should like to know who wrote that book, some Farrier I suppose.' When he is changing position, throwing back a flank, he will not allow the flank regiment to move by echelon of Troops, but makes them retire in a column of Divisions from the inward flank of the Regt. and the whole Regiment enter the new alignment at one point. You may fancy the length of time we are getting into the new alignment. If we have to manoeuvre in the presence of good cavalry they may be into us and knock us all of a heap before [we] could show a front. . . . I trust Scarlett will be allowed to manoeuvre his own Brigade and then all will go well with the Heavies, but I write this to you in order that if any mishap should occur to the cavalry, you may be able to form a

correct idea how it happened. Do not say anything about Lord Lucan unless we come to grief.

Rarely have words been so prophetic.

At the end of August the British, French and Turks began embarking the contingents that they were to send to the Crimea. Nineteen-year-old Lieutenant George John Young of 'A' Field Battery the Royal Artillery, attached to the 1st Division, was looking forward to returning aboard ship, as he explained to his mother:

> When I first embarked at Woolwich I used to consider a ship as a necessary evil on the road to glory but after having lived under canvas so long one has come to look upon a residence aboard ship as the *ne plus ultra* of comfortable living. Drinking out of wine glasses and china cups is not the least of the luxuries, among others of which may be enumerated the comfort of being able to go to bed at night without the rather disagreeable excitement of not knowing whether one's tent may not be blown down in the course of the night. Moreover in tents one cannot sleep after sunrise because of the flys which are an abominable nuisance. I think the horses too must be glad to get back to the ships because they are comfortably fed and don't sometimes go for two days without anything to eat but about five pounds of oats or barley. By the bye two horses belonging to Capt Swinton's battery encamped on the hills above Varna died in rather a curious manner. They were camped in deep sand and having very little to eat they took to eating the sand and there two died, and on a post-mortem examination about two buckets full of sand were taken from the inside of each of them.

By 6 September the British had completed their embarkation and were ready to sail to the Crimea the next day. Captain William Pollexfen Radcliffe of the 20th (The East Devonshire) Regiment looked out on the armada assembled in Baljik Bay from aboard the steamship *Colombo*. He felt great pride and confidence.

> The French are greatly astonished at the magnificent vessels our Troops are conveyed in, & well they may be, for their own are nothing more than coasting vessels. Our discipline also surprises *them much*, & they put it down & with truth, to the great distinction of classes in England. Let the Papers say what they will, 'Old England'

is superior to every nation, & I don't wonder at Englishmen being prejudiced; the more I see of Foreign countries, the more I am assured of her superiority in everything essential.

Whether his confidence was to prove justified would soon be revealed.

2

ALMA

On 7 September the combined fleet set sail for the Crimea, taking with it the diseases of Bulgaria. Trumpeter William Wharin of Captain D. W. Paynter's Battery of the 8th Battalion Royal Artillery was aboard the transport *City of Carlisle* with two companies of the 93rd Highland Regiment, being towed by the steamer *Emperor*. Fifty years later he recollected how:

> An incident occurred one day which stirred up serious thought. About half a dozen of ours and the 93rd Highlrs were discussing the prospects of the Expedition. On separating for dinner we agreed to re-assemble after the grog was issued. On doing so [i.e. re-assembling] we noticed a body committed to the deep. As Sergt McLeod had not rejoined the party I was requested to look him up, when to my surprise and sorrow I was informed that he had just been buried, having been seized with Cholera during the dinner hour.

The expedition had left for the Crimea still uncertain of where it was to land, and only after Lord Raglan had undertaken a personal reconnaissance of the coastline aboard the *Caradoc* was it determined to disembark at Calamita Bay, a long sandy beach thirty miles north of Sevastopol. The fleet eventually rendezvoused on 13 September at the small nearby port of Eupatoria – which provided no resistance – and Raglan, having explained his intentions, fixed the landing for the following day. The disembarkation would proceed, as Raglan later acknowledged, to the plan drawn up by Sir Ralph Abercromby for the landings in Egypt in 1801. Three days' rations were to be issued. Raglan, concerned about his men's debilitated state after Bulgaria, also ordered that they leave behind their knapsacks and take only blankets ashore: this was known as light marching order, although besides their rifle and fifty rounds of ammunition the troops had still to carry wrapped in their blanket a greatcoat, a spare pair of boots, socks, shirt and forage cap, as

well as part of their unit's cooking apparatus. Nor could tents be taken
ashore immediately.

'On the 14th Septbr', wrote Trumpeter Wharin,

> the disembarkation commenced, the weather was favourable, our
> Highlanders were taken off and with the assistance of Men of War's
> men the horses & guns were placed on flats formed by two paddlebox
> boats being lashed together with planking placed crosswise. We were
> then towed to the beach and with the aid of the sailors disembarked.
> My horse a Tunis Barb took the opportunity of being on terra firma
> to stretch his legs for he lashed out until he was exhausted. The
> excitement drew a crowd together amongst which were sixteen of my
> old schoolmates. We had to exercise economy with our three days
> rations, those who had acted thoughtlessly and had eaten part before
> leaving the ship were in sad plight. Some of the men made tea, but
> the foul water was more than they could drink, for it could not be
> drunk even mixed with rum. We stayed that night on a sandy strip
> of beach; a storm added to our discomfort. We lighted a bonfire with
> the wood obtained from the flats which had been driven to pieces
> on the beach and made the best of the situation, singing until tired
> out. Many laid down in the sand and endeavoured to obtain sleep;
> as we were thoroughly drenched we got used to the rain and longed
> for the morning. Our Captain had a splendid contrivance: two picket
> posts were driven into the sand and a hammock slung in which he
> lay covered with a waterproof sheet. Our Colonel [Dacres] gave a
> man a dollar for the loan of a blanket, he fared no better than his
> men.

The Russians had not attempted to interfere with the first day's
landing, which saw the British get ashore all their infantry and part of
their artillery, and only a few Cossacks were in evidence. But these were
clearly bent on denying the British and French whatever local sources
of matériel were available. Prompt action was required to prevent the
Russians succeeding, and immediately upon disembarkation, Richard
Airey, the army's Quartermaster-General, was ordering troops forward,
as his aide-de-camp, Captain Louis Nolan of the 15th (The King's)
Hussars, noted in his journal.

> A Comp[a]ny of the 23rd Welsh Fusiliers [the 23rd Regiment (Royal
> Welsh Fusiliers)] under Major Lysons ascended the hill, fired a few

Minié bullets amongst the Cossacks & captured 15 carts which they were in the act of driving off. A poor Tartar boy one of the drivers was shot in the foot, the first blood shed by our men on the soil of the Crimea. We took every care of him & had his wound dressed, though the Ass[istan]t Surgeon stated his toe sh[oul]d be amputated, but this being an *operation* he could not undertake it without orders from higher medical authority. It is to be hoped that this principle is not carried out in the case of dangerous wounds from which the Patient might die from effusion of blood whilst the authority for acting was being sought.

The British high command was determined not to treat the local Tartar population as conquerors, and in one village relations were particularly cordial, as Nigel Kingscote explained:

The people, Tartars, were very civil and offered to give the men anything they had got but we made the men pay for it. Unfortunately the French troops got into the village early next morning and ransacked the whole place committing every atrocity before a stop could be put to it.

Having left behind whatever transport they possessed in Bulgaria, the British were desperate to secure replacements. During the five days that it took to complete the disembarkation of the army's 27,000 men, with its 1,000 cavalry horses and 60 artillery pieces, no fewer than 350 wagons with their teams and drivers were gathered in. But this still proved insufficient and, before the army could move, its tents had to be sent back on board ship. The army, during its coming advance, would need to be continuously replenished from the fleet standing offshore.

The 30,000 French and 7,000 Turks had completed their disembarkation far sooner than the British. Having brought transport with them, the French waited impatiently for their ally. They, however, being as yet largely without cavalry, had carried with them far fewer horses; it was their unloading that took time.

While the Allies remained at Calamita Bay a Russian attack could not be discounted and alarms were a nightly occurrence. On the night of 16 September Trumpeter Wharin was suddenly awakened:

The outlying picquet commenced firing in the direction of the village of Sak, and were shouting 'Turn Out.' I at once sounded and Trumpeter Kerr of 'G' Battery took it up, notwithstanding the 'All's Well' which was called out before he commenced sounding. It appears that battery had its tents and the Trumpeter had orders to sound at every tent in future when an alarm was given. This he took in a literal sense and continued after the 'All's Well' was called out. The Duke of Cambridge's Marquee was close at hand and was lighted up, there being no sound to denote a false alarm. Colonels Gordon & Cunningham, the Adjutant and Quarter Master Generals of First Division, were making very impolite enquiries for the Trumpeter who started the sounding who was to be tied up to a Gun wheel and flogged. I disagreed with their ideas and told Davy Ford a comrade that I would pay a visit to the next battery, where I stayed for some time to allow things to cool down. After a while I ventured near to find out how things stood and was informed by my friend that our Sergeant Major was in arrest, as he had, like a brave soldier as he subsequently proved to be, taken the blame for ordering me to sound. My back was therefore saved the lash.

The Allied army finally began its advance south towards Sevastopol on 19 September, following the post road from Eupatoria. Even in light marching order men were soon falling out of the ranks. Cholera had not gone away. Others were tormented by a raging thirst. At the end of the war, John Fisher, a non-commissioned officer of the 1st Battalion Rifle Brigade, recalled the experience:

Water was scarce, some had little, others had none, and what there was [was] salty. We had not gone far under that boiling hot sun that shone above us with increasing intensity, when like sheep after a long journey may be seen our brave men dropping down here and there gasping for thirst. I espied a group of men round a mud hole. I made towards it but they had emptied it of all its water except a quart or so of liquid clay. This I dived after and swallowed some portion of it and set off to overtake the column, which I did by certain maneuvers as not to be seen by the officer. Some of the men was punished or threatened for leaving the ranks that same day although choking with thirst.

Storekeeper John Rowe of the Commissariat was another tempted to

steal away from the column of march, as he recollected eighteen years
later.

> At one part of the journey, seeing several persons together about a
> furlong from the road I went to see what they were doing. There
> was a well there. The water was 6 or 8 feet down. There was a stone
> work round the top, but no convenience for getting water. A bucket
> and rope would have been worth a jew's eye. They were trying what
> could be done with canteens and straps. It took three straps buckled
> together to reach the water, but fancy trying to fill a light canteen
> with its little mouth. A stone was attached to sink it under. One
> officer was there on horseback and had to fight and beg for a little
> to wash the beast's mouth. The horse seemed eager enough to go
> head for[e]most down the well to help himself. After a bit I had to
> struggle hard to get my strap back and then started off to overtake
> my party that had gone on out of sight.

Relief came in the early afternoon when, after a march of eight miles,
the army reached the River Bulganak. The troops broke ranks to slake
their thirst. Ahead of the army, on the slopes and dips in the ground
south of the river, four squadrons of cavalry under Lord Cardigan
conducted a reconnaissance. When some Russian cavalry hove into
view Cardigan wished to charge them, but Lord Lucan, who by now
had joined him, stayed his advance. However, what neither Cardigan
nor Lucan could see, although Lord Raglan, placed on higher ground
to the rear, was able to discern, was a further 6,000 Russian troops of all
arms beyond the Russian cavalry screen. Cardigan's men were in imminent danger. Raglan moved the 2nd and Light Divisions up in support,
and sent General Airey, accompanied by Captain Nolan, to order the
cavalry to retire. Nolan commented:

> At this time Ld L. & Ld C. had an animated controversy as to what
> sh[oul]d be done, Lord C wishing to ascend the height & charge the
> Enemy whilst Lord L wished the Troops to retire. The discussion was
> cut short by an order from Lord Raglan to retire. This was done
> by alternate Squadrons amidst the yells & hootings of the Russian
> horsemen who's skirmishers opened fire on ours, but their fire was
> not returned our men retiring leisurely across the Plain. A fine strap-
> ping Drag[oo]n. riding beside me said, 'It is a thousand pities Sir
> they w[oul]d not let us dash at these miserable fellows & knock them

over. It is too bad to go back before such rabble'. The retrograde
movement brought down the Russian Cavalry & Horse Artillery in
force and these latter opened fire upon our Squadrons.

One of Raglan's staff officers, Captain the Hon. Edward Thomas
Gage of the Royal Artillery, observed the Russians' rather ineffectual fire.

Not having the exactly proper range they only killed 4 horses &
wounded 5 men. Ld R sent me back instantly for the two troops of
H[orse] A[rtillery] & they fired a few rounds by which we find were
killed some 40 men 7 Horses. It lasted about ½ an hour during
which time the H.A. fired 130 rounds. By this you may judge that
there was not much time given to the Rascals to move off.

The Russians withdrew to prepared positions five miles further south
on the line of the River Alma. The British, after their exhausting march
from Calamita Bay, bivouacked for the night on the ridges above the
Bulganak. On resuming their march the following day, they had not
proceeded far when the ground started to fall away towards the valley
of the River Alma. Major-General Codrington, in a letter to his wife,
described the sight.

A few mounted Cossacks here and there were all we saw till we came
in gradual sight of the line of hills which formed the opposite side
of the Alma. Our glasses were all directed to the small but regular
lines and spots which marked something not of nature's formation
on the hillside, but which showed a great number of troops in
position. Here then was to be the fight.

The Russian position was immensely strong, and they had 39,000
troops and 96 guns with which to defend it. At Raglan's request,
Lieutenant-General Sir John Burgoyne used his practised engineer's eye
to describe the ground.

The position taken up by the enemy in rear of the river Alma, crossed
the great road, about 2½ miles from the sea, & is very strong by
nature. The bold & almost precipitous range of heights of from 350
to 400 feet high, that from the sea closely border the left bank of the
river, here ceases, & formed their left and turning thence round a
great amphitheatre or wide valley, terminates at a salient pinnacle
of the same height, from whence the descent, though steep is more

gradual, & consequently more distant from the river ... The front was about two miles in extent.

Across the mouth of this great opening is a lower ridge, at different heights, varying from 60 to 150 feet, parallel to the river & at distance from it of from 600 to 800 yards.

The river itself is generally fordable for troops, but in broken order, as the approaches & immediate banks are rugged, & in some parts steep, the willows along it were cut down to prevent them from affording cover.

In front of the position, on the right bank at about 200 yards from the river is the village of Bourliouk, & near it a timber bridge, partly destroyed by the enemy ...

It will be perceived that the high pinnacle & ridge on the right was the key of the position if attacked in front, & consequently where the greatest preparations had been made for defence; halfway down the height, & across its front was a trench of some hundred yards long, to afford closer cover against an advance up the even steep slope of the hill; – on the right & a little retired, was a powerful covered battery armed with heavy guns which flanked the whole of its right flank.

As Burgoyne identified, for a distance extending over two miles inland, the River Alma was overlooked by rocky cliffs, which were nego-tiable only by a few narrow tracks. These faced the French, who had advanced from Calamita Bay with their right flank against the sea. So confident was the Russian commander, Prince Menshikov, that the posi-tion was impregnable that he posted only a single regiment to hold his left flank. Two and a half miles inland the cliffs terminated at a feature known as the Telegraph Height, upon which the Russians disposed the main strength of their left. Adjacent it to the right, across the 'amphi-theatre' bisected by the post road to Sevastopol, was the 'salient pinnacle' of Kourgane Hill, 'the key of the position'. To protect it the Russians had thrown up a breastwork – not dug a trench – known as the Great Redoubt, behind which they placed twelve heavy guns, supported by field batteries. Further back was the entrenched battery dubbed the Lesser Redoubt, containing eight guns.

Marshal Saint-Arnaud asked Raglan whether he intended to turn the Russian right flank or assault frontally. Aware of the threat posed by the Russians' numerically superior cavalry and unwilling to subject his troops to the additional marching that a flank attack would entail, Raglan opted for a head-on assault. The army continued its advance. Arrayed in columns of battalions at a half-distance of companies, it bore down on the Russian position. Lieutenant-General Sir George De Lacy Evans' 2nd Division was on the right, with the French between it and the sea. The Light Division, under Sir George Brown, was alongside Sir George De Lacy Evans on the left. In the second line, behind the 2nd Division, was Major-General Sir Richard England's 3rd Division; and with it, in immediate support of the Light Division, was the Duke of Cambridge and the 1st Division. Major-General Sir George Cathcart's 4th Division was in reserve; Lucan and the cavalry protected the army's open flank.

Among Brigadier-General George Buller's 2nd Brigade of the Light Division was the 19th (The 1st Yorkshire North Riding) Regiment, of which Thomas Longmore was assistant surgeon. He recollected:

> Some little time before the troops deployed into line I, as surgeon of the 19th, was riding in my place at the rear of the regiment on the left flank and Colonel Shirley was immediately behind me in command of the 88th [Regiment (Connaught Rangers)] which was marching close up to the 19th. Already a few bullets from the Russian skirmishers were reaching us when one struck the spade of a pioneer who was close by my side with such a loud ping that involuntarily I turned towards the man. At the moment I did so a bullet whistled by close to my left ear, &, from our respective positions I felt sure it must have wounded Colonel Shirley behind me – the more so as I distinctly heard the bullet strike. I turned round quickly & saw the Colonel was safe, & moreover he made a movement & some remark which showed me it was his holster which had been struck.

Lieutenant-Colonel Arthur Lawrence, in command of the 2nd Battalion Rifle Brigade, was further in advance with the skirmishing line. The Russians noted the contrast that his green-jacketed soldiers made to the red coats worn by the rest of the British infantry. Lawrence informed his wife that:

> It was about 1 o'clock when the action commenced. The enemy's first fire I took for a flight of starlings passing over my head!! There was a Village immediately before hid by the nature of the slope which I believe we were all ignorant of & which we had not noticed till we saw a cloud of smoke & fire rising before it. An admirable ruse

of the enemy & a great hindrance to the Light Division & particularly the Light Brigade which I was covering [i.e. Codrington's 1st]. A shower of grape shot saluted our ears from the distant batteries while they plied us sharply out of the Village with musketry but the smoke so effectually concealed them that my Riflemen could hardly fire a shot. Finding we could do nothing but unwilling to retire we inclined to our left & got some shelter from a dip in the ground.

To the right, the firing of the village of Bourliouk caused General De Lacy Evans some consternation and he had to adjust his formation accordingly, as his subsequent battle report confessed:

At the commencement of the action, I was obliged to detach Br[igadier] Gen[era]l. Adams with two Reg[imen]ts & Cap[tai]n. Turner's Battery round the right of the Village, set on fire by the Enemy, as it was impossible to penetrate this village, it being in continuous blaze for 300 yards in front of my centre.

An officer in De Lacy Evans' division, Lieutenant Mark Walker of the 30th (The Cambridgeshire) Regiment, witnessed the resulting confusion:

The Guns opened on us [and] we discovered that the Enemy had set the village on fire which seemed to put our rulers out as we took Ground to the right then to the left, all the time under fire . . . After some fruitless moving we were ordered to lie down until the smoke cleared away. As we lay we had a few men wounded; most of the shot passed over us.

As of that moment, Raglan's attention was drawn principally to the Light Division, which he could see was taking ground too much to its right and crowding the 2nd Division. The right-hand regiment of Codrington's brigade, the 7th Royal Fusiliers, threatened to collide with the 95th Regiment, on the 2nd Division's left. He had already sent one message asking Sir George Brown to realign his division, and now he rode forward to give the order himself. Unable to find Brown, he spoke to Codrington:

Lord Raglan passed by the Brigade shortly before the attack saying orders had been given to Brown to move us to his left, [and] asked me if I had received them. 'No'; 'You are to do so, but I won't interfere with the execution of it as it is gone to him to carry out'.

He then went off to the right. We were shortly after moved in files of fours to the left.

Immediately to the front, Colonel Lawrence was moving forward.

I ordered our skirmishers to fix their bayonets & rush up to two or three houses before us, but the enemy had abandoned that part & we found a temporary shelter from the storm behind the smoking walls & were shortly afterwards joined by Gen[era]l Buller & one of the Reg[imen]ts of our Division, the 19th. Here there was a delay of some twenty minutes.

Sir George Brown now put in an appearance and gave Codrington his instructions.

I was then ordered to advance till I found troops on my front and then order the men to lie down. This brought us within a short distance of the rifles and (I believe) the 19th Reg[imen]t who were occupying the walls of the houses of the village opposite the river and banks. These were lined with riflemen apparently by the fire which came against us. The most striking thing to me in this part, in the midst of the rush of shot and shell, and also from return fire from our artillery, was the silent way in which death did its work. No sight or sound betrayed the cause; a man dropped, rolled over, or fell out of ranks to the dust. One knew the little bullet had found its destination, but it seemed to happen in mysterious silence – they disappeared, were left, as we went past them.

Lord Raglan had been prepared to wait for the French attack on his right to develop before committing his own troops to a frontal assault. If Saint-Arnaud's army was to threaten encirclement of the Russian position, as Raglan understood was his counterpart's intention, the French required a head start. Although by now General Bosquet's division had scaled the cliffs and reached the plateau, alarming Prince Menshikov to the extent that he immediately rushed seven battalions of infantry, four batteries of artillery and four squadrons of cavalry to meet the threat, the latest message to reach Raglan – conveyed by an excitable aide-de-camp – was that the French, despairing of giving their troops on the heights adequate support, were contemplating withdrawal. In response, Raglan ordered the British attack to begin immediately. It was 3 p.m.

De Lacy Evans led forward the 2nd Division, circumventing the obstacle posed by a blazing Bourliouk.

On detaching Genl. Adams to the right, I took at the same time, the 30th 55th [(The Westmoreland)] 95th & 47th [(The Lancashire)] Regiments; & a battery under Lt. Col. Fitzmayer, to the left of the conflagration, to endeavour to force, by that direction, the passage of the river & the Bridge. But this was not easily done, for we were completely under the Enemy. Every man & every movement exposed to their view, & to a continuous shower of every species of Cannon Shot or Missile, directed with too accurate aim, such perhaps as few of the most experienced soldiers have witnessed.

Lieutenant Walker of the 30th felt the full effect of the cannonade directed at the 2nd Division by the massed Russian guns which raked the Sevastopol road.

After a little we advanced to the village where the fire was tremendous. The men were ordered to shelter behind a wall. We the mounted officers sat on our horses in rear and every moment I expected one of us would be knocked over but through the mercy of God we escaped. The Artillery came up behind us and opened [fire]; they suffered considerably. Here my shako was knocked off. We were then ordered to move across a small green field. In going over it many were knocked over including Pakenham severely wounded and Luxmore killed. His servant fell with him. We then got into a vineyard on the banks of the river which was deep and the sides steep. We were ordered to shelter for a little. Many were wounded, many killed and some were drowned here. Dixon was wounded and my horse hit severely.

All this time, the 2nd and Light Divisions, ranged on too narrow a frontage, were increasingly getting in each other's way. Realizing that the same was likely to happen with the 1st and 3rd Divisions in the second line, Raglan withdrew the 3rd Division. Sir George Brown, in his battle report, explained why he had not taken remedial action.

I have already stated that a Battalion of my right Brigade extended beyond or overlapped the left Regiment of the 2nd Division. It was from this circumstance that the 7th & 95th Regiments became mixed up together in moving to the front & during the attack, for my 1st

Brigade itself completely filled the whole mouth of the Gorge or
Valley through which the [Sevastopol] road runs; to have attempted
the attack in Column with such a concentrated fire of artillery bearing
upon it would have been to expose the troops to utter annihilation.
I therefore determined to effect the passage in line & to trust to the
spirit & individual courage of the troops not only for getting over
but for subsequently carrying the Batteries & attacking the Troops
by which they were defended.

Codrington's brigade was still lying down short of the river when
Brown rode up to him once again.

After some little time spent in this way, Sir G Brown came and said
to me something about not understanding why a halt took place,
which was by his orders as English troops were in our front under
the walls &c of the vineyard and village. He then said, 'Codrington,
you will advance your Brigade in line, and not stop till you have
crossed the water.'

Colonel Lawrence and the 2nd Rifle Brigade sprang into action.

At length the Division was ordered to advance. They broke down
part of the wall & Topsey passed actively over & our Riflemen rushed
into the vineyards which concealed us from the river but Major
Norcott with the 4 Companies [of Lawrence's battalion] on the left
had attacked them with great ability & in conjunction with the 2nd
Division on our right had made the place too hot for their skirmishers & we passed through without opposition followed by the
19th Regt. It was just the ground for us the broken nature did us no
harm, but it was ruin to the compact line of the Regt behind us. The
River was far less difficult than expected, a fresh shower of bullets
saluted [us] as we passed through but there was nothing to stop
us, & we gained the other side & found a partial shelter under the
slope of a bank from the top of which about 700 yards [away]
the enemy were pouring down their artillery & musketry & half way
up the hill they had an entrenchment above which were posted their
Riflemen. In this position we were not entirely out of fire for there
was another Battery on the Enemy's left. I believe I ought to have
remained here & made long shot with my Riflemen up the hill, but
the distance was great.

As Lawrence indicated, the progress made by the 2nd Division on the right had facilitated his own advance. In his subsequent report, De Lacy Evans did not disguise the difficulties that the regiments acting under his immediate control had encountered in moving forward.

This part of the Division . . . could only advance gradually, taking occasional advantage of such little cover as the locality afforded. And then, as the shower of balls occasionally abated, making a further advance. At this time, we were greatly aided by the powerful fire of two additional batteries – one of the L[igh]t. Divn. under Capn. Anderson – the other of the 1st Divn. under Lt. Col. Dacres & Capns. Paynter and Woodhouse, who kindly offered us their assistance. We had thus at a critical moment, 18 guns, which replied to the Enemy with vigour, while our Infantry were working their way, with heavy loss, to the Ford & Bridge . . . The fire on the Bridge & causeway was very severe. Major Hume of the 95th seized a Color & led over the Bridge. Lt. Col. Daubeny's conduct (55th) has also been mentioned to me favorably. I passed the ford myself, between the 1st Brigade and the 47th Regt.

Lieutenant Walker of the 30th, for one, had a lucky escape.

After a little we got across with some difficulty and formed line and advanced steadily. During this advance a sharp fire opened on us and I was struck by a spent grape shot in the chest which nearly knocked me over but thank God I was not disabled.

Further upstream Major George Valentine Mundy of the 33rd (The Duke of Wellington's) Regiment, part of Codrington's brigade, was under a similar fire.

I had (commanding the left wing) to pass through a Vineyard with my men, & so dreadful & so *perfect* was the range of their guns, fully ¾ of a mile off, that the men fell about me like leaves, & my charger w[oul]d not move (without being shoved on behind) to cross the river with balls splashing all about. 3 of our Officers were shot carrying the Colours. My poor subaltern (Worthington) lost a leg. Montagu I passed shot through the brain, but alive three hours afterwards.

General Codrington, although unhappy at the disorder evident in his brigade, pressed on:

The line on the left was of course broke by the houses, and rough ground, that in the vineyard better but of course not in Hyde Park order; we got irregularly to the banks, somewhere steep, somewhere shelving, easily forded at one or two places, deep at others, and as the river twisted about, of course the steady line formation was entirely broke by that and by severe fire. I knew that the steep rocky bank of the opposite side w[oul]d protect us from artillery, and when we arrived there I caused them to remain and tried to re-establish the formation of 2 deep in line under its shelter. But a biting, enfilading fire from our right of musquetry . . . was telling much upon the ranks where I was; the men shrunk from it, and got under shelter, in crowds of 20 or so in a heap, of the projecting places: the line could not be formed steadily under such fire. In the mean time a column of infantry – or at all events skirmishers came down towards the top of the bed of the river on their side – and down the more flat part which led to the ford, and on which all their fire and efforts seemed to tend. The men of our side – regiments mixed up, (even those from the 19th Regt. our next brigade were with us) began to fire from these crowds up the bank against the skirmishers. I soon saw that this would never do – if the line could not really form, it was necessary at all events to advance with the bayonet against whatever was on the rising ground in front of us. So I desired all to fix bayonets and get up the bank to advance and attack. I got up with them on my little Arab, there was not much of a line formed – but a straggling uncertain one – in heaps here and there, as well as I could see – but we gradually advanced.

Lawrence's riflemen had once again to steel themselves to act as the Light Division's advance guard.

The other wing had passed on & the 19th Regt were preparing to advance, so I ascended the Bank closely followed by young Ross & called upon the men to follow. A good many did so but I don't much wonder at their requiring a little encouragement for we had passed quickly over the vineyards & they were a little done & directly we put our heads above the banks we came within a very heavy fire with nothing to shelter us till we reached the summit of the position but the redoubt.

The Great Redoubt, situated halfway up Kourgane Hill, loomed menacingly. Codrington did his best to get his men to form line and resume their advance.

The fire [was] heavy from somewhere against us, and the officers scarcely able to get the men away from those heaps into the proper formation: I was in front a good deal for [the sake of] example and to lead them on; and in this manner we gradually got up to the entrenchment, whilst a heavy column of [Russian] infantry was coming down on the Brigade in column... The men remaining somewhat in these heaps, I rode forward towards the battery taking off my cap and leading them as well as I could to the front. Many brave fellows came on, but not much in regularity.

Meanwhile, in order to witness the advance of his troops, Lord Raglan had found himself an unparalleled vantage point. After issuing the order to attack, he had quite incredibly taken himself and his staff across the Alma, ridden ahead of the 2nd Division and occupied an elevated position amidst the Russian skirmishing line. The position was a highly exposed one, as Captain Gage admitted:

It seems marvellous how one escaped. Shells burst close to me, round shot passed to the right, left, & over me. Minié & musket [balls] whistled by my ears, horses & riders of Ld R's Staff (where I was) fell dead & wounded by my side, & yet I am quite safe & can hardly realize what I have gone thro'.

Raglan ordered up General Adams' brigade of the 2nd Division. He also received the support of two 9pdr cannon, which suddenly appeared and brought a telling fire to bear on the Russian infantry formations and artillery batteries within range. Their shot had a quite disproportionate effect on the Russians, who pulled back the batteries which had been so galling the 2nd Division. Raglan was also able to observe the progress of the Light Division's attack on Kourgane Hill, three-quarters of a mile away; but this he was powerless to influence.

Climbing upwards in a thick skirmishing line, Codrington's troops were by now closing on the Great Redoubt. Before it could come to hand-to-hand fighting, the Russians, anxious to save their twelve cannon

from capture, began to pull back. Colonel Lawrence was as close to the
Great Redoubt as anyone when they fired their parting shot.

I got up unseen there till within a few yards of the redoubt when a
shower of grape shot rolled over poor Topsey who fell as for dead.
I struggled to get from under her, leaving one boot, [and] got under
cover of the redoubt, which the enemy had evacuated. Ross's horse
also fell, & he joined me, & we & our men were soon mixed up
under this low bank with our own men & a much greater number
of the 19th Regt.

General Codrington endeavoured to get his men to consolidate their
newly won position and push on.

When I got to the entrenchment, I got off my horse and showed
them they were to fire over it and were in shelter. I was close to a
large howitzer in position, not served then, and saw a large gun
attempted to be moved away with a driver and a pair of dark horses;
I made several men fire and rode my horse over the breastwork (no
difficulty) into the entrenchment from which by this time most of
the people had retired. At the same time I saw an officer on my right
go to the horses, and the driver run away: the officer, Capn. Bell of
23d, led the horses and gun round the flank of the breastwork behind
our men. On getting into this entrenchment where there were many
dead bodies and wounded of Russians, a battery opened upon us
from the front and at the same time the front of the [Russian]
infantry column was firing – it was a large company front, and the
men ran out also from the sides of the column – many were killed
on both sides – but the battery and their fire together were too strong
for us, and the men, not turning or running, yet gradually got into
the little masses, bearing back towards the entrenchment, from which
we had scarcely advanced indeed; as soon as we were borne back
over, up came those helmets again – brass helmets of skirmishers –
the Russian 31st Regt. – and at us again. I got people up again
to the entrenchment; I know I got into it twice on horseback – and
through all this firing – and mercifully not touched though as I say
I saw those brass helmets at us hard over the breastwork as we retired.

Nor was Colonel Lawrence without concern:

On our right were the 7th, 23rd & 33rd Regts, but instead of the beautiful lines 2 deep which these Regts ought to have been formed in, the broken ground, & the river they had passed through had brought them into knots & masses, & although the Officers had attempted to restore their formation, the fire was so heavy that it was but partially effected, & I was in a perfect crowd who were firing indiscriminately over the bank at a column of Russians who were coming down the hill.

Codrington desperately needed support. The two remaining regiments of the Light Division, the 77th (The East Middlesex) Regiment and the 88th Regiment (Connaught Rangers), part of Buller's 2nd Brigade, were being timidly handled and had halted at the foot of the Kourgane Hill 400 yards away to the left. What of the 1st Division behind? 'I had told the Coldstream when I was named to the [Light] Brigade,' wrote Codrington, 'that I should now and then have to look behind me – and sure enough, here it was – I did anxiously look behind me'. But the Guards were a long way back.

> I felt if not supported that we were gradually giving way from the position we had won. I therefore sent Campbell to beg the Guards to come up fast to support – the fact is they were too far [away] – otherwise the position must be lost.

That the Guards were so far to the rear was the fault of the Duke of Cambridge, who had earlier halted the 1st Division on the far side of the river. Uncertain of his orders, he had dithered, and it was only when General Airey rode up to repeat Lord Raglan's instruction that the 1st Division was to support the Light Division that Cambridge resumed his advance. This lasted only as long as it took for his men to come under renewed fire, when the division again halted. It was rumoured by A. H. Layard, watching the battle from offshore aboard Rear-Admiral Sir Edmund Lyons's flagship HMS *Agamemnon*, that at one point Cambridge had proposed withdrawal; Codrington too understood that 'some idea crossed him of retiring, when others said to him – No, Sir, rather see all the Guards die in their ranks.'

Fortunately, in addition to the three regiments of Foot Guards – the Grenadier Guards, the Coldstream Guards and the Scots Fusilier Guards – the 1st Division also comprised the Highland Brigade under Major-General Sir Colin Campbell. Unlike the Duke of Cambridge, whose first battle this was, Campbell was an experienced soldier of sixty-one who had served in the Peninsula, China and India. He was not the type of man to tolerate indecision under fire, as the testimony of his brigade major, Lieutenant-Colonel Anthony Sterling, demonstrates:

> When C[ampbell] got into the bed of the river, and could see along the left bank, he perceived that the Light Division was in a mess. 'By God!' said he, 'those regiments are not moving like English soldiers.' He immediately ordered the 42nd [(The Royal Highland) Regiment] to form as rapidly as possible on the south, or enemy's bank, and sent orders to the 93rd and 79th [the 79th Regiment (Cameron Highlanders)] to do the same as soon as they could. The Duke at this time came up to him, and C energetically recommended an immediate advance, saying that 'he foresaw a disaster unless we did so.' The 42nd was pushed on at once by him, marching over the 77th Regiment, which was lying down. The soldiers of this regiment called out to us, 'You are madmen, and will be all killed!'

While the Highland Brigade advanced on the British left, the Guards Brigade, an imposing sight in their top-heavy bearskins, stepped forward into the river. Once across, the Guards regiments halted to dress their lines; the Scots Fusilier Guards, according to Cambridge, 'alone were hurried forward rather too rapidly for formation'. This regiment found itself in the lead. Among its ranks was Lieutenant the Hon. Hugh Annesley:

> We got across the river, which was not much over the ankle, as fast as possible, in some disorder, from the difficulty of the ground; on the other side a high, sloping bank protected us and here we formed line again. There were several scattered parties of Line regiments here and a few Rifles. When formed in line, as well as the ground would allow, we got the order to advance; directly our heads were clear of the hill, the bullets came through us, and before us, at about 200 yards distance, we saw the Russian redoubt, a long low bank of earth it seemed. A Russian battalion was in square close behind it on the left, firing on the 23rd Regiment which was in a sort of irregular mass just in my front, and endeavouring to keep up a feeble desultory fire on the enemy.

At the Great Redoubt, the moment of crisis had arrived. A massive

Russian column was approaching. Colonel Lawrence described what happened next.

At this juncture a most untoward mistake occurred. Some Officer believed the advancing column to be French, & called upon a Bugler to [sound] cease firing, & shortly after the mass began to give way, whose existence appeared to depend upon either clinging to the bank or advancing boldly towards the enemy ... In vain Col[onel] Saunders of the 19th exhorted his men both by voice & manner not to retire. In vain Genl Codrington rode up to the left where I was, & made every effort under this murderous fire to check the rolling mass. But it slowly retired, and our voices were unheeded in the din. To my dying day I shall never forget following them down the hill. The men were falling fast, and I thought that all was lost.

From lower down the slope, Hugh Annesley witnessed the same events.

Suddenly the Russians seemed to line the redoubt again and their fire grew hotter and then the 23rd came down in one mass, right on top of our line. Their disorder was caused by the Colonel and both Majors and nearly all the officers being killed and no one knowing who to look to for orders. However it was, they swept half my company clean away and a great many of the next one to it, all this under a terrific fire from the redoubt.

General Codrington had seen the Guards approaching.

They came on in line – but in [the] meantime the fire had forced our men in groups to bear back, which they did in somewhat of a crowd, and thus came on the left wing of the [Scots] Fusilier Guards – bearing that Wing back with them and thus 2 or 3 companies of the Fusilier Guards were mixed with our men even as far as under the steep bank which gave shelter to our side of the river. Here I had to call upon 'you men with the bearskins, to the front, to the front, to your own regiment which is engaged – you ought not to be here with us now.'

With the remaining half of his company, Annesley continued to ascend the slope.

I kept on shouting, 'Forward, Guards', and we had got within 30 or

40 yards of the intrenchment, when a musket ball hit me full in the mouth, and I thought it was all over with me; just then our Adjutant rode up with his revolver in his hand and gave us the order to retire; I turned round and ran as fast as I could down the hill to the river, the balls were coming through us now even hotter than ever, and I felt sure that I should never get away without being struck again; halfway down I stumbled and fell, then I was quite certain I was hit again, but I got up all right, and went on. I lost my sword and bearskin here; at last I reached the river bank and got under shelter, there were crowds of soldiers here.

Annesley was in a bad way: a bullet had entered his left cheek and come out at the right corner of his mouth, carrying away twenty-three of his teeth and part of his tongue. Around him was the debris of his regiment, and that of most of the Light Division as well. Viewing this part of the battlefield, an observer might have assumed that the day was lost; it was therefore fortunate that the fighting was going better on the 2nd Division's front to the right. With the aid of massed artillery support the British had begun to gain ground, as De Lacy Evans reported:

At that time, the Enemy still showing some stoutness of resistance, Lt. Genl. Sir R. England sent to me to know if I wished any assistance from his Div[isio]n. I asked for his Artillery, which he promptly brought up himself, to the front. Col. Dacres & Dupuis also brought up rapidly theirs, as did Lt. Col. Fitzmayer. Above 20 guns were thus available, & opened their fire immediately to the right & left, against the retiring & confused masses of the Enemy, which produced a very destructive effect.

Not all the guns in this twenty-gun battery were equally well served. Trumpeter Wharin was with one of Colonel Dacres' field guns and tells a cautionary tale of the consequences of placing one's headgear on the lip of a cannon's mouth and allowing it to be rammed down the barrel. In his memoirs he had previously explained how a red night cap, part of the sea kit issued his unit when first sailing from Britain, had been retained by some as an alternative forage cap:

Jim Smith, leading driver of No 1 gun had his Chaco shot away and substituted the red night cap. On crossing the river by a ford and getting on to a rising ground forming a sort of plateau on our left where two or three batteries were crowded together doing great execution on some masses of Russians there was seen a Corporal Tom Mitchell in a desperate state of excitement because his gun would not go off. The gunners were hurrying up on foot after the guns. After pricking the vent several times, a burster used in filling the shrapnel shell was brought which after pouring some loose powder in the vent had the desired effect, for with the discharge out came a red night cap fizzing which dropped a short distance from the muzzle of the gun. Poor Jim in the excitement only then remembered that the cap was his, but dare not let on, for Tom was talking of ramming the owner in the gun in the same way.

Meanwhile, away to the left at the foot of Kourgane Hill, General Codrington was attempting to rally his brigade.

I got together as soon as I could, many men of my three Regts and some of the next brigade with whom I formed a sort of scratch Batt[alio]n having one colour of the 23d and one of the 7th: I got together about 300 men, and advanced them and halted them, occasionally getting them into 2 deep – and showing a front towards a gap between the Guards line (probably caused by the Fusiliers). Having so got them together I sent to the front to know if they wanted that gap filled up; I did not like to march up and interfere with them otherwise. They sent to say it was not necessary – so I remained getting as many together in their Regts as I could.

The self-belief of the Guards had not been dented by the disaster to have befallen one of their regiments, and the Grenadiers and Cold-streams, tramping steadily forward, were quite prepared to repair the damage themselves. When an unidentified officer rode up from nowhere and, before disappearing, told the Grenadier Guards that they were to retire, one company commander, Lieutenant-Colonel the Hon. Henry Percy, was incredulous. 'Retire! What the devil can they mean?' Percy, a relative of the Duke of Northumberland, was a truculent man: his subaltern, Captain William Cameron, described him as 'eligible for any appointment but [he] makes himself so generally disagreeable that his relations, though the highest in the land are not much inclined to do anything for him'. And it was now, precisely in this spirit, that Percy mischievously concluded 'They must mean "dress back" '; whereupon the left wing of the Grenadiers pivoted on their centre and created a flank with which to face a Russian column that was attempting to exploit the gap in the British line. It was the right thing to have done. The Minié fire unleashed by the perfectly disciplined ranks of the Grenadiers was devastating. Captain Cameron was exultant:

> I think you will find that we decided the day. We came up to a long line of earthern breastwork, from which all the most deadly fire came just as the line in front was litterally shot to pieces. It was a critical moment; the poor fellows before us were wavering and were glad to open out & let us have our turn. The work was unenclosed and our right being well thrown forward in five minutes we should have swept the whole line from flank to flank.

The punishing volleys of the Grenadiers, combined with the pressure exerted elsewhere on their opponents' line, suddenly began to tell: 'The Russians then saw the day was over & we had merely to pour our fire into immense masses of retiring columns where nearly every shot told.'

Contributing to the Russian decision to retreat was the startling success of the Highland Brigade, which had advanced up Kourgane Hill further to the left. As soon as he crossed the Alma, Sir Colin Campbell's intention had been to outflank the Great Redoubt. 'The effect of this manoeuvre', wrote Lieutenant-Colonel Sterling,

> was foretold by C before the 42nd moved, showing the advantage of a General with a true tactical eye. We made a deliberate parade movement of regiments in echelon, right in front, up the highest hill. I was sent to the left to form the 79th in column, to be safe from the Russian Cavalry. The 79th afterwards deployed. The 42nd was the right regiment, and was the first formed. I never got back from the left in time to go up the hill with it. The men never looked back, and took no notice of the wounded. They ascended in perfect silence, and without firing a shot. On crowning the hill, we found a large body of Russians, who vainly tried to stand before us. Our manoeuvre was perfectly decisive as we got on the flank of the Russians in the centre battery, into which we looked from the top of the hill, and I saw the Guards rush in as the Russians abandoned it. The Guards were not moved on quite so soon as our Brigade, and suffered far more, poor fellows . . . C had his horse shot under him, and we all had plenty bullets flying about us. I saw a Russian skirmisher, a great big fellow, come within forty yards, and take

a deliberate shot at Colonel S.* He made two or three men on the right of the 42nd turn to their right and fire at him; but the fellows missed him. Our Brigade lost one officer, and about one hundred men, which was very fortunate, as some regiments lost as many as ten officers.

The three battalions of the Highland Brigade, deployed in line to maximize their firepower, had overcome no fewer than twelve Russian infantry battalions drawn up in column.

With the Highlanders dominating Kourgane Hill to the left, the Guards in possession of the Great Redoubt, the 2nd Division pushing up the Sevastopol Road in the centre and the French, by now securely possessed of the cliff tops above the Alma, looking down from Telegraph Height, the battle was won. It was 4.30 p.m. John Fisher, in reserve with Cathcart's 4th Division, heard the sound of cheering:

The final charge comes and all is hushed to a comparative calm. The day is ours. The Russians fled leaving the heights in our possession. Now another shout resounds from Hill to hill. Victory, Victory. Hip! hip! hip! hurrah! which is taken up by one and all, the living, even the poor wounded soldier found his feeble voice as well, and many a dying man's spirit though too faint for mortal ears shouts Victory.

Now was the time to commit the cavalry against the fleeing enemy. According to an exasperated Captain Louis Nolan, it had already required the sending of one aide-de-camp to get Lord Lucan across the River Alma.

On the left the Cavalry was at last found 40 min:ts from the time it had been sent for. The Q[uarter] M[aster] G[enera]l [Airey] desired them at once to advance when the officer in Com[man]d said 'Oh the Russians are still in great force over the brow of the hill'. The QMG[enera]l rode & looked over the brow. I was with him & not one Russian soldier was in sight!!

Although Raglan, unsure of the intentions of the French, and anxious that his small cavalry force might over-reach itself, subsequently sent orders prohibiting a pursuit, it was towards Lucan that Nolan directed his resentment.

---

* Identity uncertain.

An enterprising leader w[oul]d have crossed, gained the heights in the right rear of the Enemy & when the Inf[an]t[r]y had driven them from their Redoubts the Cav[a]l[r]y sh[oul]d have prevented them from carrying off their Guns . . . but no attempt was made to cross the River early in the day by our Cav[alr]y. The best proof of their culpable inactivity is that neither horse or man was wounded even by a stray shot during the day. To the gallant spirit of which our Cavalry is composed their having no share in so glorious a victory was most galling. The deeds of our horsemen in India of late years prove what they can do when led by men like Cureton, White, Smyth, Lockwood & Pearson and many others whose glorious feats of arms were all performed with but a handful of horsemen compared to what we had in the field of Alma, therefore the plea of want of numbers is inadmissible. At no time sh[oul]d Cavalry stand fast to count the opposing squadrons. Frederick the Great gave an order that any Cav[a]l[r]y Officer meeting the Enemy & not charging sh[oul]d be cashiered! When a routed army was in full retreat what excuse can any one find for those horsemen who did not do their duty & whose chief replied to an order to advance that the Russians were very numerous!!

Two thousand British and a good proportion of the 5,700 Russian casualties were strewn over the hillside above the Alma, and the preoccupation of the wounded among them was naturally rather different from that currently felt by Captain Nolan, for they faced an uncertain future. The British had left their Ambulance Corps and its wagons along with the rest of their transport in Bulgaria. Simply in order to move the men that he was treating, the surgeon of the 46th (The South Devonshire) Regiment, present with an advance party of his unit, had to entreat the Commissariat to lend him one of the locally acquired arabas or carts being used to carry spare saddlery. After some debate, Storekeeper John Rowe obliged by emptying the cart and transporting the wounded. He then returned to recover his cargo.

I was not long in making my way back for saddlery &c. but met with an incident. I came upon a party of three or four, two of which were wounded officers. An officer of the 30th with a damaged arm was partly supporting an officer of the Scots Fusilier Guards. This officer was leaning forward and dripping blood from his mouth. He could not speak but wrote with a pencil in a small book that he was the Honble — Annesley and that a ball was lodged in his throat after having knocked away some of his teeth and part of his tongue. He wanted to know in what part of the field (if I may so call it) the Fusilier Doctor had his stand and whether I could convey him there. I could not tell him anything of the Doctor though several Doctors' standings appeared still scattered about on the near side of the river. I also told him I had no discretion as to the use of the mule cart but to fulfil the duty I was there upon.

Annesley was left to find his own way to treatment. John Rowe's dedication to duty, even so, went unappreciated.

Getting in with the saddlery, I was met by one of the higher officers of Transport, who questioned [me] roughly about where I had been &c. I explained. He condemned the lending of the mules.

Not surprisingly, the Russian wounded had to wait longer than the British for attention. Colonel George Bell of the 1st Regiment saw them:

I visited the field at dusk with water; most of the English had been carried away. I gave it to the poor Russians & how thankful they were, carrying my hand to their lips, & then pressing it to their foreheads.

Reports were made that some Russians had fired upon those who tried to help them. A few British soldiers complained to General Codrington: 'They wanted me to have a man killed who was brought to me as having fired in this manner, but I told them I would kill no man as prisoner in such cold blood.'

Although he was an old Peninsular veteran, and in measure inured to the sight, the lack of treatment available to the British wounded could still cause Colonel Bell concern:

24 hours had passed over & many of our own men had not their wounds dressed, no accommodation was prepared for the wounded, not one of the ambulance carriages ever left Varna after all the noise, trouble & expense about that celebrated corps. Officers were having their limbs amputated behind walls in the open air. Sailors landed from the fleet brought up their hammocks and with a pole passed through them carried the wounded miles to the coast. Jack is

a good natured fellow with all his drollery & although he returned
to his ship careful of his charge his head was covered with a Russian
helmet, a sword by his side or a good firelock slung over his back.
Few returned without some trophy! The heaps of dead collected was
incredible. They were laid close together in rows of 50 & 100ds. A
long trench was dug at their feet & they were packed close together,
until the trumpet sounds. The Redcoats were put into pits by themselves, as well as the French.

Some of the dead were afforded special treatment. During the battle
Private John Pine and the 1st Battalion Rifle Brigade had remained in
reserve. Not so his brother Tom, whose unit, the 2nd Battalion Rifle
Brigade, had been in the forefront of the attack on the Great Redoubt.
John Pine had sad news for their father.

I must now inform you my beloved father that my poor beloved
brother Tom is no more in this world. It was my painful duty to
throw the cold cold earth over his blessed remains yesterday and I
sincerely hope and trust he is in a better world where wars and all
such things are unknown. I hardly know how to write my beloved
father my tears will not allow me. Poor dear Tom fell in action whilst
storming the Russian entrenchment, a short distance from Sebastopol.
Poor fellow he was the bravest man in the field on that dreadful day.
He was the leading man of the leading regiment and would had he
have lived been immortalised for his gallant and daring conduct on
that awful day. He fell at the very muzzle of one of the enemy's guns
on the battery at the very moment of victory. He was shot right
through the breast on the right side of the body and fell to rise no
more. This was on the afternoon of the 20th of September and the
next morning we found him among the slain and buried the poor
dear fellow as well as laid in our power. Although my dear father
there was no minister to bury him still there was as sincere a prayer
offered up by me and his comrades as if there had been one, and we
are taught to understand that God despiseth not the prayer of the
humble.

Another unit heavily involved in the fighting was the 95th Regiment,
part of the 2nd Division. Lieutenant George Carmichael wrote home
that:

We lost 5 officers killed and 12 wounded, and 240 men killed &

wounded out of 650 men . . . Our brigade was in the centre, & were exposed to a terrific fire from the enemies batteries. My escape was wonderful, a ball passed through my trousers close to my heel without touching me.

As Carmichael intimated, many of his fellow officers of the 95th had not been so fortunate. Among them was the regimental adjutant, Captain James Kingsley, who had so welcomed the outbreak of war just a few months before. Major J. S. Adamson of the 38th Regiment wrote to his sister:

I convey to you the sad tidings of the death of dear James Kingsley who fell while behaving in the noble & gallant manner in Cheering on his Regiment. Such is the account I have heard from the soldiers of his Regt, one of whom spoke for many that I saw . . . I have two or three locks of hair cut off in my presence from his poor head which I hope to have an opportunity of sending for his poor Father & Mother.

The Battle of the Alma was a qualified victory. It was widely felt that more could have been achieved. True, Raglan had checked his own cavalry's pursuit of the Russians; but he had been ready to send forward the 3rd Division, which had not seen action, in order to exploit victory in conjunction with the French. Saint-Arnaud informed him however that his infantry had to return to collect their knapsacks, of which they had divested themselves at the start of the battle.

In a private letter written to the Duke of Newcastle four days later, Raglan expressed disappointment with his ally:

The French Army accomplished what they undertook perfectly well but Lord Burghersh will tell you *confidentially* what is the general conviction in the English Army that if Marshal St Arnaud had kept moving on after he had turned the Enemy's left, the results of the victory would have been immediate, large bodies of prisoners would have fallen into our hands and the dispersion of the Russian Troops would have been extensive.

I have reason to believe that the same feeling is prevalent amongst the Officers of the French Army. This may be gathered too by the pains that have been taken to impress upon me the belief that they have lost in killed and wounded at least 1600 men. This I hold to be impossible and I have just got a note from Sir Edmund Lyons in which he says 'Mr Layard heard yesterday from the director of the French Ambulance that their killed amount to about 60 and their wounded, to 500, but our Officers who were on the beach do not think that so many men were embarked.' This in my opinion is conclusive.

Captain Gage, writing home the day after the battle, found the attitude of the French towards the two guns captured by the British a subject for equal disbelief:

Ld R[aglan] sent this morn to have the guns *we* had taken brought down & parked close to his Tent, can you conceive the *French* having the bad taste to send two limbers with 6 Horses to take them away? Ld R could not help laughing at their impudence ... They give us the brunt of the Action, & when we take the Battery (they being two miles to the right & not mixed up with us at all) have the face to attempt to take the Guns *we* captured away from us the next day.

But not everyone with the British army was ready to exonerate Raglan from blame for an incomplete victory. Austen Henry Layard, who had been with the army since August, gave his fellow Member of Parliament H. A. Bruce the benefit of his opinion:

Lord Raglan & his staff behaved with great courage & were under the heaviest fire, but something more was wanted. Unfortunately the Russians were allowed to retreat unmolested. Had the defeat been followed up, which it might have been done as two divisions, the 3d & 4th, had not been in action & were quite fresh, the Russian army would have been completely destroyed & during the panic we might have taken Sevastopol. Not a deserter or prisoner since taken who does not confirm this. A perfect panic appears to have seized the Russians. Menshikoff as we know from an intercepted dispatch, believed he would hold the position for weeks – the boasted power of the Russians had been exposed in three hours! At such a moment as this the man of genius – a Wellington or Napier – was wanting. We lost two days in looking after the wounded & dead ... Our mismanagement was astounding.

The sentiments of A. H. Layard concerning Lord Raglan – and those expressed by Captain Nolan with regard to Lord Lucan – were to prove of unexpected significance in the months ahead.

3

SEVASTOPOL

After two days spent clearing the battlefield of the wounded, on 23 September the Allied army marched from the Alma to the Kacha, the next river to the south. Although appealing, the countryside here hid dangers, as Nigel Kingscote commented: 'This Valley is most luxuriant, grapes, peaches, pears, apples, and every sort of fruit in profusion; our troops regularly surfeiting in them. Very conducive to Cholera I am afraid.'

The next day's advance took the Allies to the River Belbek. Reconnaissance showed that the mouth of the river was commanded by Russian gun emplacements. Behind them lay the Star Fort, an outlying defence work of the Severnaya, the district to the north of Sevastopol's harbour. Marshal Saint-Arnaud, on whose front stood the fortifications, did not wish to attack them. While Raglan, given the situation in which the Allies now found themselves, would have preferred the more direct course of attacking Sevastopol from the north, he was prepared, as an alternative, to resurrect a previous proposal of his, that Sevastopol be attacked from the south. This would enable the Allies to use nearby harbours in the Chersonese Peninsula for resupply; Sevastopol could also be approached from a direction that was relatively undefended. Sir John Burgoyne, daunted by the apparent strength of the fortifications protecting the Severnaya, agreed. 'I have always been disposed to consider that Sebastopol should be attacked on the south side', Raglan wrote to the Duke of Newcastle, 'and Sir J Burgoyne tended strongly to the same opinion and prepared a memorandum on the subject which I caused him to confer with the French Engineers upon.'

Saint-Arnaud endorsed the proposal to attack Sevastopol from the south. It was to be his last act of command. Two days later, in the terminal stages of cancer, he handed control of the French army to General François Canrobert. Within a further three days he was dead.

According to Captain William Radcliffe of the 20th (The East

Devonshire) Regiment, the night before what came to be known as the 'Flank March' around Sevastopol was a disturbed one.

> About 1 A.M. we had to stand to our arms, as some musquet shots were heard in front. After waiting an hour we were told to lie down again and the Camp were all gently asleep when we were suddenly roused once more by the sound of a horse at full gallop & the cry 'Look out, look out'. We expected nothing less than an attack from Cossacks and were ready in less than a minute, but it turned out to be nothing more than a runaway horse and the voice was calling out for the sleepers to get out of the way. Of course there was no more rest that night, for it was nearly day break & the men set to work to relight their fires, which are always put out on the slightest alarm, that there may be nothing to direct the fire of the enemy.

Lieutenant Mark Walker of the 30th Regiment felt equally out of sorts.

> We passed last night a wretched time of it. Twice we were obliged to stand to our arms for nothing. Hundreds were dying round of cholera. Poor Johnston who carried the colors all day took ill at 5 o'clock pm and was buried at 7 am. He lay beside me and his groans were dreadful.

At 8.30 a.m. on Monday 25 September the army, with Lord Lucan and the Cavalry Division in the van, commenced its flank march round Sevastopol. Until it could reach the clearing at Mackenzie Farm – named after an eighteenth-century Scottish settler – the going through heavily wooded terrain proved difficult. Captain Nolan, well forward with Lord Raglan and the Headquarters Staff, described the conditions:

> The roads were very intricate and we were quite in the dark as to what might be in front or on either side of us for the Country is covered here with a thick forest of young oak almost impassable except on foot and singly. We had no Guides we could trust and the Q[uarter] M[aster] Gen[era]l led the van with a compass in his hand to which he frequently referred to see that the head of the Column was moving in the proper direction.
>
> About ½ past 11 o'clock I was ordered to push ahead with a few of the Escort & keep a look out in front & at the same time a report

from the Cavalry reconnaissance came in to the effect that the roads
were clear in front & to the opening of the Valley and that the English
Cavalry [under Lucan] were then halted on a road a little to our
right & running parallel to our line of march.

Having rejoined Raglan's Headquarters party, what happened next
took Nolan by surprise:

About 10 minutes before twelve I came to the clearing at Mackenzie
and on debouching from the wood saw the Enemy in some force.
They had one Regt. of Cav[al]ry one batt[alio]n Inf[an]t[r]y some
guns and a large convoy of carriages & carts under their charge. We
were jammed up in a narrow road & had they with common courage
placed their guns in position to command the outlet & supported
them with Cav[al]ry & Inf[an]t[r]y it w[oul]d have cost many many
lives to push through in sufficient force to drive them off. They
however appeared only anxious to make their escape & I requested
permission to take out the Escort & Capt Maude's Troop [of horse
artillery] and at once attack them before they recovered from their
surprise. This was however not allowed for fear of exposing our
artillery without sufficient support but the Cav[al]ry on our right
were immediately sent for with orders to move to the front with the
utmost speed.

Lord Lucan, who should have been ahead of Lord Raglan's advance
party, was now behind it, having taken a wrong turning. Lieutenant-
Colonel Arthur Lawrence and the 2nd Battalion Rifle Brigade
accompanied the Cavalry Division:

Our Staff soon lost the way & we found ourselves threading our way
amidst the bushes & in no pleasant position for the Cavalry who
w[oul]d have been entirely dependent on us for protection had
we been attacked while Ld Lucan was consulting his map & his
Compass & almost despairing of finding a road. We heard the rumble
of Cavalry & shortly afterwards an ADC rode up to hasten us to the
front. Our guns were unsupported as they had been moving in a
road parallel to us & Ld Raglan & his Staff had with them stumbled
upon the tail of a Russian Division.

By one of those accidents of war, just as the Allies were marching
around Sevastopol, Prince Menshikov – with the intention of both threat-

ening his opponent's communications and receiving reinforcements – was leading the Russian field army out of the town. Nolan, with the rest of Raglan's staff, was now confronted by Menshikov's rearguard:

> The Enemy now showing a disposition to advance Capn Chetwood led his Troop* out of the road into the open and the guns of Capn Maude's Troop H[orse] A[rtillery] were unlimbered & placed ready to sweep the road. Capn Chetwood's Escort retired again to our guns the Russian Cavalry having advanced upon them at a Trot and now the English Reg[i]m[en]ts of horse came up & were led out into the open by Ld Lucan. Maude's Troop with the foremost at once galloped forw[ar]d, unlimbered & fired down the road by which the Russian guns were retreating with the Convoy & the Inf[an]t[r]y, the Regt Cavalry in the confusion making its escape to the right by another road where they were not pressed, why I do not know!

Once again, Nolan's implication was that Lucan missed his opportunity. He continued:

> The Russians now retreating in confusion were followed full speed by our H[orse] A[rtillery] under the gallant Capn Maude who's fiery zeal led him on to pursue the Enemy with his guns & waggons whilst the more cool & collected horsemen of England followed the Artillery until brought to the front by degrees by Genl Airey who mounted on a fleet tho[rough]bred horse was at one moment leading the pursuit, at the other bringing up Cav[al]ry or himself driving the Russian soldiers for shelter into the wood.
>
> A great part of the 8th Hussars had now headed the guns when in a small clearing the Russian battalion formed in confusion to receive us. The Hussars sword in hand were galloping at them when an order to halt was given by Ld L[ucan] who shouted for the Guns to come to the front whilst the Inf[an]t[r]y gave us a volley in our faces. Maude's Troop rode up unlimbered & with a volley from the guns scattered the battalion who threw themselves into the wood both sides & then fired upon their pursuers.
>
> The guns limbered up, the pursuit continued whilst a Troop of the Scots Greys [2nd (Royal North British) Regiment of Dragoons]

---

* Captain George Chetwode and a troop of the 8th Hussars provided Raglan's escort.

dismounted & went into the wood to keep the Russian Inf[an]t[r]y going which they did without much hustling.

At about one mile from Mackenzie we came to the crest of the Plateau we were on and looked down upon a most animated scene. The guns which had escaped were tearing along the road below with some of the few carriages of the Convoy which had managed to escape. Disbanded Inf[an]t[r]y were running down the sides of the steep descent without arms without helmets whilst a few shots from our guns hastened them along towards a Russian Army formed in dense Columns below. Two Reg[i]m[en]ts of our Cavalry moved along the road down the Valley for some distance picking up carts & horses of which we captured in all 22, amongst them Genl Gortschak-offs travelling carriage with two fine black horses.

Colonel Lawrence and the Rifle Brigade had by now caught up.

We shared some of the baggage & the amusement of the soldiers decking themselves in the finery of some of the Russian Officers. We also took ammunition, horses & carriages & I have since been riding on different pieballed Russian Troopers.

The flank march continued that day from Mackenzie Farm as far as the River Chernaya and the Tractir Bridge. The army bivouacked that night on the heights above the Chernaya. Captain Nolan, while full of praise for the strategic boldness of the march, was also aware of the risks that had been run:

Our Army drawn out to a narrow thread by the difficulties & impedi-ments in the road could have been cut through at any time by a bold & resolute Enemy. Our men were exhausted, our artillery horses actually dropping down & dying on the roadside; our communi-cations were joined on by the thread of the Column only; we had but one line of march. The road on our right lay under the Guns of the Enemy, the country on our left was occupied in force, thus this movement hazardous at all times was 'neck or nothing' in our case, and a little dash a little daring on the part of our foes might have brought our expedition to an earlier & less glorious close than we now proudly anticipate.

During the course of the march the army had once again been pushed to the limits of its endurance. There had been little to drink throughout.

'I assure you some men were offered a guinea for half a pint of water & would not give it', wrote Private Henry Smith of the 21st Regiment (Royal North British Fusiliers). Colonel Bell related how:

> Hundreds of men lay down exhausted by the road side & resigned a life they would no longer convey to the next camp. No help, no carriage to carry them on. They threw away their blankets, & lightened their kitts, to keep up, night came with its very heavy dews and cholera took possession when the Blanket was gone. A peculiar sort of cholera, a total prostration at once without any pain, gradually sinking in a few hours.

The next morning the army resumed its march. Its goal, the small virtually land-locked harbour of Balaklava, overlooked by an old Genoese Fort, was within reach. The fleet, it was anticipated, would be waiting. Colonel Lawrence wrote to his wife:

> We were within 4 miles of the port of Balaclava where we were to re-establish our communications with the sea but to approach it we had to pass thro' a narrow gorge with high bare mountains on either side. I was ordered to send the Regt in advance. Norcott went to the right, Bradford to the left & I kept the centre with four Companies. We met with no opposition till we got some way when a fire of musketry made us cautious but the enemy appeared to be only a few men of the hills & having driven them in a Staff Officer reported to Ld Raglan that the coast was clear. He rode to the front & was entering the gorge when I took the liberty of remonstrating, telling him that I still saw some of the enemy up the heights & begged that I might at least send one of my companies in advance. He assented to this but when he turned a corner of the road & approached the Fort we were saluted with a couple of shells which marvellously did not hurt a creature of the 200 people on the road. The Staff turned quietly back. We went skirmishing up the hills & more troops were sent to crown the heights on both sides. From the heights in front I witnessed this mimic fight for the fort was so small it hardly deserved the name. Our artillery battered it on one side & the 'Agamemnon' fired into it from the sea, while the Rifles fired into it from the heights on both sides. After one or two ineffectual attempts to attract notice, a white flag on a bayonet was observed & the Rifles rushed in to take possession of this petty post & 4 small mortars which

might however have cost us our C[ommander] in Chief. We entered
the small town [and] found our ships waiting for us.

When the first of the French arrived in Balaklava the next day, the
British were already in full occupation. The harbour was too small to
cater for both armies and General Canrobert offered Lord Raglan the
choice of its exclusive use or, if he relinquished it to the French,
the opportunity to shift the British base to the harbours of Kazach and
Kamiesch, further round the coast but nearer Sevastopol. Advised by
Admiral Sir Edmund Lyons, Raglan opted to retain Balaklava. This was
a mistake. Although no one could foresee that the campaign would not
be concluded within a matter of weeks, by choosing Balaklava the British
had placed themselves on the combined army's open flank. With Prince
Menshikov's field army in close proximity, this was the post of danger.
Moreover, the distance from Balaklava to the British encampment outside
Sevastopol was six miles. To maintain a line of communication of even
this length, the ramshackle British transport system would need to
improve significantly. The French, mounting the Left Attack against
Sevastopol, were in contrast within three miles of their base. But as
Raglan informed the Duke of Newcastle:

> I consented to take the right attack, desiring to retain Balaklava,
> and I was not ignorant when I did so that the labouring oar would
> rest with us. But the French maintained, and with some reason, that
> as they were obliged to land their material in a bay within Cape
> Kersonesus [Chersonese], it was absolutely necessary that their
> Troops should be placed in immediate connection with the place
> of debarkation.

On 27 September, the day that the French arrived in Balaklava,
Sevastopol was reconnoitred for the first time. Raglan was for an
immediate assault, but Sir John Burgoyne advised against. He wished
first to subdue the enemy's fire with siege guns. Sir George Cathcart, in
command of the 4th Division, strongly disagreed. 'Land the siege-trains!
But, my dear Lord Raglan, what the devil is there to knock down?' he
expostulated. He wrote to Raglan explaining that his troops had taken
post on what became known as 'Cathcart's Hill'.

> If you & Sir John Burgoyne would pay me a visit you can see every
> thing in the way of defences, which is not much. They are working

at two or three redoubts but the place is only enclosed by a thing like a loose park wall not in good repair. I am sure I could walk into it with scarcely the loss of a man at night or an hour before day break if all the rest of the force was up between the sea & the hill I am upon. We would leave our packs & run into it even in open day only risking a few shots whilst we passed the redoubts.

The French, however, agreed with Burgoyne, and rather than risk an immediate assault the Allies settled down to landing their siege artillery. This was a lengthy process, as Captain Gage, who was detailed to super-intend the disembarkation, discovered: 'I had no idea what it was to land 80 heavy Guns with their materials out of Ships, & the quantity of Horses & fatigue Men it requires is surprising.' The delay, moreover, gave the army an opportunity to contemplate its discomfort. Its officers felt particularly aggrieved, as Lieutenant-Colonel Anthony Sterling admitted:

As to us, the common decencies, not to say comforts, of life are denied, and many of the officers grumble openly. They have no transport, and have to march loaded with heavy cloaks, besides provisions, and till yesterday had no tents. Now an officer's duty begins when the march is over; for he has then to look after his men, and he cannot do it efficiently if he is fagged.

Captain Nathaniel Steevens of the 88th Regiment was in full agree-ment:

We all feel much disgusted when we, officers, see how comfortable the French are in comparison with us; we are obliged to load ourselves like donkeys with provisions, heavy cloaks &c, so that really at the end of a day's march I feel more fit to sleep than attend to the many duties around me; the French have mules provided for them; Sir Geo B[rown] says he pities us much & never saw such a thing in any previous campaign.

For a man in his sixties, like Colonel Bell, it was even worse:

We have been settled in Bivouac up to this 4th of October when tents have been sent up from Balaclava & we are now under cover after 20 days of the damp sod without a change of garment of any kind & 'tis no joke sleeping in one's boots & a big pair of epaulets for

3 weeks! We are still without any baggage & in great need of some change of clothes.

'No army was put to worse shifts than this has been, very trying for the officers too, more so than the men', was Captain Nigel Kingscote's verdict; in fact the other ranks would not receive their tents until 9 October. Disease, meanwhile, did not discriminate. On 7 October, Captain William Cameron wrote to his father:

> I would to God that he might please to spare us from all this grievous sickness. The misery one sees quite hardens the heart. I now am so accustomed to see horrors, that I think nothing of it. Propriety of arrangements for the sick and dying in a civilised land soften the shock to the beholder, but in a camp or bivouac without a tent, as it has been a great part of the time, human sufferings and horrors have no mask and appear in all their nakedness. No one I firmly believe but those who have seen it can realise the horrors of war. The Cholera is still doing its work.

His regiment, the Grenadier Guards, now numbered only 530 of the 1,000 men with which it left England.

Unable to secure French agreement to an immediate assault, Lord Raglan had hoped to push his siege batteries as close as possible to Sevastopol without the time-consuming undertaking of digging approaches. But when, on 7 October, he put this proposal to his divisional commanders 'they were unanimous in opinion, that without cover they could not maintain an advanced position.' The batteries would have to be sited fully three-quarters of a mile from Sevastopol. Sir John Burgoyne was despondent. This was beyond breaching distance. All the British batteries would now be able to do, he claimed, was support the French by bombardment.

The Russians meanwhile, mobilized by Admiral Kornilov, the inspirational Governor of Sevastopol, and instructed by Colonel Todleben, his highly capable chief engineer, were putting the southern fortifications of the town – initially so weak – into an impressive state of defence. Nigel Kingscote, writing home on 8 October, felt uneasy:

> I really know not the opinion of those who are able to judge, how long they think it will take to get into Sebastopol. I don't believe anyone can judge until after we have had 24 hours peppering at

them, but all I know is that the more you look at it the worse it seems, like a big fence out hunting.

A. H. Layard, writing to his parliamentary colleague H. A. Bruce the same day, was more concerned at the mismanagement that he saw about him: 'Lord Raglan is a gallant English gentleman – kind hearted, sincere & honorable – but he wants the energy & vigour of intellect which an expedition of this kind demands.' He continued:

I have been greatly struck at the great superiority of the navy in all that relates to details & management & in energy – enthusiasm – to the army. This may be a good deal owing to the want of a military leader who can inspire troops with confidence and inject into them a part of his own spirit. Both the commissariat & medical arrangements are exceedingly bad. The men are exposed to great unnecessary suffering and the ravages of the cholera have been doubled by the want of common precautions. Up to this day the men have not had their tents and the officers only received them two or three days ago. You would be surprised at the state of things. The fact is there is no master mind to grasp the whole subject, to give orders and to see that they are carried out. I could not put my finger upon one man (with the exception perhaps to *a certain degree* of Sir Colin Campbell) and say 'there is a man to command an expedition'.

Layard's critique encompassed Raglan's personal staff:

There are a number of red waistcoated gentlemen, with their hands in their pockets, cousins & nephews of Lord Raglan, or officers in the Guards, idling about. Men of undoubted gallantry, but without a spark of enthusiasm or energy, all voting the thing a great bore and longing for Pall Mall. At Varna what with this spirit & the terrible ravages of the cholera the army was well nigh demoralised . . . Being at headquarters I have had an admirable opportunity of seeing everything. I wish Sydney Herbert* could have some such experience . . . it is laughable to see how all his grand descriptions of ambulances, comforts for the troops &c are but a pure myth. There is not one cart for conveying the sick or wounded in the whole army! & then the heads of the Commissariat & Transport service – Filder & Christie – the Lord deliver us!

* The Secretary at War.

On the night of 9 October the French broke ground on Mont Rodolph, a thousand yards from Sevastopol's Flagstaff Bastion. By daylight a substantial entrenchment had been constructed. The British followed suit the following two nights, siting batteries on the Green Hill (the Left Attack) and Vorontsov Height (the Right Attack); but partly because of the rocky ground these were further away. Captain Radcliffe of the 20th Regiment described the operation:

The working parties generally number 500 men on each attack. I ought to have said, the whole of the operations are divided into two, viz the left attack & right ditto & these are guarded by an arm'd covering party more than double their number to prevent the enemy making Sortie to destroy the works. This makes the duty very hard for all of us as we are seldom off duty, 12 hours out of 36 but all work most cheerfully, well knowing the sooner we open our Fire the sooner 'twill be over & it is most astonishing what can be done in one night. I came off duty this morning at 4 a.m. after 24 hours guard in the trenches. I'll endeavour to give you a short account of that 24 hours. We marched from Camp (got our tents 3 days ago) before daylight, but did not get to the works soon enough for we were seen from the Batteries, & they showered Shot & Shell at us in such a manner that I thought we must have suffered severely, but as it was we only lost 2 men kill'd & two wounded. Rotheram was among the latter, but only a contusion in the calf of the leg from the bursting of a Shell. He will be all right again soon, but the pain is great & he is put aboard Ship. When we got under the Breastwork that had been thrown up in the night we were pretty well under cover, but were obliged to lie down all the time for this of course was the target for the Enemy's Artillery day & night & the Trench was only half made. However a few men were placed on the look out their heads a few inches above the work, to give notice when they fired, by watching the smoke from their Guns by day & the flash by night & calling out 'Shot' when all in the Trenches lie down & get under cover of the breastwork till it has pass'd & then resume their work. By attending to this we only lost 1 man during the day; he was killed by a round Shot. When it was dusk the working parties were relieved by fresh men & except an occasional shot they left us alone pretty well until between 12 & 1 but then they opened on us very briskly & stopped our workmen for some time. Neither

Officer or men are allowed to go to sleep for a minute, all sit up or lie with their *Arms* within *hands* ready in a moment to repel an attack. It was a *real relief* this morning when we were *relieved* & we moved off before they could see us & in consequence got away without any damage a Shot or 2 only falling in our direction.

Captain Cameron of the Grenadier Guards, displaying an anxiety to satisfy the high standards of his father, wrote home at the same time:

I can thank God give you the welcome news, that I am in a fair way of doing something better than a subaltern's duty. My name has been sent in as a volunteer for engineering work and this time to some purpose as I am now appointed temporarily to do the duty of an engineer during the siege.... I have now only to pray for one of those lucky chances that now & then come in one's way and without which there is little chance of being singled out from the crowd.

He continued:

The placing all our heavy ships guns in position has been most tedious and the rest will be comparatively easy. The ships guns have to be taken all to pieces, as the carriages, having only small rollers, as wheels, cannot be moved along by themselves, whereas the regular siege guns can be wheeled into their places, as they stand. We have just completed a battery of 5 68lb guns of 95 cwt each. All ships guns, which will tell more than any battery ever heard of at a siege before. The ground is dreadfully rocky, so that a great part of the earth for the parapet has to be carried.

He then explained his position in the engineering hierarchy.

There are to be two points of attack each under an engineer officer, who is called director of trenches and has 5 brigades of officers under him, each brigade consisting of two officers. I am in Capt Gordon's brigade. Capt Chapman is the other director.... The general commanding the engineers (Tylden) died of Cholera the day after Alma and a Col. Alexander has succeeded him. A more fussy little crotchetty chap exists not and a difficult matter I can assure you it is to understand his half finished directions.

By Sunday 15 October final preparations were being made for the bombardment of Sevastopol, as Captain Samuel Enderby Gordon of the Royal Artillery wrote:

We have been since the 26th – the day we took Balaklava – landing and putting in position our siege train. It is now nearly completed and Tuesday will see us open a very heavy fire on the Enemy's works. They have been firing incessantly at us with very little damage. We have in position 6 68Pr 95 cwt guns – 2 of them Lancasters – 20 8 Inch guns, 30 24 Pounders & 7 32 Pounders, besides Mortars, 10″ & 8″. The distances are however proportionately great, 1400 yards. The French are within 900 yards with a heavy siege train, but the ground favours them more than us.

The bombardment of 17 October was intended to prepare the way for an assault. The French on Mont Rodolph would engage Sevastopol's Flagstaff Bastion, and the British the Redan, with subsidiary fire being directed at the Malakhov. Captain Gordon assessed the result:

At 6½ AM to day we opened our fire and the French theirs. The roar of some 300 Cannon and smoke created by them was incessant for about an hour and a half. The smoke then began to clear off and the Round Tower [the Malakhov] opposite us struck work being battered about the Top and the guns dismounted, not so the Batt[erie]s underneath it. About 10 a French magazine blew up and 'on dit' killed & wounded 100 men. They continued firing slowly and about 12 another of their Magazines blew up and destroyed their Batt[erie]s so much that they ceased firing for the day and are I believe going to make new ones tonight. About 3 we blew up a large Magazine in the Redan, a strong work filled with Art[iller]y and it fired but little after that. A little while after we blew up another magazine in the Town Batt[erie]s, but it still kept some 6 guns going . . .

I cannot tell what the End of this affair will be. I suppose they will have to assault, as to this Art[iller]y fire as much as we are superior to the Russians they are superior to the French, so we shall not gain much by that.

The cooperation of the combined fleet was also secured to stand in and attack Sevastopol's sea forts. This was as much as could be done, for the Russians had sunk blockships in the harbour mouth. From the outset the attack was compromised by a belated French insistence that the Allied fleet begin its cannonade late in the morning, and their announcement they would anchor a mile offshore. Only a portion of the British navy could get within 800 yards of Fort Constantine. Henry Ridley James was an officer of the merchant navy on board the *Colombo*, a Peninsular and Oriental Company steamship taken up from trade to act as a transport. He described the events of the day in his journal:

Got under weigh at 3.30 A.M. and ran down to the Fleet. At 7 anchored with the Fleet. We sent on board different transports to borrow what sails we could as the Captain had volunteered the ship (without the consent of his officers) to tow a line of battle ship into action & the sails were wanted to protect the engine room . . . The Captain called all the men aft & asked if they would all go with him & that whoever was wounded would receive the same that any one in the Navy would if of their rank. All hands said that they would go. After the men had gone forward he called the officers aft & asked who would go. The 1st [Officer] said that he would not go & made the objection that he did not consider the ship safe to stand fire being iron. The 2 & 3rd the same but they said that they would go & offer their services on board Men of War so it was not funk on their part. Pearce, Duncan & myself were the only ones that would go. The Capt[ain] said that those who did not wish to go were at liberty to leave the ship as soon as we had got under weigh, but after all our preparations for action we were told that our services were not wanted as the Admiral did not consider our ship a safe one, but were told to cruise off & if we observed a signal hoisted by any of the Men of War we were to go in & tow her off. The fleet went up to the Harbour of Sevastopol & we cruised about at the dist[ance] off land of 4 to 2½ miles. The sight was one of the most awful in the way of guns. Several of the liners kept up a heavy cannonade & it could be compared to the rolling of a huge drum. The brass guns with their sharp report & the peculiar sound of one ship's that went 'tong-tong' something like a flat bell. We could see showers of shot striking the water at the foot of the forts & flying up in heaps at the walls. The Russians kept up a very good fire. The 'Agamemnon' ran close in till she had only 1 or 2 inches of spare ground under her bottom. During part of the time most of the vessels were hid from sight by the smoke. Several shot passed over us between our fore & main mast. A shell burst 6 or 8 yds in the water from me & several

others not very far off. Several shells passed close astern. There was
a heap of stones at the foot of Fort Constantine after 3 hours firing.
About 5 the ships came out [and] returned to their old anchorage.
Forts along the coast blazing away at us. I hear that the Albion has
40 killed & wounded. The Brittania 4 wounded. Retribution loss of
main mast.

The navy had suffered severely in a futile attempt to silence Fort
Constantine. Two ships were so badly damaged that they had to return
to Constantinople to refit. The outcome on land, in contrast, was mixed.
After the second explosion on Mont Rodolph, the French ceased fire
altogether and did not resume until two days later. The British meanwhile, firing at a greater range though with heavier ordnance, had caused
such damage to the Redan that the Russians were in imminent expectation of an assault. Admiral Kornilov had been killed in the Malakhov
and 1,100 casualties inflicted. But Lord Raglan would not assault without
the French, whose misfortunes, he considered, were attributable to their
chief engineer, General Bizot, who 'committed an error in concentrating
all his Guns, and thus enabling the Enemy to direct the whole of their
fire upon one spot in the trench line.' Although Raglan was happier with
the contribution of the British artillery, the performance of the new and
much vaunted 68pdr Lancaster gun, with its elliptically bored rifling,
was questioned.

> The Lancasters are represented by Captain Lushington [of the Royal
> Navy] to be a failure, and to be very wild and ungovernable in their
> flight. I am inclined to think that the mode of loading and firing
> them is not as yet perfectly understood by those who served them
> yesterday.

Although no assault took place on 17 October, there had still been a
role for the infantry, as Captain William Cameron explained in writing
home.

> I had nothing to do in the engineering line today and hearing that
> an Officer was required to volunteer from our Reg[imen]t to take
> command of a party of sharpshooters I offered my services, which
> were accepted and I received my instructions from the Duke of
> Cambridge personally. The object was to advance under the fire
> of our own guns and pick off the enemy's Artillerymen at their guns,

but not to make a fight of it with Infantry as our party was very small. No one knew the ground and all was left to my own discretion. They sent me down to a place where I found no artillery opposed to me, but instead, a long wall across the valley with a large force of Russians behind it and stretching along the heights to the left. I maintained myself, after having driven in a Russian picket, for two or three hours and killed some of the enemy, but finding that a large party was sent round to the heights on the right and that we were consequently between three fires and in danger of being cut off, I retired as nothing was to be effected and the real object of disabling the enemy's artillery was impossible. This was perfectly approved of so all has turned out well. I hope it may do something towards promotion. My brother officers all wished me luck and if successful thought it might be promotion. I hope it may. I am ready for anything to put me in the way of doing credit to myself & family.

The next time Cameron wrote he was nursing an arm broken by a Russian bullet.

I am well out of the sharpshooting business. I think my last letter was written after my first day's expedition in which I showed the utter absurdity of the whole scheme. However the next day I was put in command of the sharpshooters of the whole division and told to proceed down another ravine more direct upon the enemy's works and to see whether from that point we could reach the Enemy's embrasures with our Minié rifles. I was again left entirely to my own discretion, as no one knew anything of the ground. As it was the day before so it was again and before I could get within reach of the enemy's batteries, there stood the Russian skirmishers under a long line of cover in considerable force. My party was small but I knew that if the men would only obey my instructions I could keep the enemy in check for a long time, from behind some large heaps of stone and quarries. I established the main body behind this cover but am sorry to say that I had the greatest difficulty in making a few men move to either flank, to prevent my position being turned, because they were obliged to cross under the enemy's fire. I had to keep continually on the move to place all the men, which was not my business, as intelligent sharpshooters are supposed to know how to take advantage of the ground. The British soldier who is never left to himself and to whom self-reliance is unknown is quite unfitted for a sharpshooter, who may be a hundred yards from his next neighbour. I impressed upon them all the necessity of reserving their fire unless they saw an enemy much exposed, instead of which those who were out of my reach blazed away at anything. The Russians thinking at last that our ammunition must be running short advanced upon us with loud hurrahs and I am ashamed to say that all the fellows in rear of me took to their heels. I saw that we should be decimated if we retired down the ravine with the enemy firing at leisure into our crowded ranks. I drew my sword, ran to the foremost of the fugitives, swore I would cut any man down who did not come on and ordered a charge. Though in great disorder directly the Russians saw us make something of a front and prepare for some sort of a charge they in their turn turned tail and we followed so close that not having time to load, some men had recourse to large stones which they pitched into the quarries and hollows now full of the enemy. It was here at these close quarters that I got shot at the head of my men but had the satisfaction of seeing that the game was now in our hands. On my way back to the camp, I gave directions to a picquet I came across to support if necessary with men and ammunition the officer I left in command of my party. I was lucky enough after going about a mile to get a stretcher and found on arriving at my tent a medical man who soon did all the needful. I, next morning, dictated a letter through the deputy Adjt: Genl. to the Duke of Cambridge shewing the uselessness of sending out such small parties of sharpshooters to pick off the enemy's artillerymen at their guns when you have not the whole ground up to the walls in your possession. I heard next morning that my opinion was favorably listened to and the volunteers ordered to return to their duty.

Over the next few days the Allied bombardment continued with diminishing effect; yet some retained their optimism. Gunner Charles Branton of the 4th Company, 12th Battalion Royal Artillery wrote to his wife on 21 October:

I now lay down on my Belley to write these few lines to you hopeing to find you in good health as it leaves me at present thank God for it. Dear wife i ham sory to hear that my dear son his dead but God knowes best. But i expect that i shall be home in about 2 months and be happy together once more. We have fighting ever day from daylight until sunset and i think that about 4 days more will do it.

1. The Grenadier Guards encamped at Scutari, with Scutari Barracks, later notorious as the Barrack Hospital, on the skyline.

2. The campaign in *Punch* to rid the soldier of the leather stock and to lighten his load gathers momentum.

STRIKING EFFECT OF CHOKING AND OVERLOADING OUR GUARDS AT A LATE REVIEW.

3. Crisis at the Alma.
With the Light Division ahead
wavering, the Brigade of Guards
presses forward.

4. 'You men with the bearskins,
to the front, to the front'.
General Codrington,
under pressure at the Alma.

5. Clearing a path at the Alma: 9pdr cannon of the 3rd Division.

6. The cramped confines of Balaklava Harbour.

7. A Russian shell explodes behind a British breastwork outside Sevastopol.

8. The Green Hill Battery, British Left Attack.

9. Captain Louis Nolan: 'What excuse can anyone find for those horsemen who did not do their duty?'

10. The Charge of the Heavy Brigade.

11. The Charge of the Light Brigade.

12. Officers and men of the 13th Light Dragoons, survivors of the Battle of Balaklava.

13. The Guards in action at Inkerman, painted by Colonel the Hon. George Cadogan.

14. A hero in his own imagination: Sergeant Poolfield Davies saves the colours at Inkerman.

THE GREAT GRENADIER.

...ing represent one of those scenes of daring and deter-
...vith which the story of the campaign in the Crimea

...rgeant Davies of the Grenadier Guards, affords a most
...ery instance of preservation in battle, rendered more
...t by the Herculean frame of the soldier. Both at Alma
...reman he was the first in the fray—towering above his
...onspicuous in every sense of the word—yet returning from
...unscathed. He stands six feet four inches high, present-
...hat prominent target for Russian marksmen, yet while
...flying in every direction and bayonets glistening on every
...aped unhurt.

...devoted band of 500 Grenadiers, in the midst of thou-
...e Russian infantry, and without ammunition, having fired
...charge, yet determined to sell their lives as dearly as
...avies defended his colours with the utmost tenacity, and

literally mowed down the enemy, who made a rush to capture them.
On this occasion, Col. Hamilton, who commanded this legend of
the heroic Grenadier, seeing that there was nothing left for his
men but the bayonet, ordered them to form four deep and charge.
The order was, of course, instantly obeyed, and in a few minutes a
clear gap was visible in the Russian columns, and our gallant men
quickly regained their comrades. Amidst dead and dying, first
among the bayonet, then the bullets of his musket, with his arms
unriveted from close to range of mighty down the enemy, this sergeant, who, according to the letters of an eye-witness, arose like a
giant above the surrounding level of heads, and to men whom would
appear an utter impossibility, appeared at the roll-call after the
terrible engagement without a wound, and with scarcely a single
scratch upon him. To enumerate the enemy killed and put to
...de conduct by the single arm of Davies would appear almost incredible; suffice it to state, following the relation of trustworthy
witnesses, that he performed the greatest prodigy of valour.

In furnishing some details of the battle of Inkerman, Sergeant

Davies says: "Our heroic dreadful. The bridge...
up very much, and the poor third battalion all to...
longer a regiment, but a skeleton, and doing duty...
unfeeling stores, &c. Let any person who was...
London nine months ago, look at us now; and if...
bleed, he has one mass of ailment. We have lost...
five of the brave fellows called in the London pa...
"the flower of the country;" and yet Sebastopol...
Bombarding has been carried on continually; and...
doubt, the army is destined to winter here, for...
our position; that we must hold—at least if w...
take Sebastopol. The barracks at Scutari are...
wounded."

Colour-sergeant Davies has been in the army seve...
entered the Grenadier corps when only fifteen...
at Scutari his gigantic size attracted a great deal o...
the "Great Grenadier" became the theme of...
ration.

15. French Zouaves, eager for a fight.

16. Inkerman: the Sandbag Battery after the battle.

We begin on the 17 of October to take Sebastopool and i expect it will last 9 days for they are getting tired now but hour men is as fresh as ever. Hour lost is not more then about 100 but the Rushians is thousands ... Dear wife we have lost many lives through the Corora they are dieing like rotton sheep but we have plenty to eat and drink. We have two Gills [10 fl oz] of rum a day plenty of salt pork and a pound and a ½ of biskit and i can a shore you that if we had 4 Gills of rum it would be a godsend for it is very hot by day and cold by night so the dew falls like rain and only you Blankett to cover us.

Major George Mundy of the 33rd Regiment, writing to his mother the same day, was less sanguine. He was a convert to Sir George Cathcart's view that Sevastopol should have been stormed at the outset.

We have now been at the Town like 'Blazes' since the 17th & with very little Effect. The Lancaster Guns are a *failure*, & we are bombarding a place like Woolwich, cram full of Cannon, shot &c &c, & beautifully served. I believe we shall take it in time but not with Artillery, the Bayonet I fear will have to do the work. Would that we had been permitted to go strait at the Town, the day after we arrived here, & I feel convinced that we should have been able to force our way right into the Town, with very little assistance as the Enemy were then panic stricken & there were then but very poor fortifications on this side; but now we have been delaying here so long that we have permitted them to erect the most formidable entrenchments which our Guns seem to have but very little effect upon.

... Talking of the Navy, they have turned out very like Lancaster Guns; perfectly useless here. On dit if the other ships had come in as close as the Agamemnon did to Fort Constantine that they c[oul]d have battered it to peices. The French also at present have been of very little use to us. They built their batteries so badly, & made their magazines so slight, that they were both blown to bits, & instead of having about 80 of their Guns to back us up, we have had from 12 to 16, by which we have had the concentrated fire of most of the Enemy's Forts at us.

... The long & short of the Matter is this, we must settle the Town somehow *very* shortly, for winter is fast approaching. The morn[in]gs are very cold, & such hard work as we Officers & men now have, (*one* night in tent out of *three*) in the batteries & throwing up Entrenchments would kill hundreds, if the cold were intense. The men too, are not only getting very much knocked up for want of proper rest, but they are getting depressed in spirits, slovenly, grumbling, & look all eyes & bones . . . The men are so overworked, that they constantly sleep on their posts, & are obliged to be visited every hour. I suppose 40 or 50 men have already been *flogged* for that crime.

Lord Raglan was not unaware of the problems facing the Allies following the initial failure of their bombardment. On 23 October he informed the Duke of Newcastle that the British infantry's other ranks barely exceeded 18,000, and when guards and working parties were deducted there only 8,000 men left to act as a reserve. He had been warned too by Charles Cattley, the erstwhile British Consul at Kerch, that the Crimean winter could be severe.

We have been fortunate in having very fine weather, and Mr Cattley encourages us to hope, that this may last till nearly the middle of next month. Then we must be prepared either for wet or extreme cold, and in neither case could our Troops remain under canvass, even with great and constant fires, and the Country hardly produces wood enough to cook the Men's food.

Sevastopol had to be taken, and taken quickly. But the Russians had other ideas.

4

BALAKLAVA

For nearly two weeks after he marched out of Sevastopol, Prince Menshikov had kept the Russian field army to the north of the town in the vicinity of the River Belbek. Chastened by defeat at the Alma, it took him a considerable time to act on the news that the Allies had marched south of Sevastopol, abandoning in the process the commanding Mackenzie Heights to the north-east. Russian patrols began to press into the valley of the Chernaya. Lord Raglan, to protect the port of Balaklava and his lines of communication to Sevastopol, deployed the 1,500 men of Lord Lucan's Cavalry Division (augmented by the recent arrival of the Heavy Brigade), 1,200 Marines and the 93rd Regiment. These were the troops available when, on 7 October, the Russians crossed the River Chernaya in strength and pushed forward onto the Plain of Balaklava. Captain Nolan confided to his journal the following view of events:

> Saturday the 7th Oc[tobe]r. I was awoke at 6 o'clock am by a report brought by Mr Woomwell 17th Lancers [17th Regiment of (Light) Dragoons (Lancers)] that the Russian Army had forced our Picquets in the Valley & were marching in great force on Balaklava. Rec[eive]d orders to go on & sh[oul]d the attack be pushed home to withdraw the 93rd Highlanders from outside Kadikoi & let them occupy the conical hill in the Gorge.
>
> The Cav[a]l[r]y Div[isio]n to oppose the advance of the Enemy but if driven back by superior force to retire throwing back its right so as to fall back towards our own position.
>
> I found the Cav[a]l[r]y drawn up on the heights facing the Gorge leading to the Bridge on the Tchernaya through which the Russians had advanced & subsequently retired unmolested by our Cavalry though their retreat was hurried by a round from each of Capt Maude's guns of the H[orse] A[rtillery].
>
> The Russians could be seen with the Telescope on the farther side of the River. I asked Ld Lucan had he pushed forward any force to

watch their movements. 'No but look at the disposition of my Troops is it not good.' His troops looked very well but they were a long way from the Enemy. I told him I wished to go for[war]d & see what they were doing when he offered me two Regm[en]ts but I contented myself with one squadron of the 17th Lancers with which I pushed across the near chain of heights & the River & counted 8 Bat[talio]ns Inf[an]t[r]y and five Regm[en]ts of Cavalry. These retired up the Valley towards Mackenzie.

Nolan, to his disgust, discovered what had happened when the Russians made their initial advance:

It appears meanwhile that Lord Lucan advanced with the Lt Cav[alry] Regm[en]ts *to this ridge saw the Russians and gave the word 'threes about'.** The Enemy perceiving Troops on the heights in their front close enough to com[man]d the Gorge through which they came with Artillery began to think they had got into a scrape & made the best of their way back again hurrying their Artillery to the rear followed by masses of Inf[an]t[r]y then the Cav[al]ry & leaving five Squadrons as a rear Guard.

Ld Lucan now came up on the heights with the whole of the English Cav[al]ry & Capt Maude['s] Troop H[orse] A[rtillery] who asked leave to open fire but was not allowed to do so for some time. At last leave being granted he fired a round from each gun which greatly quickened the movements of the Enemy. Capt Maude then wished to push on nearer but was ordered to stand fast. The 6 Pdrs could not range far enough to do harm from the hill. The English Cav[al]ry Div[isio]n was not considered strong enough to attack & drive the 5 Russian Squadrons in disorder onto their other Troops now choked up in the Defile thus the Enemy went off leaving on the field such arms & accoutrements as they had thrown away in haste as a Trophy to the Victors, who calmly sat on their horses & looked at them from above! thus contributing a strong case in favor of the Russian assertion that our Cavalry are very cautious a quality quite unknown to the British Drag[oo]n of former days who's rash & headstrong courage was his only fault.

Nolan did not condemn the passivity of Lord Lucan solely in the

---

* The italicized passage is crossed out in Nolan's original text.

pages of his journal: reports had it that he remonstrated with Lucan at the time. But it was not only Nolan who was disenchanted with the leadership of the Cavalry Division. Writing home on 12 October, Major William Forrest of the 4th Dragoon Guards was more even-handed in his criticism:

> We have no faith in the generalship of my Lord Lucan. We all agree that two greater muffs than Lucan & Cardigan could not be. We call Lucan the cautious ass and Cardigan the dangerous ass. Between the two they got us into two or three very awkward positions at Alma and also on the previous day [the Bulganak] & then began to dispute who commanded the brigade. Cardigan abused the officers of the 11th [11th (or Prince Albert's Own) Hussars] & called them a d—d set of old women. The officers sent Douglas to remonstrate with him, when Cardigan asked him what he meant by speaking to a Major General in that way. In the evening he sent for Douglas and Peel to his tent and said that under the excitement he had made use of some hasty expressions. He is now on board a ship with a touch of diarrhoea and we hope he will remain there.

Nor was the cavalry's opinion of Lord Lucan to improve. 'Some wag in the Division has given our Commander the name of Look-On,' Forrest informed his wife twelve days later.

In response to the increasing threat, Raglan decided to position at Balaklava 4,400 newly arrived Turkish troops. In addition, six redoubts were constructed on the line of a low ridge, known as the Causeway Heights, which ran from east to west and bisected the Balaklava Plain. These the Turks would man. Nigel Kingscote was reassured:

> We have got most of our Cavalry, some Turks and Marines with one Highland Regt. to protect Balaclava, and having thrown up works I hope and think it is quite safe, but fully expect if they are not shocking muffs the Russians will attack it when we begin our fire [on Sevastopol].

Rather less content was the man chosen by Lord Raglan to take command at Balaklava – Sir Colin Campbell. 'We have made lots of redoubts, but C does not like them,' commented his brigade major, Anthony Sterling. The six redoubts were strung over a distance of a mile. For the number of troops available to man it, Balaklava's defensive

perimeter was over-extended. To maintain a successful defence, everything depended upon the British troops before Sevastopol sending
reinforcements in time. But, taxed as they were by their unremitting
labours in the siegeworks, could their prompt appearance be guaranteed?

It did not help that the defenders of Balaklava were subject to
innumerable false alarms, as Lieutenant Edward Seager of the 8th Hussars
complained to a friend:

> The cavalry have been worked very much, as we do all the outpost
> duty, night and day. We cover Balaklava, being encamped in the
> valley leading to the town and we have to find patrols, pickets, and
> vedettes for all the country around our position. We are protecting
> the rear of our position from attack, and what annoys us the most
> is there is scarcely a day passes that it does not sound turn out the
> whole, and away we have to go to look at a few cossacks; perhaps to
> remain there for many hours.

Major William Forrest was equally frustrated by the fruitless alerts.
He wrote to his wife on 24 October:

> The last time the enemy appeared Lord Lucan had the whole division
> out, & had them out 14 hours; had them standing to their horses all
> night or rather gave that order and sent for his own waterproof &
> blankets so I sent for my waterproofs & I allowed our men to cloak.
> It was a very cold night they say it killed poor Willett of the 17th
> Lancers who was taken ill the day following & died in a few hours, &
> it sent lots of men into hospital.

By now the threat to Balaklava was becoming serious. On 13 October
Menshikov had occupied the village of Chorgun in the Chernaya Valley.
Ten days later an army of 25,000 men under General Liprandi assembled
in the vicinity. On the night of 24 October a spy came to British
headquarters and announced that the Russians would attack the following day. Lord Raglan, having sent a thousand men of the 4th Division
down to Balaklava from the siegeworks in response to a false alarm but
three days previously, failed to react. At 5 a.m. on 25 October Liprandi
commenced his attack. Thirty Russian guns bombarded his first objective,
No. 1 Redoubt on Canrobert's Hill. The 500 Turkish defenders put up a
gallant resistance until, at 7.30 a.m., the redoubt was stormed at the
point of the bayonet. Seeing this, the Turkish garrisons of redoubts 2, 3

and 4 ran away. Seven British cannon which had been lent to the Turks were lost.

Lord Lucan had been early in the field with the Cavalry Division and attempted to menace the Russian advance. Major Forrest was present with the 4th Dragoon Guards:

The Russians then brought up their artillery & pounded away at us, who were drawn up down in the Plain. We had one troop of Horse Artillery, Maude's, but they were of no service against the Russian guns, which were very much heavier, . . . poor Maude being the first man wounded. A shell entered his horse, exploded & severely wounded him in the arm.

Sergeant George Cruse of the 1st Dragoons also felt the enemy fire:

The Russian guns began to advance and several round shot fell into [our] ranks, breaking the legs of two Horses and one large ball struck a man named Middleton right in the face, of course killing him instantly. The shot began to fall so thick around us that the Men began to bob their heads which made Lee and I pitch into them for being so foolish, just as if they could avoid a thirty two pound shot by moving their heads one way or another. Just about this time the Turks fled in confusion down the Hill towards us, abandoning the redoubts in a shameful manner. The Russians came up in dense Masses and bringing up their heavy guns with them (besides turning those which the Turks had abandoned) they opened such a fire upon us that we could do nothing but retire which we did about half a mile behind our encampment. Our tents had in the meantime been struck but because of the confusion they could not be packed up and we had the pleasure of galloping over all our little property.

Lord Raglan had been roused from his headquarters at the first alarm and, from his vantage point on the Sapoune Heights, at the western end of the Balaklava Plain, witnessed the fall of the redoubts. Seeing the seriousness of the Russian attack, he ordered to the scene the 1st and 4th Divisions from before Sevastopol. The Duke of Cambridge complied dutifully, but Sir George Cathcart's response – his men had only just returned from a night in the trenches – was grudging and the subsequent approach of the 4th Division painfully slow. The British infantry would not arrive on the battlefield until 10.30 a.m. and this gave Liprandi his window of opportunity. A decisive move against Balaklava could yet sweep aside its defenders. Raglan, in preparation for bringing on a general engagement, had withdrawn the Cavalry Division from the position taken up by Lucan in front of Balaklava. This left on the ground only the 93rd Regiment, who occupied a hillock in front of the village of Kadikoi, and two battalions of Turks. The way to Balaklava was apparently clear. Major Forrest, having fallen back with the British cavalry, saw the enemy make its move:

> Upon our retiring, the Russians advanced their Cavalry. They came on in great strength & with great boldness, & one body charged our 93rd the only English Regt. we had on the ground. 'Bedad, they must take them for Turks' said one of our men.

Lieutenant-Colonel Anthony Sterling was with Sir Colin Campbell, who to escape the effects of Russian artillery fire had temporarily withdrawn the 93rd to dead ground. 'C told the 93rd they must die there; and he looked as if he meant it,' Sterling wrote. He then went on:

> As soon as the Cavalry began to charge, C advanced his men to the crest again, and opened fire. The Turks ran away to the rear, into the village of Balaklava, crying, 'Ship, ship!' However, the Commandant, an old officer of the Royals (Lieutenant Colonel Daveney), put a sentry to stop the vagabonds. One of my native servants (all trembling) went off with two of my horses, and was not found for hours afterwards.
>
> The little 93rd [only six companies were present] stood fast, and fired away. The Cavalry could not bear the fire, and swept off to their left, trying to get round our right flank, and cut in on the Turks. But C. wheeled up the Grenadier Company to its right, and peppered them again, and sent them back with a flea in their ears.

The journalist William Howard Russell likened the 93rd Regiment on this occasion to a 'thin red streak tipped with a line of steel', a description that was later altered to the more familiar 'thin red line'.

The main body of the Russian cavalry, meanwhile, began to move across the Causeway Heights from the North Valley to the South Valley. Simultaneously, in response to an order from Raglan to go to the support of the 93rd Regiment, eight squadrons of the Heavy Brigade were moving across the Russian cavalry's front. Seeing the Russian lance tips rising above the crest of the Causeway Heights, General Scarlett's aide-de-camp pointed out to him the imminent danger and the British cavalry wheeled left. In their first line were 300 troopers – two squadrons of the 2nd Royal North British Regiment of Dragoons and one squadron of the 6th (Inniskilling) Dragoons: facing them was a massive column of up to 3,000 Russian horsemen. The enemy had the advantage of the slope but did not use it. Instead, the Russians halted and extended their flanks, hoping to envelop their opponents. Scarlett led the British Heavies into the midst of the enemy. Although the charge lacked impetus, the 2nd Dragoons (the Scots Greys) in particular having to pick their way through the ropes and tents of the Light Brigade camp, the British were soon hacking their way through the Russian column. Nigel Kingscote, with Lord Raglan on the Sapoune Heights, was an enthusiastic spectator. The Scots Greys, so distinctive in their bearskin caps, caught his eye:

> This charge was out and out the most exciting thing I ever saw or shall see again. Being on high ground and close by one could see the fellows coming to hand to hand blows beautifully, and our fellows did not spare them. We had to charge up hill and had not room to get our men into a swing or we should have shaken them still more. The Greys did their work well, so they all did, but the Greys looked beautiful.

Major William Forrest, in support with the 4th Dragoon Guards, was more critical in his appraisal. He noted how the Greys, having fought their way into the column, eventually began to fight their way back, and mistook this for a retrograde movement.

> Another body of cavalry came down towards us, the Heavy Brigade & was charged by the Greys, & I think the Inniskillens [who] were in the first line. The Russians met them well & outflanking them, wrapped round both flanks, & took them in front, flank & rear. Our front line upon this retreated, at least we saw the greatest part of the men come back, upon which we the 4th charged the Russians in flank, some other Regt. immediately afterwards charged them in front.

The 4th Dragoon Guards, in common with the other squadrons advancing in support, were able to catch those Russians attempting to envelop the British first line at a disadvantage, slicing into their flanks and rear. Even so, in the combat's confined spaces there was not much room for swordsmanship. As Forrest admitted, it was simply a question of laying about with one's blade.

> My own attention was occupied by the hussar who cut at my head, but the brass pot stood well, & my head is only slightly bruised. I cut again at him, but do not believe that I hurt him more than he hurt me. I received a blow on the shoulder at the same time, which was given by some other man, but the edge must have been very badly delivered for it has only cut my coat & slightly bruised my shoulder.

It was immediately after this that Forrest became aware the enemy had fallen back.

> The Russians stood a few minutes, & then retired precipitately but reformed in good order on the top of a hill; but on getting one shot from our Horse Artillery away they went. Lord Raglan, who by this time had arrived on the heights in our rear, sent an Aide de Camp with this message 'Well done the Heavy Brigade,' but for my part I think the Heavies might have done much better. The Greys charged at a trot, & our pace was but very little better, but we had very bad ground to advance over, first thro' a vineyard, & over two fences, brush, & ditch then thro' the Camp of the 17th & we were scarcely formed when we attacked, & had but very little good ground to charge over, still we did not go in at so good a pace as we might have done. Once in we did better, but the confusion was worse than I had expected. The men of all regiments were mixed, & we were a long time reforming. If we have to do it again I hope we shall do it better. I do not know what the loss of the Brigade was, but we had only one man killed, & 5 wounded & I did not see more than 2 or 3 English on the ground. We had one horse killed & 3 wounded. There were about 20 Russians on the ground or perhaps rather more; they were Hussars & well mounted, fought in great coats, having their jackets in their valises.

The Heavy Brigade had scored a significant success but it was far from decisive. The Light Brigade, all this time, had stood inactive only 500 yards away. Lord Cardigan, displaying a lack of imagination that bordered on the obstinate, had chosen to interpret the last set of orders which he received from Lucan as meaning he was not to move from his current position on any account. Nor had the Heavy Brigade been able to inflict many casualties. Just as the bigger horses and longer reach of the British cavalrymen had afforded them a certain immunity, so too had the Russians' greatcoats, which were discovered to have the texture and consistency of India rubber. Few sword thrusts could penetrate them. Colonel George Bell, walking the terrain in the wake of the action, found so few fatalities that he was able to describe the wounds suffered by them on an individual basis.

> Now look over the ground, that part in our hands, & see what is here. That Russian Dragoon shews how far they advanced, nearly up to the Tents. He lies quiet on his back, with a sabre cut almost through his head, and his long beard is matted in crimson gore. He sleeps soundly. That man is more hideous to look upon, a sabre point let out his life blood under the Bridle Arm & he is smashed too about the face with the broad sword of England. Here's another lying on his back in a bath of his own blood, both hands clenched tight in the agony of his departing spirit. This man's Bridle Arm is cut in two and hangs by his grey coat sleeve, a home thrust through the abdomen finished his career. There lies a fair haired younger man in blue Hussar uniform, his sky blue chako lies beside, uncrushed, it fell off in the charge. He tried his skill in fruitless combat against one of our *Heavies* whose greater power of Arm first gashed him about the head and then let out his life below the left arm. See what blood the frame contains, clotted all about his corps[e] and [which] deeply dyes the cold grey sod on which he rests. I need not go any further. Only one red coat lay here.

The shaken Russians had withdrawn their cavalry from the South Valley. They had also retreated from Redoubt No. 4 on the Causeway Heights. Raglan wished to exploit his advantage but the infantry he had called for from before Sevastopol were not yet in position. He decided to use the cavalry again. Lucan was sent the following order: 'Cavalry to advance & take advantage of any opportunity to recover heights. They will be supported by Infantry, which have been ordered. Advance on two fronts. R Airey'. The order was not well drafted by General Airey, who wrote and signed it. It meant to convey the information that the infantry – the 1st Division in the South Valley and the 4th Division along the Causeway Heights – would advance on two fronts in support of the cavalry. But even with its incomplete sentences, this much could perhaps have been inferred. Lucan, however, took it to mean that he was to await the support of the infantry before advancing, and of these he could see no sign. Three-quarters of an hour passed. Then it was noticed by Lord Raglan's staff, standing 600 feet above the Plain of Balaklava on the Sapoune Heights, that the Russians were removing the British guns from the captured redoubts. It was imperative to prevent this happening. Raglan dictated to Airey another order for Lord Lucan, renewing the injunction that he advance. General Airey's aide-de-camp, Captain Nolan, was chosen to carry the order to the plain below. As he rode off Raglan called after him: 'Tell Lord Lucan the cavalry is to attack immediately.' Here was Nolan's opportunity. At last he possessed the authority to make Lucan act. No longer would the cavalry remain idle under his hand. He found Lucan standing between the Light and Heavy Brigades on the lower slopes of the Causeway Heights. In a letter addressed to Lord Raglan the following month, Lucan described what happened next:

> The Cavalry was formed to support an intended movement of the infantry, when Captain Nolan, the aide de camp of the Quarter-master-General, came up to me at speed, and placed in my hands this written instruction:–
>
> 'Lord Raglan wishes the cavalry to advance rapidly to the front, follow the enemy & try to prevent the enemy carrying away the guns. Troop Horse Artillery may accompany. French cavalry is on your left. Immediate. R Airey'
>
> After reading this order I hesitated, and urged the uselessness of such an attack, and the dangers attending it; the aide de camp, in a most authoritative tone, stated that they were Lord Raglan's orders that the cavalry should attack immediately. I asked him where? and what to do? as neither enemy nor guns were within sight. He replied in a most disrespectful but significant manner, pointing to the further end of the valley, 'There, my lord, is your enemy; there are your guns.'

Nolan's gesture, rather than pointing towards the Causeway Heights, indicated a battery of twelve Russian cannon over a mile distant, behind which had regrouped their defeated cavalry. On either side of the North Valley, on the Causeway Heights to the south and the Fediukine Heights to the north, the Russians had further batteries as well as riflemen. Attacking in that direction was surely suicidal. Yet Lucan, as he told Raglan, felt he had no choice.

> So distinct in my opinion was your written instruction, and so positive and urgent were the orders delivered by the aide de camp, that I felt that it was imperative on me to obey, and I informed Lord Cardigan that he was to advance.

Cardigan, in a memorandum for Lord Raglan of 27 October, described his response.

> On the afternoon of the 25th Inst. when in sight of the Russian Army, I perceived that our Cavalry were on the point of being employed, I sent my Aide de Camp L[ieutenan]t F Maxse to the L[ieutenan]t General Com[mandin]g the Division to say that the heights which flanked the valley leading to the Russian battery of heavy guns was covered with Artillery & Riflemen. The answer was we were going to attack. A few minutes afterwards the Lt General came in front of the Brigade, ordered the 11th Hussars to fall back in support and told me to attack the Russians in the Valley, about ¾ of [a] mile distant with the 13th Lt Dragoons [13th Regiment of (Light) Dragoons] & 17th Lancers. I answered 'certainly but allow me to point out to you that the hills on each side are covered with Artillery & Riflemen'. The Lt General replied 'I cannot help it, you must attack, Lord Raglan desires the L[igh]t Brigade immediately to attack the enemy'.

The Light Brigade, with the 13th Light Dragoons and 17th Lancers in the first line, the 11th Hussars immediately behind, and the 4th (Queen's Own) Regiment of Light Dragoons and 8th Hussars constituting the third line, were ordered to head the attack. Lucan would lead the Heavy Brigade in support. Taking up position in front of his brigade, Cardigan ordered the advance. The light cavalry had not proceeded far and had barely broken into a trot when Captain Nolan, who had joined the 17th Lancers in order to share in the advance, suddenly rode out of the ranks. Cardigan was appalled by the breach of etiquette: 'whilst advancing Capt. Nolan came in front of the Brigade with a view as it appeared of hurrying it on.' Knowing as we now do the contents of Nolan's journal and how he had seethed at the inactivity of the cavalry ever since the Alma, this interpretation of his actions appears not unlikely.

In later years, however, it was claimed that Nolan, having realized that the advance was heading the wrong way, was simply attempting to redirect it. The truth shall remain forever unknown. At that moment, as Cardigan wrote, 'A shell burst between him & me which was the cause of his death'. For Captain Gage of Raglan's staff, however, in common with other observers, the headstrong aide-de-camp's intentions were plain: 'Capt Nolan was killed by the 1st shot, screeching like a madman to the Brigade, "Are you not coming on, follow me" he received a shot in the breast & fell dead.'

The Light Brigade continued to move forward. Lieutenant Edward Seager was with the 8th Hussars in the third line, and the following day penned this account of his experiences.

About 3 o'clock pm [actually 11 am] by some mistake, the Light Cavalry were ordered to attack the Russian Cavalry and we had to proceed down the extent of a valley about a mile long, at the other end of which the Russians were posted, in force. On the hills on each side of the Valley, the Russian guns, and also on our right a line of Infantry, armed with Minié Rifles. The whole of this force we had to pass before we got to their cavalry. We advanced in three lines, the 8th the last line went in support. There were only about 100 of our regiment in the field. We advanced at a trot and soon came within the Cross fire from both hills, both of cannon & rifles; the fire was tremendous, shells bursting amongst us, Cannon balls tearing the earth up and Minié balls coming like hail. Still on we went, never altering our pace or breaking us up in the least, except that our men and horses were gradually knocked over. Our men behaved well. Poor Fitzgibbon was shot through the body and fell, he was supposed to be dead. Clowes's horse was shot under him and the last that was seen of him, he was walking towards where he started from and we suppose he was taken prisoner or killed. Up to this time I was riding in front of the men and on the right of the line of officers, and Clutterbuck, who was on my left, got wounded on the right foot by a piece of shell that must have passed me, and Tomkinson who commanded the squadron had his horse shot under him. I then took the Command of the squadron and placed myself in front of the centre. Malta had just previously got a ball through her neck, just above the windpipe, but we went bravely on.

The Russian fire was intense. 'I have heard say of a person walking through drops of rain,' wrote Sergeant William Williamson of the 11th Hussars: 'it is the only thing I can compare it to for the Balls of all description whistled like putting your head into a hive of bees.' In an effort to bring the ordeal to an end, the Light Brigade inexorably quickened its pace; but by the time the first line reached the guns at the end of the valley, only sixty men of the 13th Light Dragoons and 17th Lancers remained. Having outstripped their supports, they were quickly swallowed up by the Russian cavalry behind the guns. Cardigan had survived the charge and, finding himself isolated behind the gun line, turned his horse about to ride back up the valley and complain about the conduct of Captain Nolan. At that moment the 4th Light Dragoons smashed into the Russian guns. Major Alexander Lowe told General Codrington afterwards that 'he met Lord Cardigan going out of the fight, as they, the 4th Light Dragoons, were *going in*, and he was riding back as hard as he could go.' The Light Dragoons cut down the remaining gunners and passed on in an attempt to link up with the 11th Hussars.

Ahead of them both, the remnants of the 13th Light Dragoons and the 17th Lancers were attempting to extricate themselves from an unequal combat with the hordes of Russian cavalry that had assailed them. Private Edward John Firkins of the 13th was among those desperately trying to cut their way free.

> By this time I could not see three men of our Regiment. I of course thought I was lost but I turned my Mare's Head to try to get back if I could. I had only got a few yards when I saw two Russian lancers coming towards me with clenched teeth and stareing like savages. I prepared to meet them with as much coolness and determination as I could command. The first one made a thrust at me with his Lance. It is a heavy weapon and easily struck down which I did with my sword thrusting it at the same time through the fellow's neck. He fell from his horse with a groan. The shock nearly brought me from my saddle. The other fellow wheeled round his dying comrade and made a thrust at me. I had not the strength to strike down the blow for my sword fell from my grasp, but my time was not yet come. One of our Lancers seeing the attack made on me came to my assistance and thrust his Lance clean through the fellow's body at the moment I lost my sword.

The 13th and 17th fell back until they came upon the 8th Hussars. Having been kept to a rigid pace throughout by Colonel Shewell, the 8th had fallen well behind the rest of the Light Brigade and passed through the Russian guns after they had been silenced. Now they were in equal danger of being cut off, as Lieutenant Seager realized:

> About this time we discovered a large body of Russian Lancers coming on in our rear to attack us; we immediately wheeled about to show fight and we advanced upon them. The Colonel and Major got through them somehow but I think did not come in for the shock. I kept with the squadron, Clutterbuck the left troop, Phillips the right, me in front of the squadron leading. The men kept well together and bravely seconded us. We dashed at them, they were three deep with lances levelled. I parried the first fellow's lance, the one behind him I cut over the head, which no doubt he will remember for some time, and as I was recovering my sword I found the third fellow making a tremendous point at my body. I had just time to receive his lance point on the hilt of my sword, it got through the bars, knocked the skin off the top of the knuckle of my second finger and the point entered between the second and top joint of my little finger coming out at the other side. I shall most likely be returned wounded in the Gazette but you see I have only got a slight scratch that might look interesting in a drawing room.

On the other flank the 4th Light Dragoons and the 11th Hussars were also fighting their way back. Like their comrades, the 4th and 11th found the Russian cavalry unwilling to bar their path if ridden at with determination. General Codrington reported more of his conversation with Alexander Lowe to his wife:

> He describes the affair of the fight as like the noise of so many tinkers at hammering work! But few men were killed by the cavalry of the enemy – they did not stand the attack, and he says, cannot ride at all well.

Lying before the fugitives of the Light Brigade now was the long ride home. Their passage was assisted by a brilliant charge of the French *Chasseurs d'Afrique*, which silenced the Russian guns on the Fediukine Heights. There was also the Heavy Brigade, with which Lord Lucan had intended supporting the Light Brigade. What had happened to it? According to Sergeant George Cruse of the 1st Dragoons, at the commencement of the advance 'the light Brigade went so rapid that we almost lost sight of them.' The Heavy Brigade nevertheless had continued to move forward. 'Just as we got under the cross fire,' Cruse went on,

> I could see *the remains* of the Light Brigade returning, scarcely a mounted man and dozens of poor fellows crawling along on foot to the rear. Lord Lucan saw that a great error had been committed as we were under the fire of fifty heavy guns and just within range of the Russian riflemen, who poured in their shot like hailstones. We were I should say steady under this horrible fire for upwards of half a minute and how a single man of us escaped is quite a mystery . . . Mr Robertson's horse was shot dead just on my right, little Trumpeter Stacey was severely shot just on my left, and a young lad named Aslett had his arm blown off by a cannon shot just in front of me.

The 1st Dragoons alone had sustained twenty-one casualties, far more than they had suffered charging in the morning. Lucan decided to withdraw the Heavy Brigade: 'They have sacrificed the Light Brigade: they shall not have the Heavy, if I can help it,' he told an aide. His role now was simply to discourage pursuit of the Light Brigade's survivors, among whom was Lieutenant Seager, running the gauntlet of the Russian fire for a second time.

> After I found myself through the Russians, I saw the Colonel and Major a long distance ahead going as fast as their horses could carry them, the Batteries and Rifles peppering at them in grand style. As we had to go back through the same fire, a great number of men and horses having been killed, we did so in a scattered manner so as not to give them so great a chance of killing us. On looking to see what had become of my men, I found they had got through and had scattered to the right to get out of reach of the Rifles, and a large body of Lancers were coming on my left to cut us off. I put Malta to her speed and she soon got out of their reach, but the shot and rifle balls flew in great quantities, shells bursting just over my head with an awful crash. Through all this fire I returned, sometimes galloping and sometimes walking my horse, until I got out of reach of the fire, and found the remains of the regiment collecting gradually and counting over the missing. That any of the Light Cavalry Brigade returned through the crossfire kept upon us, was through the great

providence of God to whom I am grateful more than I can express. Many a poor fellow was laid low. We had 26 men killed and 17 wounded, 38 horses killed and a number wounded. The Light Brigade is now a skeleton, as all the regiments suffered more or less. They give us great credit for wheeling about and attacking the Lancers, it enabled the other regiments who were previously broken to get through them much more easily. The Colonel gets all the credit for it, but Phillips who was riding next to me could tell you who it was who called to the Colonel to let us wheel about and attack them, but I will tell all, please God, when I get home, and it is well known in the Regiment.

The compensations of a bloody action were the opportunities for promotion that it gave to the survivors. Writing home on 1 November, Seager was not above admitting this:

Those that were left collected, shook hands and congratulated each other on escaping. We, about 5, sat down on the grass, and fared sumptuously on salt pork and biscuits, washed down by rations of rum, all brought on the ground by our quartermaster. Poor Captain Lockwood of our regiment was killed, he was aide de camp to Lord Cardigan, and all his kit and Fitzgibbon's was sold by auction yesterday. I shall get my troop by poor Lockwood's death and I had rather I got it under less melancholy circumstances, as he was always particularly friendly with me. It was his fate poor fellow, and I have this satisfaction that I ran the same risk that he did and earned my promotion on the field of battle and through God's assistance did my duty there. I wish to think and I am sure if it were possible that could he have known what was to be the consequence of that Battle to him, he would have told me he was not sorry to resign the troop into my hands ... We sent a flag of truce to the Enemy on the 29th to find out the number of prisoners they had taken, and out of 11 officers missing belonging to the Light Cavalry Brigade only two were prisoners, all the others killed and buried by the Russians.

Seager did not mention that one of the two officers taken prisoner was Cornet George Clowes of his own regiment. Although communication between Clowes and his brother officers did not prove easy over the coming months, he asked for money to be forwarded to him. A letter written from Simpheropol and dated 8 December was also sent on to his father:

> You will all be glad to get a few lines from me to hear I am all right and very comfortable. I heard from the camp that the Colonel had written to tell you I was taken prisoner and you will have seen in the papers a full account of our fatal charge, so there is no use in my taking the trouble to tell you again. I will only say I am very thankful that I did not share the fate of many of my brother officers for I had a pretty narrow escape, being hit hard in the back by a grape shot, but it only skimmed across, taking a few splinters of bone off my right shoulder blade. However I am nearly all right again now.

The following month, still at Simpheropol, he wrote again:

> We are very comfortable here and the people here are *excessively* kind to us. We have lots of English books and go where we like, only with a soldier to accompany us. There are two other English officers with me, the Adjutant of the 17th Lancers, and a Mr Duff of the 23rd Fusiliers, who is an old school-fellow of mine. We were in the same house at Rugby together.

While Clowes was desirous to pay for the hospitality afforded him, Major Rodolph de Salis of the 8th Hussars explained for the benefit of Clowes's father some of the problems that this posed:

> Your son on being first taken prisoner, wrote for £10 to be sent to him. I had it increased to £25, this being about the pay then due to him, and I believe it reached him safely. He has since written twice for more, but so many objections were made by the parties concerned, that I have myself advanced this additional money 50 sovereigns. He states he had borrowed money from Prince Menshikoff's A.D.C. and was anxious to repay him, as well as to get more. This £50 will be sent through Prince Menshikoff and will, I make no doubt, reach him safely, though naturally there is *always* a risk.

Cornet Clowes was eventually exchanged for a Russian prisoner of war and had returned to Scutari by September 1855.

Notwithstanding the heroics of the 93rd Regiment and the Heavy Brigade during the morning, there could be no denying that the Battle of Balaklava had ended as a defeat. Captain Gage admitted as much when he wrote to his mother two days later:

> Our position has been much too extended for the number of troops & our little disaster has been the result. We are now taking up another position & have not deemed it expedient to attempt to turn the R[ussians] out of the 3 T[urkish] forts.

Writing the same day, Anthony Sterling agreed. The loss of the three redoubts had necessitated the drawing in of Balaklava's defensive cordon. Yet the port remained at risk:

> We are in a predicament, our English force to hold this place being very small, and the courage of the Turks being mild. The defence of Silistria becomes to me more and more a mystery.

The Light Brigade too had been destroyed. Of the 673 men who charged, over 260 had become casualties. Even more crucially for the brigade's operational effectiveness, 475 horses were lost. Someone had blundered, but who? Publicly, the ever-emollient Raglan was unwilling to apportion blame. In his official dispatch on the Battle of Balaklava of 28 October he contented himself with observing that 'from some misconception of the instruction to advance, the Lieutenant-General [Lucan] considered that he was bound to attack at all hazards.' However, in his private letter of the same date to the Duke of Newcastle, Raglan acknowledged that in the transmission of the order, hot words had been exchanged between Lucan and Nolan:

> I have heard that there was some bad feeling between Captain Nolan and Lord Lucan, and that the former entertained it on account of the latter having spoken disparagingly of the horses he had pur-chased in Syria.*

There the matter rested until Raglan's dispatch on the Battle of Balaklava was published in London. When he saw it, Lucan was furi-ous. There had been no misconception on his part. In ordering the Light Brigade forward, he pursued the only course open to him. On 16 December he wrote a letter of protest to Raglan, requesting him to forward a justification of his actions which he had prepared for the Duke

---

* Nolan had been sent to Syria to buy cavalry remounts in June 1854.

of Newcastle. Raglan was taken aback. 'I was by no means prepared for his communication,' he wrote to Newcastle. 'On the contrary I rather expected that he would be satisfied with what I had said in my dispatch, and would have thanked me for it.' Lucan's insistence on complete exculpation forced Raglan to throw off his self-restraint. Writing to Newcastle, he reiterated his belief that Lucan had misconstrued the order conveyed to him by Nolan:

> In his lordship's letter, he is wholly silent with respect to a previous order which had been sent him. He merely says that the cavalry was formed to support an intended movement of the infantry.
>
> This previous order was in the following words: – 'The cavalry to advance and take advantage of any opportunity to recover the heights. They will be supported by infantry, which has been ordered to advance on two fronts [sic].'
>
> This order did not seem to me to have been attended to, and therefore it was that the instruction by Captain Nolan was forwarded to him. Lord Lucan must have read the first order with very little attention, for he now states that the cavalry was formed to support the infantry, whereas he was told by Brigadier-General Airey, 'that the cavalry was to advance, and take advantage of any opportunity to recover the heights, and that they would be supported by infantry', not that they were to support the infantry; and so little had he sought to do as he had been directed, that he had no men in advance of his main body, made no attempt to regain the heights, and was so little informed of the position of the enemy that he asked Captain Nolan, 'where and what he was to attack, as neither enemy nor guns were in sight?'
>
> This, your Grace will observe, is the Lieutenant-General's own admission. The result of his inattention to the first order was, that it never occurred to him that the second was connected with, and a repetition of, the first. He viewed it only as a positive order to attack at all hazards (the word 'attack,' be it observed, was not made use of in General Airey's note) an unseen enemy, whose position, numbers, and composition, he was wholly unacquainted with, and whom, in consequence of a previous order, he had taken no step whatever to watch.

Viewing the dispute, the authorities in London naturally sided with Raglan. On 27 January 1855 a dispatch was sent from the War Office recalling Lucan from his command. He had, by then, forfeited what little sympathy he possessed. Nigel Kingscote was glad to see him go: 'I always knew he had not a leg to stand on. He was *hated* here.' Lucan had nonetheless lasted longer in the Crimea than his brother-in-law and rival, Lord Cardigan, who had left for home on medical grounds the previous December. Captain Seager was just as happy to see his departure:

> We have got rid of Lord Cardigan. If pomposity or bluster are the requisites for command, he is the man. He went up to the Guns gallantly enough on the 25th but finding it no joke, he bolted and left the Brigade to get back the best they could. I suppose he found his courage something like 'Bob Acres'.*

With these words Seager summed up both Cardigan's glory and his tragedy. On his return to England he was fêted for his leading of the Charge. But many of his fellow soldiers, like Seager, continued to believe that he had left the fighting too early and should have remained to rally his men. In December 1856 the Hon. Somerset Calthorpe, who like Nigel Kingscote was a nephew of Lord Raglan and had served as one of his aides-de-camp, published his *Letters from Headquarters*, implying that Cardigan had withdrawn from the battle prematurely. Some indeed were by now prepared to believe that he never took part in the charge at all. Cardigan eventually sued Calthorpe for libel. Although it was proved that he had reached the Russian guns, the exposure of Cardigan's apparent indifference to the fate of his men thereafter did him no good and he never recovered his former standing with the public. To that extent his reputation proved just another casualty of the Charge of the Light Brigade.

---

* The character in Sheridan's *The Rivals.*

5

INKERMAN

Inspired by their relative success at the Battle of Balaklava, the following day – 26 October 1854 – the Russians in Sevastopol launched a sortie against the right flank of the British army on the Inkerman Heights. They met stiff resistance from Lieutenant-General De Lacy Evans' 2nd Division. The determination of the outlying pickets to hold their ground was especially noteworthy. Among them was Private George Burdis of the 47th (The Lancashire) Regiment. 'I was on outline Piquit when they turn'd out,' he wrote to his family the next day,

> and a very severe engagement we had 1 Man killed and 7 wounded that was on the same duty that I was on but thank God I escaped and a very narrow escape it was but I had to fight my way through sending Prince Menshikoff home with a broken head & wounded arm.

De Lacy Evans elected not to support his pickets but to allow the Russian columns to press forward. This drew them onto his artillery, ranged along Home Ridge. The fire of eighteen guns soon dispersed the enemy. Burdis described the aftermath of their retreat:

> We took a great many prisoners of the Russians amongst them was a German officer and the accounts he gave Prince George Duke of Cambridge was that they were obliged to come out of Sebastopol on account of the disgraceful smell that was in the town and his oppinion was that the town would soon fall into the Hands of the British as the killed and wounded was laying in the streets.

Paymaster Lieutenant Godfrey Mosley of the 20th Regiment was not impressed with the condition of the Russian prisoners.

> The Army that came out of Sebastopol to attack us the other day were all drunk. The hospitals smelt so bad with them, that you could not remain more than a minute in the place and we were told by an

officer who they took prisoner, that they had been giving them wine till they had got them to the proper pitch and asked who would go out and drive the English Dogs into the sea, instead of which we drove them back into the town with the loss of about 700 in a very short time. The same officer told us that we might have got into the town when we first came here very easily, but now we should have some difficulty. The cool way we all take it here, there might be no enemy near us instead of one some little way in our rear and another in front.

But the coolness of which Mosley wrote was deceptive. After Liprandi's success on 25 October and the continuing threat posed by his army, Lord Raglan had contemplated abandoning the port of Balaklava. He would attempt instead to draw supplies through the French-held harbours at Kamiesch and Kazach. Commissary-General William Filder, however, claimed that without Balaklava he could not guarantee to keep the army supplied, and so the British remained. Their resources were nonetheless stretched to the utmost. Everything now depended on the French mounting a successful assault against Sevastopol. With reinforcements, they had 40,000 troops available, whereas the British still possessed only 25,000. Their siegeworks were also far better placed. 'The F[rench] are creeping nearer & nearer their attack,' wrote Captain the Hon. Edward Gage on 3 November,

> & we earnestly hope as the cold is evidently setting in, that it will not be long before a lodgement is made on the bastion Dumas [Flagstaff Bastion] which it is expected will tend to the speedy fall of the place. *We* are making the *false* attack on the place, & have nearly expended all the Am[munitio]n. The R[ussian] Batteries are very quiet now & do us little harm. For the last three days there has not been a casualty, but 6 were killed & wounded this morn[ing], by some of the men lighting a fire, & thus drawing the E[nemy's] attention to them.

In fact, the Allies had fixed a conference for 5 November to agree the final plan of assault. But the Russians were aware of the vulnerability of the Flagstaff Bastion and, using the reinforcements that had now reached the Crimea from Odessa (giving them a total of 120,000 troops in and around Sevastopol), decided to smash the Allies without delay. Their strategy was to have the garrison of Sevastopol and the 22,000 men of Prince Gorchakov's (late Liprandi's) army north of Balaklava make feint attacks against the Allied armies on the Chersonese uplands. The real thrust, however, would be delivered by 40,000 troops under General Dannenberg, attacking over the same ground as 26 October. Nineteen thousand infantry under General Soimonov would sally forth from Sevastopol. Another 16,000 infantry under General Paulov would leave the Mackenzie Heights and attack across the River Chernaya. Both Russian corps were supported with a numerous artillery. To oppose them were the 3,300 troops and twelve guns of the 2nd Division. On the foggy night of 4/5 November the Russians began their advance. Their immediate objective was to establish themselves on the northern edge of the Chersonese plateau, in particular the 600-foot-high Shell Hill. Thirteen hundred yards away to the south was the main British position on Home Ridge, of approximately the same elevation. Slightly lower, and running between the two, was a narrow ridge, Saddle Top Reach; this was flanked on either side by two ravines, the Mikriakov Gully to the west and Quarry Ravine to the east. Through the Quarry Ravine ran the post road to Sevastopol. Where this emerged from the ravine, 600 yards north of Home Ridge, the British had constructed, from stones, the 'Main Picket Barrier'. Much of the ground was covered by oak brushwood, which lay especially thick in the gullies and ravines, but was rather sparser on the ridge tops.

With the pickets of the 2nd Division that night was Lieutenant George Carmichael of the 95th Regiment. Some years later, he recollected the events of the day to come:

A portion of the Shell Hill picquet came down to my surprise on to the road, and I ascertained in conversation with Vialls, that his Field Officer was withdrawing his chain of sentries from the brow, to the base of Shell Hill, on account of the fog, that they had got somewhat astray in the dark, and amidst the brushwood, and that they had struck the road in order to make sure, that the new and retired line should be properly placed. Unless my memory fails me, there was an instruction to this effect in the Field Book of those days, the idea being that the Enemy would in foggy weather be better observed on the skyline from the base, than from the top of a hill. This was of course wholly inapplicable under the circumstances, and the change was certainly contrary to Vialls wishes & opinion.

Vacating Shell Hill meant that the Russians found it possible to make their initial approach without detection. Carmichael did not yet think anything was amiss.

> Tho' I laid down on the ground, I slept very little. I remember hearing the clang of the church bells in the town, and the rumble of wheels in the valley, but the latter noise raised no suspicion in my mind, as it was a nightly occurrence and had been reported previously, and it was well known to all, that the Enemy used the road during the night.

An hour before daybreak he was relieved by pickets of the 41st (The Welsh) Regiment and returned to the 2nd Division Camp on Home Ridge. 'I found, that the 2nd Division which was always under arms for an hour before daylight had been dismissed, and the wood, and water parties had been sent out.' He had only been in his tent three minutes when he heard firing. The shooting got heavier and heavier and was sounding from all directions. He called out his company and they formed line in front of the camp behind the crest of Home Ridge.

The initial firing that Carmichael could hear came from thirty pickets of the Guards under Captain Gerald Goodlake. Looming out of the fog, they had seen the leading elements of Soimonov's corps, supported by thirty-eight guns, coming towards them out of Sevastopol. This was the right-hand thrust of Dannenberg's attack, moving onto and across the front of Shell Hill from the west and heading for Saddle Top Reach. Within half an hour the Russians had twenty-two guns on Shell Hill. They were soon engaged in an artillery duel with the twelve guns of the 2nd Division deployed on Home Ridge.

Already in the field was Lieutenant Frederick Elton of the 55th Regiment. He wrote to his father two days later.

> The 4th had been wet and dark the whole day and the arms were piled in the open air as they always are in camp and of course wet through when it was my lot to go out-lying picket with my company the next morning at 5 a.m. I happened to be nearly junior and so I stayed with the reserve under the field officer of the day. About an hour after we had been on we heard firing from our advanced pickets and soon after the word was passed to 'stand to our arms for the enemy were coming in force'. I was sent on to support the advance and on trying the muskets, to my horror I found that only 15 out

of the company would go off and out of those 15, only about six
men would follow me to the front. However there was nothing to be
done but push to the front and we soon joined the advanced picket
which I found in much the same state with regard to the arms as
my own. We retired gradually before them as they were coming on
in Masses of Columns supported with a very powerful artillery and
soon had most desperate work, almost hand to hand in the thick
brushwood with the guns playing on us in a most fearful way, and
ours answering them over our heads, while we were firing musketry
into each other at between 15 and 30 paces distance now and then
charging and driving them back and then being driven back by
superior numbers again.

Further to the left, posted on the Victoria Ridge, was General
Codrington's brigade of the Light Division protecting the extreme right
flank of the British siegeworks. Codrington was already on horseback,
as he wrote to his wife.

As far as I was concerned, I had as usual gone to the front about an
hour before daylight. I went to our redoubt and the old picquets had
just come in: and having waited till near dawn I heard firing begin
on the brow to our right – first a little, then rapid increase – in
short, I then knew at once an attack had begun. I kept the troops
on our brow, of course; Sir T[homas] Troubridge was the new field
officer and was in the battery. I sent a company down there to his
support, and sent 3 companies to line our brow of the hill above the
valley to fire across it on their skirmishers and troops. I then galloped
in myself to get the remainder under arms and to the front. I
remember now I had already sent in the old picquets to camp; it was
a dull, half rainy morning: I got out all the troops I had, advancing
them as they were ready. There were however only about 2 companies
of rifles and about 4 companies of the others altogether. On getting
out towards the redoubt I saw, and heard the shouting of, columns
and troops advancing in skirmishing order, and a great many guns
took up their position on the rocky height to our right (in front of
the 2d. Division) [Shell Hill] in a similar manner to the attack of the
other day. Their fire advanced and advanced – the English picquets
were of course driven in and the columns keeping over towards the
further side of the brow principally, but in great force. Their artillery
any number – and firing severely – their skirmishers in thick order

however came on and on, lining the brow opposite our battery and firing into it, our skirmishers also firing much upon them, and their artillery, but this was rather far. The columns occasionally might have given one the opportunity of using artillery against them, if I had had any there. But the artillery of the Light Division was in demand to our right.

The Light Division positions on Victoria Ridge were not in fact the Russian objective. They made only one small thrust across the Careening Ravine which, as Lieutenant Edward Newdigate of the 1st Rifle Brigade explained to his father, was repelled:

We had very hot work, 2 only of our Companies lined the top of a ravine which runs between us & the 2nd division, the other Companies being on piquet & 4 Co[mpanies] at Balaklava. The Russian skirmishers came in crowds to the opposite side, firing very heavily & field artillery were showering us with grape. They came down into the ravine & just as they came up our side Elrington with ½ doz men rushed up to them, fired his revolver & away they skuttled. A lot of skirmishers who hid themselves on the opposite hill kept up a steady fire but made no other attempt to turn us out of our position.

The real threat was on the front of the 2nd Division. The Russians had placed a twenty-two-gun battery on Shell Hill and were subjecting Home Ridge to an intense bombardment. Lieutenant Carmichael witnessed the unequal attempt to make a reply.

Shortly after we had formed line (the centre of the regiment being about astride the [post] road,) the two (or three) guns belonging to the Artillery of the Division, which were always horsed and in readiness on the road day and night came up, and Ens[ign] Brown, who commanded the left centre company, and myself opened out to let them come through, and they came into action on the rising ground just to the right of the road, and directly in front of my company. They were commanded by Lieut. H T Arbuthnot, with whom I had been stationed at Woolwich the previous year . . . They fired, I should judge at the flash of the Enemy's guns on Shell Hill, and drew soon a heavy fire on themselves in return. Some of their men fell, and we also suffered, altho' we had been ordered to lie down to obtain what shelter we could from the ridge. One round shot I remember tore into my company *completely severing* the left arm and both legs off a man in the front rank, and killed his rear rank man without any perceptible wound . . . The guns, I have alluded to came into action short handed, and were firing as fast as they could load, and each successive discharge and recoil brought them closer to our line. Arbuthnot asked for assistance, and I called upon some men of my company, and we, including my Col[our] Sergt Jno M Sexton assisted the gunners to run the guns into their first position, and some men also aided in carrying ammunition.

Sir George De Lacy Evans was ill and so the 2nd Division was commanded by one of his brigadiers, Major-General John Lysaght Pennefather. The day after the battle Pennefather reported to Raglan that at 6.30 a.m., on hearing musketry to the left, he had got his men under arms. The point of attack was across Saddle Top Reach between Shell Hill and Home Ridge. Word was sent to the Guards Brigade and General Bosquet requesting their support.

Meanwhile the action went on in the bottom between the Russian Infantry which every moment increased in numbers and my Picquets, which I fed by reinforcements from my line, and who for a long time held their ground between the two positions.

Unlike De Lacy Evans, who on 26 October had drawn the Russians on to Home Ridge, Pennefather wanted to keep the Russians at arm's length as long as possible, to give time for reinforcements to arrive. Hence his tactic of reinforcing the picket line. Moreover, as he admitted, little was possible beyond improvised defence: 'the Enemy's guns, being of so much heavier metal than ours, severely played upon our position, paralysing all our arrangements for formation or attack.'

Sir George Brown had also been alerted by the firing. He first rode to Victoria Ridge and consulted with General Codrington. 'After he had been out to me on this front, and said "Well, Codrington, you will do the best you can?" he left, and I heard went to the 2d. Division front.' For Codrington, whose relations with his superior, never good, had deteriorated after Brown criticized the dispositions made by him on 26 October, this was of a piece with the short-sighted Brown's behaviour at the Alma: 'he always will go riding about (not seeing) any where in fire or any where but with his own people.' Nonetheless,

Brown felt that his presence was needed. 'They could not have taken us at a greater disadvantage,' he wrote afterwards to Lord Raglan,

> for at the moment they attacked both the old & new Picquets & Guards of the trenches were at their posts, & we had scarcely anybody in Camp. The consequence was that the aid we were enabled to send up consisted of Detach[ment]s of two or three Companies only for we had not a complete Batt[alio]n to send!

That this was the case was to some extent Brown's own fault. Having ordered George Buller's brigade of the Light Division, four companies each of the 77th Regiment and 88th Regiment and a battery of artillery – some 650 men – to Home Ridge, he fell in with Sir George Cathcart, engaged in sending forward detachments of the 4th Division. The two of them then encountered General Bosquet. Gorchakov's feint attack on the Balaklava front had proved so unconvincing that the Frenchman had immediately sent two and a half battalions to aid the British at Inkerman with more to follow. Brown and Cathcart nevertheless told Bosquet that his assistance was not required.

The demonstration mounted by the garrison of Sevastopol on the French front was vigorous enough to detain Prince Napoleon's division until 11 a.m., but the British were not deceived and this was the reason Buller's brigade and the 2,200 men of the 4th Division had been released in good time. First into action was the 88th Regiment. Sent forward by Pennefather from the western end of Home Ridge across the Mikriakov Gully, they soon lost all cohesion amidst the fog and thick brushwood. Captain Joshua Crosse, in a letter written in 1876, described what befell him.

> The Picquet of the 2nd Div. passed through as we came upon the advancing Russians and an order was given to retire which I thought was for the Picquets & I called out to our men 'Don't retire, stand your ground', but the men did retire and I found myself close to a knot of 6 Russians who were advancing to attack me. It passed through my mind at once 'It is all up with me but I will sell my life as dearly as I can.' I had my pistol in my hand as I had taken it out to save one of our men, I think his name was Lance Corporal James McDonagh No 7 Co – it was the man who got the Distinguished Conduct Medal and a fund got up in Ireland for him as he was supposed to have saved my life: instead of which I saved his. I shot

four of the Russians, the fifth bayonetted me & fell pulling me down
on the top of him, the sixth then charged on me & [with my sword]
I cut down his firelock on to his hands & he turned back. I at once
got up and made my way off but I turned almost immediately after
as I thought this man might charge me again, which he did & I
rushed at him as the best way of saving myself & he again turned.
I retired and after a few yards I met Colour Sergeant Cooney . . .
[and four others], they had come back to look for me.

Crosse afterwards wrote a testimonial for the Deane Adams Revolver
Company, stating that with its automatic cocking, the weapon was far
superior to the rival Colt.

In the wake of the retreat of the 88th Regiment, three of the Light
Division's newly arrived guns were overrun on the Mikriakov Spur.
The situation appeared desperate. It was now that the 259 men of the
77th Regiment under Lieutenant-Colonel Thomas Egerton made a telling
intervention. As Brigadier George Buller reported subsequently:

That Regiment made a charge of the greatest consequence which
drove back a *very strong column* of the Enemy who had penetrated
under a dense mist, which made it impossible to discern objects until
within a few yards, within 200 yards* of the *front of the Camp* of the
2nd Division, which had they succeeded in – and the moment was
critical – would have placed the Column of the enemy in rear of our
position of the Ridge.

Egerton's men had routed no fewer than 1,500 Russians of the Tomsk
Regiment, pushing them back as far as the foot of Shell Hill. The
Katerinburg battalions of Soimonov's column also retired, surrendering
the captured British guns. Canister fire and a charge of the 49th (Princess
Charlotte of Wales's) (or the Hertfordshire) Regiment repulsed the
Russian assault on Home Ridge. General Soimonov was killed.

By now, however, the other Russian corps under General Paulov had
crossed the River Chernaya and was ascending the plateau. Six thousand troops began to emerge from the head of the Quarry Ravine. The
Taroutine Regiment saw a stray Katerinburg Battalion of Soimonov's
column moving eastwards across the front of Home Ridge and followed
it round the ridge's northern edge. The remainder continued their

---

* Buller meant 20 yards.

advance along the post road. Two battalions of the Borodino Regiment were confronted by 200 men of the 30th Regiment, among whom was Lieutenant Mark Walker. The description in his journal of the onset of combat is reminiscent of Frederick Elton's recollection:

> At 6½ this morning just after I returned to my tent an alarm was given, this time not a false one. The Russians had advanced in great force to attack our position. We reserves were sent to the front to support the Picquets which we found when we got down retiring. About 7 we got under fire from a column of Russians. Unfortunately after the night's rain the firelocks would not go off. At first we were obliged to retire. We then rallied and charged them.

The 30th succeeded in driving the enemy back across the Main Picket Barrier. Their opponents had been roughly handled at the Alma and did not fight well; nor were the Russians well served by fighting in company columns. The Taroutine Regiment, meanwhile, having felt its way past the British right flank, was met by 500 men of the 41st Regiment under Brigadier-General Adams. Here too the Russians were forced back. It was now 7.30 a.m. In the course of an hour's combat no fewer than 15,000 Russians had been repulsed by fewer than 4,000 British troops. Whereas the fog had favoured the Russians initially, enabling them to make a close approach, they soon became disoriented and were caught at a disadvantage by the soldiers of the British 2nd Division, who knew the ground. Indeed, so badly beaten was Soimonov's corps that no further attacks would occur from the direction of Sevastopol for the remainder of the battle. Nevertheless, that still left General Dannenberg with 20,000 fresh troops; and by now no fewer than 90 of his 135 artillery pieces were in action. The outnumbered British were tired, hungry and short of ammunition.

Dannenberg committed 10,000 troops against the British centre and right. Pennefather, once the men guarding his left and various scattered units attempting to re-form were discounted, had 1,400 with which to oppose them. Reinforcements were desperately needed and were, at last, beginning to arrive. The Duke of Cambridge, having decided that Gorchakov's feint from the direction of the Plain of Balaklava was nothing more than that, had brought forward 700 men of the Grenadier and Scots Fusilier Guards; another 300 of the Coldstreams would soon follow. General Cathcart was bringing up the 4th Division: the 21st and the

57th (The West Middlesex) Regiment were already taking up position on Pennefather's left. The arrival of two regiments of French troops – sixteen hundred men – which Bosquet had decided to send, contrary to Brown and Cathcart's opinion, was imminent. There were also three batteries of field artillery from the British 1st and Light Divisions close to hand. Cambridge's deployment of the Guards would prove not to be ideal, however. To the north-east of Home Ridge was a British gun emplacement. It faced east and had always proved something of a folly, as Lieutenant the Hon. William Amherst of the Coldstream Guards had explained in a letter home a fortnight earlier:

> The Russians got two guns in Battery near the ruins of Inkerman.
> An Engineer was sent to erect a Counter Battery but they chose a
> man who knew nothing of the localities to superintend & who built
> a very good Battery no doubt but one from which our guns could
> no more reach the Russians than if they had been at Woolwich.

The two 18pdr guns had been removed, leaving behind the imposing Sandbag Battery, with its twin embrasures and ten-foot-high parapet. When, earlier in the morning, the Taroutine Regiment had followed the stray Katerinburg Battalion round the British right flank, it had seen the battery, imagined the emplacement to be a key defensive work and occupied it. Brigadier-General Adams and the 49th Regiment then ejected the Russians. Dannenberg's latest assault, spearheaded by the Okhotsk, Yakutsk and Selinghinsk Regiments, had now recaptured the Sandbag Battery. Adams was wounded. In his battle report, the Duke of Cambridge described his appearance on the scene:

> The 2nd Division was already hotly engaged & the Brigade of Guards
> with the two Field Batteries were pushed forward, the latter to the
> support of the 2nd Division, the former to the extreme right of
> the position. Other troops then came up & the Brigade of Guards
> advanced most gallantly led by Major General Bentinck & attacked
> & took the 18 lb Battery opposite the Inkermann Ruins.

Cambridge had not yet had the opportunity of discovering that the Sandbag Battery was a useless prize: lacking a banquette it could not be readily defended by infantry. The Grenadier Guards and Scots Fusilier Guards were also facing east: Cambridge did not realize that the chief threat lay in the north where what General Pennefather called 'The Gap'

– which was currently undefended – had opened between the Sandbag Battery and 'The Barrier' on the post road. Only as Russian troops continued to appear from the north on the Guards' left flank did Cambridge begin to understand his predicament; he hurried to get reinforcements.

Cathcart's 4th Division constituted what reserve Pennefather possessed. John Fisher was among 300 men of the 1st Rifle Brigade which had been hurried up:

> On we marched through a dense fog and up to our knees in mud, passed the Old Windmill. The Roll of musketry and great guns, bursting of shells. Shouting could be distinctly heard not far from us but we could see nothing, save the objects near us, so dense had become the fog. Now we pass some Turks lolling about quite unconcerned as though it was nothing to them. Now we reach the tents occupied by the Tars also the Guards.

Cambridge was given the 1st Rifle Brigade and half the 20th Regiment of the 4th Division, as well as half of the 95th Regiment from the 2nd Division. As he neared the Sandbag Battery, George Carmichael of the 95th was made forcibly aware that, to his left, 'The Gap' remained unfilled.

> We wheeled in open column to the right, and as we approached it, we could hear the cheering or hurrahing of the Russians over the din of the fight. We were I should think about 60 or 70 yards from the Battery, and I was in my place on the left of the Company trying to keep my distance and covering from the front as well as the ground would permit, when an exclamation from one of my men drew my attention to my left, and turning round, I saw thro' the mist and smoke a line of the Enemy's skirmishers close to my left flank. I wheeled my company at once to the left and opened fire. At this moment the Duke of Cambridge rode up to me, and not having I suppose noticed the Enemy's skirmishers told me to take care, or that I should fire into the Guards. I pointed out who we had got in front of us, and he then rode on towards the left. Our fire drove the skirmishers, who were quite close to us back, and some of the men including Pte Timothy Abbott, began to follow them with the bayonet, but I got them back, and we went on to the Battery, as having both Colours with me, I felt anxious as to their safety. Directly

we got to the Battery we formed up to the assistance of the Guards who were hotly pressed on all sides. My men showed front chiefly to the left of the Battery, and the Sergeant with the Colours stood close to where those of the Guards were standing, carried by two young officers, to one of whom I was speaking for few moments. I think his name was 'Disbrowe' and that he was at Harrow with me, altho' some years my junior. Our other two companies seemed to me to have formed towards the right, but the men of different corps were very soon intermingled. The rifles of many of the men, who had been out the previous night would not at first go off from their damp condition, but the rifles of fallen men were to be had. My Colour Sergt Sexton (subsequently commissioned) was one of those in this predicament, but I handed him one thrown down by a gigantic Guardsman, who was shot through the mouth by my side, and who reeled off to the rear choking with blood.

The 1st Rifle Brigade, meanwhile, had gone some way towards filling the Gap and was trying to prevent the Russians emerging out of the St Clement's Ravine from gaining a foothold on the plateau of the Kitspur, which lay to the north of the Sandbag Battery. John Fisher later recalled the experience.

Now fizz! fizz, fizz flies the bullets about our heads. Whack goes a shell in the ground, then a bang and the lumps of iron go burning through the air like some horrid demon. Now we come to some bushes on the slope of a hill. This is Inkerman. Between those bushes may be seen figures groping about hardly knowing which way to turn. These are the enemy. Pop, bang, pop, bang, pop! pop, pop we are at them. Like good soldiers we dashed amongst the bushes in skirmishing order, and soon they begin to retire on their main body which we could observe through the fog on the top of the hill in thousands. We lay down under cover as we had no support. The Russians still blundering about in front of us, our men seemed to loose all patience. I remember having a feeling somewhat allied to madness coming over me. I jumped up not aware that Major H[orsford] was so near and said come on let us give it to them. Lie down says the major in an undertone until you get the order. At last we did up and at them again and soon made them retire over the brow of the hill and down into a hollow and up the opposite side. Here they would take courage and having the advantage of their reserve, and that of being on the highest ground, would turn about and cause us as if of pure discretion to retire to the top of our own hill. This sort of manuvering we continued for a length of time.

George Carmichael was still heavily engaged back at the Sandbag Battery.

I cannot say how long this fight lasted, but I went backwards & forwards between the flanks of the battery several times, as at one moment one would be implored to bring assistance to the right, at another time it was the left that was pressed, and could not hold out any longer without help. The men behaved with great pluck and tenacity. I saw no flinching, altho' we were several times outflanked. At one time, I thought we must be driven out, as they penetrated into the battery as far as the left embrasure, but the leading men were shot down, and the others drew back. At this time I fought with a rifle, as many other officers did during the day. Soon after the incident just mentioned, a wing or some portion of the 20th Regt. came down to our support in the Battery, and they mingled at once with the other defenders. They were armed with the old Brown Bess, and were able to give their fire with far greater rapidity, than those armed with the Minié, which was always difficult to load rapidly.

Until now, most of Sir George Cathcart's 4th Division had been committed to action towards the centre and left of Pennefather's defensive line. Colonel Charles Ash Windham now appeared at Cathcart's side with a further 400 men from the 46th Regiment and the 68th (The Durham) Regiment (Light Infantry), part of Arthur Torrens' brigade, which he had brought up from camp. Both Cambridge and Pennefather asked Cathcart to use these men to help fill 'The Gap'; but he was determined to launch a counter-attack against the Russian left flank. Even when given a positive order by Airey, the Quartermaster-General, to face to the north, Cathcart chose to disregard it. Instead, he sent his men careering down the eastern slopes of the Kitspur. The example was immediately followed by the defenders of the Sandbag Battery, George Carmichael amongst them.

As it seemed to me shortly after their [the 20th's] arrival that the Enemy's hold of the ground round the Battery was less firm, and their fire had most decidedly slackened, I proposed to an officer of the 20th (who I think must have been subsequently killed, as I never afterwards met him) that we should try and drive them off the hill altogether by a charge. He agreed, and we got together what men we could, Guards, 20th & 95th & forming them up advanced with a cheer out of the left of the Battery. The Enemy turned at once, several of those overtaken threw away their arms, and knelt down asking for mercy mentioning the name of Christ (Christos). These were taken prisoners and sent to the rear, but the pursuit was continued down the hill, and into the ravine. I thought the battle was won, and the men were also exultant. A fine young soldier of the 95th L[an]ce Corp[ora]l Purcell came up to me, saying, 'We are driving them again Sir' alluding to the repulse of the sortie on the 26th October, and at the same time was about to run his bayonet into a Russian's back whom we were overtaking. I cried out 'Don't kill him,' and he then instead seized him by the belt behind, and flung him to the ground, and took his weapon off him. I don't know what became of Purcell subsequently, but he never came out of the fight, and his body was found months afterwards on the other side of the hill facing the ruins. We pushed the pursuit down the hill, and partly up the other side, and others followed the fugitives down the hollow or ravine itself. The men had got very scattered, and were beginning to run very short of ammunition. Pte Bernard McEntee of the 95th who had been amongst those foremost in the advance reported to me that he had fired his last round. I noticed just at this time, and the men near me also remarked that those following us, but a good deal further to the rear, were turning back, and soon after cries were raised, evidently for us, 'Come back, you are cut off.' I could see no cause for retreat, and stopped those near me who began to retire thinking it was a false alarm, but the smoke and mist rolling away for a minute, a heavy Russian column became visible forming to our left on the high ground covered by a strong fringe of skirmishers, extended at an interval of only two or three paces. Three or four of their companies were already formed and in order, and the officers were busy marshalling the remainder, as they streamed up out of the ravine. Not a moment was to be lost, and it seemed to me more than doubtful if we could reach the Sandbag Battery before them.

Further to the right, the 400 men of the 46th and 68th under Cathcart

had just discovered that they were in a similar predicament, as Charles
Ash Windham subsequently reported:

> The 68th Regiment were led into Action by Br. Genl. Torrens, who
> fell severely wounded when in the act of trying to restrain their
> ardour after driving the Enemy before them. Sir Geo. Cathcart
> expressed himself to Br. Genl. Torrens lying wounded on the ground
> as highly pleased at his conduct, and then with his Staff continued
> to advance until he saw the Enemy in full occupation of the heights
> above him, which he had previously thought were in our possession.

This was the consequence of Cathcart's insubordination. Two thousand men of the Russian Iakoutsk Regiment, emerging from the
Quarry Ravine, had found the Gap undefended and now stood in the rear
of the British troops in the valley below. Cathcart vainly attempted to
reclaim the situation, addressing Windham:

> He immediately ordered me to get back the Wings of the 20th and
> 68th and tried to show front with the few skirmishers around him
> and with them drove back the Enemy twice, but I regret to say he
> was shot through the heart.

Writing home afterwards, Brigadier-General Airey found it hard to
muster much sympathy.

> Poor Cathcart – so wild and inconsiderate, was always for performing
> some action without reflection or knowledge. What he attempted
> quite wrong & against the orders I had positively given him 5 minutes
> before – so sad!!

Cathcart was dead; the men stranded in the valley floor had now to
save themselves. George Carmichael began to retrace his steps.

> Their skirmishers saw the false position we were in, and pushed on,
> some of those also we had been following turned again. With great
> coats on, and pretty well blown, and impeded by the stiff oak brush-
> wood, we made but slow progress back. My first idea was to climb
> up the side of the hill on the base of which we were standing, to pass
> in front of the Battery, and to get into it by its right; some appeared
> to be doing this, when recalled, and may have succeeded but the
> brushwood was so thick and the hill so steep, that I gave it up, and
> determined to follow those who were making for the left of the

Battery by a narrow winding little footpath which had been worn by
the picquets. Up this we travelled in single file. I believe I was the
last of the string, the man just in front of me being a Guardsman,
who I thought went very slow. In this manner we ran the gauntlet
of their skirmishers, and passed into the left of the Battery, within
six paces of their muzzles. Once there, I hoped we should find
support of some kind, but there was no one there but killed and
wounded.

Captain William Radcliffe of the 20th Regiment also headed for the
Sandbag Battery initially before taking a more circuitous route to safety.

Butler, James & I were coming back slowly & had just mounted a
very steep hill where there was an Earthwork, which we expected to
find occupied by our Troops, when to our extreme *surprise* & dismay
we saw a large body of Russians in it & extending some way outside
it to the right. We had not more than 100 men of different Corps in
sight & they were scattered about the face of the hill. I thought if we
were not shot we must be taken Prisoners & so [would we] had the
Russians come down (I was within 20 yds of the Redoubt) but they
contented themselves with firing at us & we sheltered ourselves as
well as we could under the hill which rather favor'd us & made our
way to where we expected to find our Troops. Up to this time I had
carried a Minié Rifle which I pick[e]d up at the commencement &
[had] been most diligently firing & intended to carry home, thinking
all was over, but I was too done to carry it any further & so dropp'd
it & drew my Pistol. I fired one barrel at a man who was in the act
of firing & then [we] hastened on all of us running the gauntlet of
their fire for nearly a mile (it seemed longer to me).

After the 20th, 95th and most of the Guards had followed Cathcart's
example and charged down the hill, all that remained on the Kitspur
were the Duke of Cambridge and some 150 men. Confronted by 2,000
Russians, they attempted to extricate themselves. A day later, Cambridge
made his report to Lord Raglan:

The 4th Division came up in support but made a flank movement
down the valley to the right of the ground held by the Guards.
Unfortunately there was no support on the left & the mist being very
thick & the ground extremely difficult to the eye from the thick
brushwood the Brigade [of Guards] was entirely cut off from the 2nd

Division & it was with great difficulty that I was able myself to get back accompanied by my ADC Major Macdonald. Major General Bentinck had been previously wounded. I had endeavoured to get our men back but could not manage this as so many had advanced down the hill with the 4th Division. I saw no men of the Guards till I rallied them in rear & on the right flank of the 2nd Division. Here I must record the noble conduct of Assistant Surgeon Wilson of the 7th Hussars attached to this Division. He was the only Officer at hand & rallied the few men we could get together & then held the ground to the right for some time preventing the Russians from getting through & enabling a great many of our men otherwise cut off to get back.

The opportune appearance of the French 6th Regiment of the Line was also crucial in stemming the Russian advance. A critical moment of the battle had passed.

Some six weeks afterwards, Cambridge felt compelled to write to Raglan both rephrasing and elaborating upon his account of this phase of the battle. He deemed it necessary because the reception afforded the publication of Raglan's dispatch describing the Battle of Inkerman had, in some quarters, been decidedly lukewarm, as he explained:

The Brigade of Guards are a little annoyed that it should be supposed that they were *driven back* by the enemy & forced to retire & reform *behind the 2nd Division*. . . . After maintaining their ground for a very long time & indeed many of them having even gone far beyond the two gun battery, the Brigade was suddenly & completely cut off from the position of the 2nd Division by a violent attack on the part of the Russians who drove back the troops on the *left* of the Brigade of Guards, but not the Guards themselves, [who] with a large portion of the 4th Division were engaging in a hand to hand contest, when they suddenly perceived what had occurred on their left & it was about that period that poor Sir George Cathcart fell. After this the Guards had nothing left for it but to be completely surrounded or to force their way back through the Russian masses now on their left & pushing on towards their rear. They at once went at them with the point of the bayonet, not a man having a round of ammunition left, as we were in the act of serving this out when the above occurrence took place. Therefore though the Guards actually retired they did so *facing* an enemy in their left flank & rear & litterally at the point of the bayonet, therefore in fact never retiring before the enemy at all but forcing their way through him till they reached the breastwork or position of the 2nd Division . . . I feel it my duty to represent these circumstances to you, as I fear from my want of detail I may have unintentionally been the cause of that which has pained many of my gallant friends, the idea that it could be supposed that they had been *driven back*. Possibly if you could do anything to place the Government in possession of these facts it would be gratifying to these fine fellows.

This was not the only 'misrepresentation' published in the newspapers to exercise members of the Brigade of Guards. When the Duke of Cambridge and the 150 men left with him on the Kitspur had found themselves outnumbered thirteen to one by the Russians, the saving of the Colours of the Grenadier Guards became one of the battle's most celebrated incidents. The role of Colour-Sergeant Poolfield Davies was given especially prominent coverage, Cassell's *Illustrated Family Paper* of 27 January 1855 lauding 'The Great Grenadier'. 'Both at Alma and at Inkermann he was first in the fray,' the newspaper continued; on the latter occasion,

> Davies defended his colours with the utmost tenacity, and literally mowed down the enemy, who made a rush to capture them. . . . Amidst dead and dying, first using the bayonet, then the butt-end of his musket, with his arms unnerved from the sheer fatigue of striking down the enemy, this sergeant . . . arose like a giant above the surrounding level of heads. . . . To enumerate the enemy killed and put *hors de combat* by the single arm of Davies would appear almost incredible.

In fact, his exploit was – quite literally – impossible. Colour-Sergeant Davies was not even present at Inkerman. The Adjutant of the 3rd Battalion Grenadier Guards, Captain George Higginson, who had himself been heavily involved in the defence of the Colours during the battle, confirmed as much to the regimental adjutant back in England, Captain Villiers Hatton, the following February.

> There is another Sergeant of the 3rd Battalion who is the source of much annoyance to us all: I allude to Sergt. Davies and his correspondence with the Newspapers regarding his exploits, &c. Now we

all know very well that he saw less of the fighting at Alma than any soldier in the Battalion as he chose to remain at the rear with Burgoyne who was severely wounded early in the action. He was sent on board ship two days before the battle of Inkerman, and yet he actually has the impudence, in one of the letters I have read in a Newspaper, to say that he was present in all the affairs from the 20th Sept. to 7th November!!* The N.C.O.[s] of the Battalion are furious, of course. I should be inclined myself to laugh, and let the great overgrown brute swagger a la Bobadil were it not that I hear people are making him presents & writing him flattering notices on his prowess, his claim to which he has not the candour to disavow.

Although Higginson's letter was passed to the Adjutant-General, it was too late for action. In England, the commemorative mugs celebrating Davies' achievements were already on sale.

During the desperate fighting at the Sandbag Battery, the situation in front of Home Ridge was almost equally fraught. The 30th Regiment had performed repeated charges but had eventually been forced back behind the low breastwork which provided a modicum of protection for the British artillery atop the ridge. Pennefather was forced first to commit 140 men of the Rifle Brigade and 200 of the 95th to stabilize the line, and then a few hundred more of the 20th Regiment and 57th as well. The pressure was relentless, as Lieutenant-Colonel Frederick Horn of the 20th later explained:

> A succession of retirements were alternately made between the Allied forces & that of the Russians according to their respective numbers brought to the front. . . . At the gorge of a valley down which winds the Sebastopol road, my small force which consisted of about 150 men of the 20th Regt., with a few others from other corps intermixed, . . . I was compelled to order to retire in consequence of being outflanked by two dense columns of the Enemy's infantry.

Pennefather had been unable to close the Gap and this was the reason that the Iakoutsk Regiment had been able to get behind Cathcart. By 8.30 a.m. the Russians, in spite of severe losses, still had 10,000 men engaged with another 9,000 fresh troops in reserve. The British had over

---

* Davies' absence from Inkerman is confirmed by the Crimea War Medal roll: he was not awarded a clasp for the battle.

3,000 troops available but many of these had been drawn out of position. The right wing was regrouping after Cathcart's charge down the Kitspur; the forces on Home Ridge were marshalled chiefly towards the left flank. The centre remained relatively undefended. Sir George Brown was aware of the danger.

> I had gone along the line with Major General Pennefather & had made arrangements with him for bringing up the 20th Regiment to support our Artillery in the centre, for both the Foot Guards & the other Battalions of the 4th Division had been carried off to the right & that portion of our line consequently was greatly denuded of troops. We found however that the 20th had also been carried away, & it was that circumstance which some time after enabled a few of the enemy to break through, to take temporary possession of three or four of our guns, which rendered the arrival of the French Infantry so opportune. It was in leading on these that I received a musket ball in the left arm which compelled me to quit the field.

The French troops that Brown led into action and who succeeded in recapturing the guns were later identified as sixty Zouaves who had gone absent without leave in order to join the fighting. Yet in spite of this exploit, on Home Ridge as a whole the Russians continued to gain ground. Their progress was aided by the heavy fire brought down by the ninety Russian guns on Shell Hill. Lord Raglan had been on the battlefield since 7 a.m.; one of his first acts had been to send a message for two heavy 18pdr cannon to be brought up from the artillery park to try and counter the Russian barrage. The message unfortunately miscarried and they had not yet arrived. Otherwise, Raglan had been content to allow Pennefather to have management of the battle: it was this lack of active intervention which gave rise to the legend that Raglan had not appeared on the battlefield until half the morning had gone. But Raglan's watching brief did not mean that he was not as exposed to danger as anyone else. His aide-de-camp, Captain Gage, related in a letter home what happened when Brigadier-General Thomas Strangways, the commander of the Royal Artillery, lost his leg to a Russian shell:

> Ld R[aglan] had a narrow escape the other day for Gen[era]l S was not a foot from him when he received his wound & not a muscle of his (Ld R's) countenance moved, tho 3 were sprawling on the ground close round him from the effects of the shell [Strangways; Colonels

Somerset and Gordon also lost their horses]. Another burst just in front of the Staff, & I c[ou]ld feel the wind as a bit flew past my eyes close enough to make me blink & another bit at the same time grazed my left boot.

Colonel George Bell of the 1st Regiment, whose men arrived during the course of the battle to reinforce General Codrington on Victoria Ridge, also paid testimony to the power of the Russian cannonade.

Their Artillery is the very best, & [of the] largest guns. Their shells were exploding amongst our Tents and the havock & destruction soon became alarming. . . . We *cannot* compete with the Rus artillery. They have unbounded resources & mighty guns which they can bring into the field besides the vast weight of shot they send from the Fortress. . . . They fire shot of all sizes & they come hopping & bounding along at from 50 to 150 strides at a bound. We can see them as distinctly as a cricket ball but a column of men cannot get out of their way. Poor Alix was nearly cut in two.

It was at around this time that the hundred men of the 55th Regiment in position on Home Ridge were surprised by the sudden appearance of a strong Russian column and forced back. All that stood between the enemy and the camp of the 2nd Division was the French 7th Léger Regiment, one of the two regiments (in company with the 6th of the Line) sent forward by Bosquet earlier in the morning. This regiment did not share the martial ardour exhibited by the sixty Zouaves, as Lieutenant Mark Walker of the 30th noted:

An immense force [of Russians] supported by numerous artillery drove us to the Camp where a Regt of French were drawn up. They flinched and also turned then I thought it was all up with our position. Fortunately they rallied and fresh bodies coming up we on the right drove them back with dreadful slaughter.

The return from their earlier highly successful charge by the 200 men of the 77th Regiment under Colonel Egerton served to stiffen the French; a seemingly suicidal flank attack on the chief Russian column by the remnant of the 55th Regiment, which had by now rallied, caused the enemy their final discomfiture. Frederick Elton survived the action and wreaked some execution, although not as much as he had hoped, as he explained in a letter to his father eight weeks later.

One of our officers who was wounded while fighting close to me at Inkerman sent me a present of his revolver as he is going to England but hopes to fight another battle by me some day. I tried to do great executions on the 5th with it after he was wounded, but after the battle I found that only two out of five [shots] had gone off as it had been a long time loaded and often wet so my intentions rather failed.

It was a similar story further to the British left. Here were posted 600 men of the 21st and 63rd Regiments, part of the reinforcements brought forward by the 4th Division. The preparation for combat of the 21st Regiment (Royal North British Fusiliers) had not been auspicious. 'I assure you our case was pitiful on that dreadful morning,' wrote Private Henry Smith of No. 10 Company to his parents some months later.

We were often being 24 hours in the trenches, & I believe there was not an hour's drying in the 24, so that when we came to camp we were wet to the skin & all over mud even to the shoulders, & in this very state we had to march to Inkerman battle without as much as a bit of bread or a sip of water to satisfy a craving hunger & thirst.

Six years later, Lieutenant-Colonel Frederick Haines of the 21st described for the benefit of the historian Alexander Kinglake the sequence of events that followed:

Being under a very heavy fire from the artillery posted on Shell Hill both regiments laid down. At this moment the right flank was threatened by a body of Infantry and the Brigade was on the point of changing position to the right, when a cloud of skirmishers almost like a line four deep appeared in our front. Leaving our flanks to take care of themselves, both regiments dashed to the front . . . charging side by side along the face of the hill towards the Post road. The Russians were driven before us like sheep. It was a weird journey down that hill, with we knew not what before or behind us; the mist was too heavy to allow us to see much in any direction, but away we went, the men evidently caring for none of these things. It was Donnybrook Fair revived. I have never seen troops behave better, my great anxiety was to steady and keep them together, the thick brush tending to break our formation.

The charge took the British fully 500 yards down the post road beyond the Barrier. By now they had dispersed into small parties. 'The leading stragglers observed the advance in compact order of a Column of the Enemy,' Haines continued:

> The small party (under forty men) formed up across the road taking advantage of such cover as the rugged bank on the left and the large stones on the outer edge of the road afforded, kept up a brisk fire on the head of the advancing column, dropping a few deliberate shots into a column which was pushing up the bed of the Ravine to the right. The column on the road was checked in its advance and lost many men from the effect of our fire. After a time Lt Col Ainslie who had collected a few men at the Barrier came forward in support of this advanced party, but was immediately mortally wounded.
>
> After holding this position for about half an hour a few skirmishers who had been thrown out to cover the left, & observe the enemy without direction, were driven in. Thus threatened from the high ground on the left, it became absolutely necessary to retire. The small party retreated to the barrier after having for the space of half an hour occupied *the most advanced position* held by our Troops at any period of the action. At the Barrier scattered men of the 21st & 63rd were gradually collecting together with stragglers from other Corps.

Among these stragglers were men of the 68th Regiment and 1st Rifle Brigade, also of the 4th Division. Although the Rifle Brigade troops all possessed Miniés, among other regiments of the division only thirty-five picked men were issued with them: the remainder still had percussion muskets. Haines took stock:

> At the Barrier, finding I was the senior officer, I at once busied myself in making the post secure ... on the left I posted a small party of the 68th with an officer, under cover of a broken wall. Some of these men had Minié rifles, they were directed to fire deliberately on the Artillery on Shell Hill, and to observe any movement in that direction. We were subject to a very heavy cannonade, and were attacked frequently both by the road and the ravine, but no attempt was made on our left. After we had repulsed the first of these attacks, I asked Major Roper [r. Rooper] of the 1st B[attalio]n Rifle Brigade to report our position to General Pennefather, and to request support, as our ammunition was nearly expended. He begged me to send someone else as he did not know the ground. I told him I would go myself

and handed over the post to him as next senior officer . . . I had no difficulty in finding the General. I explained to him the state of the case, the importance of the post, our want of ammunition and our weakness in numbers.

While Haines was absent, the men at the Barrier continued their gallant defence. John Fisher, in common with others of his wing of the Rifle Brigade, had by now worked their way across the battlefield from the Kitspur and joined the defence of the Barrier.

I fell in with a small party who had taken cover under a low wall. I dropped on my knees and in a few moments a large body of Russians showed themselves, coming right straight for the wall. I fired we all fired on they came close to our barrier. We had not time to finish loading. Up we jumped, threw stones, bayonets, any thing we could lay our hands on, right at them. This we continued until quite a young officer with a Red jacket ran up seeing our fix and shouted, charge them lads. With this he jumped on the wall, we followed and let drive amongst them which laid them in heaps dead & wounded. Some of the wounded tried poor fellows to crawl away but was soon stopped & brought in. One man got up and was walking off quite well. I jumped over the wall again, behind which we had once more taken cover owing to our small number and took him by the collar and brought him in. His wound was a slight one.

The reinforcements for the Barrier procured by Haines included a company of the 77th under Lieutenant Molesworth Acton; a company of the 49th under Lieutenant Richard Astley would also prove invaluable. Haines expressed satisfaction:

This small reinforcement had the best effect, for it showed we were in communication with our own people and not cut off as the men were beginning to imagine . . . Brigadier-General Goldie . . . joined us here – I explained to him how we were posted, that I should like to visit the party on the left and that I would report to him in ten minutes. I found the party all snug, but no firing from it, it appeared that they had been so plied with grape in reply, that the officer in charge had ordered the firing to cease – in this he was right for the position was exposed and valuable merely as a lookout. On my return to the Barrier I found Brigadier-General Goldie mortally wounded.

At 9.30 a.m., on Home Ridge itself, the two 18pdrs first requested by Raglan over two hours earlier had finally arrived. The weight of their shot, in opposition to the Russian 12pdrs on Shell Hill, soon began to exert a disproportionate influence on the course of the battle. One by one the Russian cannon were either silenced or forced to move their position. At 10 a.m. Bosquet reached the battlefield with over 2,000 troops; his twelve heavy guns added their weight to the British ordnance on Home Ridge. With his infantry, however, Bosquet felt the fatal lure of the Kitspur and the Sandbag Battery and bent his path towards the extreme right of the British position. True, the 6th of the Line and the 7th Léger, which had gone to its support, needed his assistance; but having stabilized the situation, he then proceeded to take up a position on the Inkerman Tusk facing north, leaving his flanks exposed. Bosquet's deployment was as faulty as the Duke of Cambridge's had been earlier when he took up a position facing east. The result was predictable: Russian columns emerging from the ravines on either side forced a hurried retreat, almost capturing Bosquet in the process. The Sandbag Battery was once again lost to the Russians. Bosquet made a desperate effort to recover his ground. General d'Autemarre had come up with another 2,300 troops; Bosquet immediately launched a counter-attack with two battalions of Zouaves and Algerians. Lieutenant George Carmichael of the 95th witnessed their assault:

> At this juncture or very shortly after, the French bugles rang out the charge and a battalion of the Algerian Indigenes in column advanced at the double close to where I was standing. A big black or negro with his musket held in the middle and high over his head led the column by some paces waving his weapon in the air. The French officers & N[on] C[ommissioned] officers were all shouting 'En avant, En Avant.' I advanced with the Indigenes who charged into the Battery, and drove out the Enemy, a French Officer jumping on the parapet, and waving a tricolour flag for a few minutes. The Indigenes swept down into the ravine, where I did not at first go, thinking if possible that the same incident might happen to them as had befallen us. I went instead to the left to see if there were any troops occupying that ground, I saw none but came across an English Staff Officer mounted (I believe Armstrong of the 49th) and pointed out to him the necessity of supporting that part of the line. He told me that other troops were coming up immediately. Just as we had

17. The Siege of Sevastopol. Tired men return to camp, drawn by Captain Henry Wilkinson, 9th (The East Norfolk) Regiment.

Left. 18. The ragged sentry, painted by Captain the Hon. W. J. Colville of the Rifle Brigade.

Right. 19. 'Cannot Government be persuaded to send out a more efficient Corps of Ambulances?' Captain Arthur Layard makes his protest.

20. British cavalry convey the sick to Balaklava. A drawing by
Captain Henry Wilkinson.

21. By February 1855 warm clothing had begun to arrive. Men of the
77th (The East Middlesex) Regiment pose for the camera.

22. Snug attire helped to make trench duty more endurable. A drawing by Captain Henry Wilkinson.

23. A hospital ward at Scutari. The radically improved conditions bear testimony to Florence Nightingale's influence.

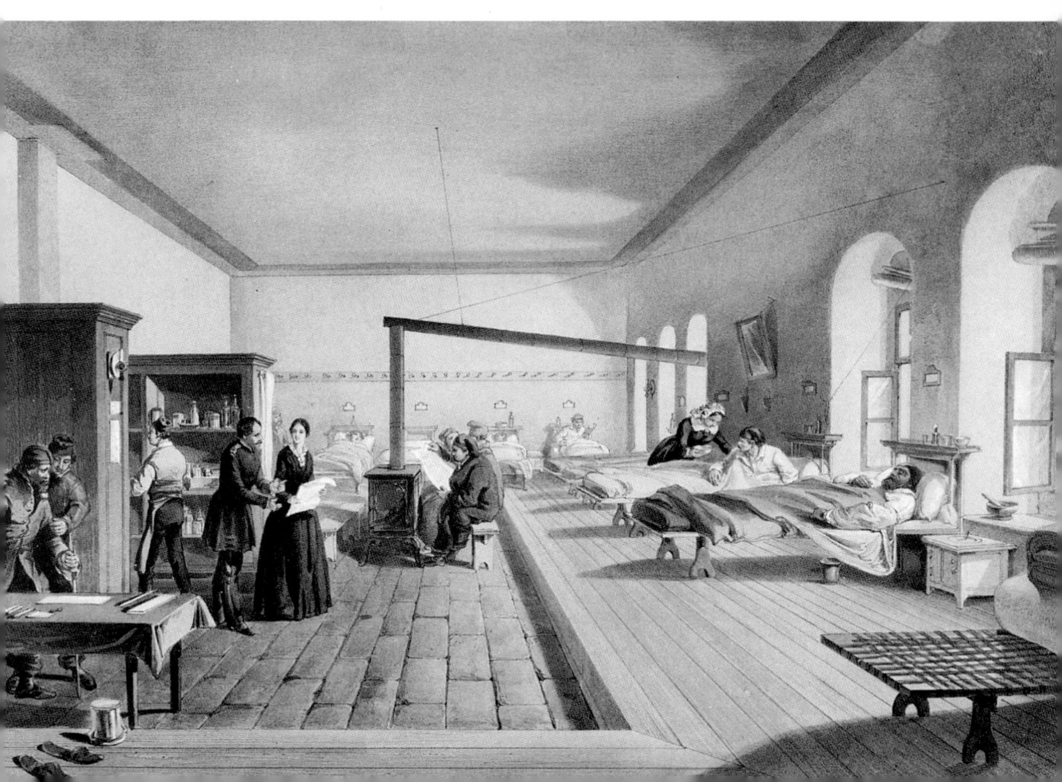

24. Florence Nightingale.

25. Officers of the 4th Division, including (second from left) Captain Maxwell Earle.

26. General Estcourt.

27. The staff at headquarters. Nigel Kingscote is on the far left.

28. 'It was hazarding your reputation every time you went into the trenches'.
Major Robert Campbell, 90th Perthshire Volunteers (second from right), voices his concern.

29. Led by an intrepid Albanian – 'a coarse reprobate looking fellow' – the Russians surprise
the mortar battery's sleeping sentries. A drawing by Lieutenant H. D. Radcliffe.

30. The truce of 24 March 1855, painted by Captain W. T. Markham,
Coldstream Guards.

31. 'I'll have none of your damned fancies'. Sir George Brown, flanked by his staff,
lays down the law.

32. Turning a captured Russian rifle pit.

33. Officers and NCOs of the 88th Connaught Rangers, April 1855.
Captain Nathaniel Steevens is sixth from the left.

34. 13 in mortar battery, painted by Lieutenant Henry Alderson, Royal Artillery.

35. The burning of the government buildings at Kerch.

done speaking, Genl Canrobert with his arm in a sling, Lord Raglan & their staffs rode up to the left of where I was standing, and halted facing Shell Hill. Genl Pennefather came up and was in conversation with Lord Raglan. I noticed that the General the whole time, kept touching his charger with the spur, so that his beast was constantly on the move.

It was now 11 a.m. The British and French had got stronger and now had up to 13,000 men in the field. In contrast, the Russians were spent: Dannenberg had no more than 14,000 battleworthy troops left. He was anxious lest the Allies might go over to the offensive: with his numerous artillery to protect and the steep slopes falling away to the Chernaya behind him, the Russian position was perilous. General Canrobert, however, who had been present much of the morning, had no wish to attack. Raglan possessed fewer than 5,000 British troops with which to act, but he was determined to prevent the Russians retaining a foothold on Shell Hill and the Chersonese Plateau; the British troops which had until then so resolutely defended the Barrier were to prove the instrument of achieving this goal. Colonel Haines sensed his opportunity:

> Feeling strong and that the enemy was becoming decidedly weak, an aggressive movement seemed feasible. The men armed with the Minié were collected and placed under the command of Lieutenant Astley of the 49th who had orders to advance in skirmishing order through the brushwood towards the artillery posted on Shell Hill, and harass the gunners as much as possible. I have always ascribed the retreat of these batteries and the abandonment of eight ammunition waggons to the very efficient and enterprising manner in which the duty was carried out.
>
> Towards the close of the action when Shell Hill was but feebly held by the enemy, the senior officer on the spot ordered Major Horsford of the 1st B[attalio]n Rifle Brigade to advance with his own men & such of other Corps as were armed with the Minié, to take up the ground now almost evacuated by the enemy, & which had been held in the morning by our own Pickets. This Major Horsford accomplished, taking possession of such trophies as the Russians left us, and thus prevented their falling into the hands of our Allies, who, very shortly after Major Horsford, advanced over the same ground with great parade, but with no real effort.

In this advance, Lieutenant Acton's company of the 77th Regiment also played a significant part, and by 1 p.m. the Russian retreat had commenced in earnest. Their artillery was nonetheless still capable of baring its teeth, as Lieutenant Carmichael discovered when the 95th Regiment began to re-form behind Home Ridge.

> Every one I think thought the day's work was done, and began to congratulate each other on the escapes of the day, and to relate incidents of the fight, when the Enemy suddenly opened again with a heavy fire of cannon. The Grenadier standing in the front rank of our line Patrick Doyle had his right leg taken off by a cannon ball. Vialls gave his handkerchief (a red silk one I remember) to Pte Martin Urell another Grenadier to tie tightly over the stump. This ... he did, and with a few words of encouragement to his comrade was taking his place in the ranks, when his own hand was taken off by another cannon ball.

Without the participation of the French there could be no active pursuit. The Russians had lost 12,000 men, the British 2,500 and the French 1,800. Thanks to the fog which shrouded the battlefield, particularly in the struggle's early stages, the British had fought in happy ignorance of the true odds against them. Pennefather's tactic of feeding the pickets had been vindicated. On such broken terrain the inability of the Russians to manoeuvre in anything other than heavy columns told against them. Yet, as Brigadier-General Airey admitted in a letter to Major-General George Wetherall back in England, it had undeniably been a close-run affair: 'What a fight on 5th!! Defeat perfect and entire, still touch and go!! If they had succeeded in establishing themselves on our heights we should have gone! Nothing but the sea to fall back upon!' The nerves of others were even more strained: 'A Royal G[enera]l lost his head they say & is still in a state of ex[citemen]t & going home for [a] change of air,' commented Colonel Bell. General Codrington elaborated upon Bell's observation in a letter to his wife:

> The D[uke] of Cambridge went away unwell 2 days after the action. He seemed to me very much excited the evening of the battle when I met him as I was going to the field of battle on that front; I never heard anything like his loud and excited talking about it and the whole business – I really believe he is seriously unwell. I scarcely think he will come back again here. I told you of Sir G. Cathcart

having taken part of his division down the slope – well the Duke was wild about it. We saw of course many soldiers about, among them one of the 41st whom he talked to. 'Good God! my man, what could have taken you down the hill, what could possibly have made you go?' Of course the man didn't know what to say except that he went where he was ordered. 'But Codrington, what could induce my poor dear friend Cathcart to go down' – then breaking off about some wounded guardsman, or some Russian prisoner – he was full of all sorts of exclamations and talk, in a loud voice before all soldiers about the expedition, &c &c. It really was a relief to me when I was able to get away.

The dogged tenacity of the Russians had impressed some. Nigel Kingscote wrote: 'Their great strength is in Artillery which is of very heavy calibre, but their Infantry fought better than I thought, but then they were fresh troops.' Paymaster Mosley of the 20th Regiment advanced another reason for Russian pertinacity:

An officer we took told one of our Generals that the Russian General had issued an order the night before the battle that all the troops would march next morning to attack the Turks, who he told them were in position on our right, and they thinking they could easily thrash the Turks as the latter had run away so soon down at Balaklava . . . came on as if they were not to be stopped by anything, and we going out in great coats (which are something like the Turks',) as it was a cold wet morning, they did not find out their mistake for some time. At least that is what this officer told us and he said if we had gone out in Red they would have stood an hour instead of seven.

Assistant Surgeon John Scott of the 57th Regiment learnt much by examining the clothing and equipment of the Russians:

Little doubt can be entertained that the enemy were chosen men as they were better dressed than most Russian soldiers. Their guns were longer than ours and remarkably clean, but are made of bad material, a single blow breaking the stock and bending the barrel. Thousands of muskets were broken by our troops lest any might be carried off or used by the wounded on the field.

I was certainly amused on the day of the battle at our own men when no ammunition could be procured, they cut the pouches off the wounded Russians and there found an abundance, but the balls were too small.

The field is covered with broken arms of every description – swords, heavy and not well made; musquets, long but not substantial. They are however beautifully clean, particularly the locks and nipples.

Every man had rum in his water, also a small bag of bad meat, and a supply of leather, awls, needles and sundry other things making up his pack. Many of them were well clothed, within and without. The officers wore the same great-coat as the men, but were richly dressed inside. Many of the men had gold pieces in a leather bag buckled around the knee.

But Scott's opportunity for observation was limited; as he noted in his diary on 6 November, his professional duties beckoned:

The medical duties were hard and dangerous yesterday, but today they are laborious in the extreme – amputations, extracting balls, dressing wounds &c. Our men are mostly wounded in the upper part of the body with gunshot. This probably arose from the close proximity of the enemy. We have only two or three bayonette wounds, and those were given after the men had fallen. The Russian prisoners however had many bayonette wounds, but indeed few compared with the number I expected. However, the enemy don't like too close quarters.

Scott's observation regarding the injuries most widely inflicted on British casualties was borne out in the instance of Lieutenant the Honourable William Amherst of the Coldstream Guards, as Colonel Lord Frederick Paulet wrote to Amherst's father, Lord Holmesdale:

I regret to have to tell you that your son was wounded yes[terda]y. . . . He was struck just under the shoulder blade, as he was raising his arm, and the ball taking an upward direction came out at the neck. Nothing is broken and from the closeness of the fire there is less laceration than is usual in gun shot wounds. He walked from the field, to the general Hospital, and then back to his tent, I undressed him and put him to bed, his patience, his resignation, his thankfulness for any attention, and his fear of giving trouble showed such a total absence of all selfishness, he quite won my heart . . . He is better off than some, as he has a bed instead of the ground to sleep on . . . We have suffered a fearful loss as the returns will show you. I have just returned from burying 8 Off[icers] of the Coldstreams killed yesy. Two out of my own tent in my own mess, 'tis sad indeed!

Casualties among divisional and brigade commanders were also high. Sir George Brown had been wounded and would eventually leave the Crimea to recuperate. The Light Division also lost one of its brigadiers, George Buller taking temporary command of the 4th Division in place of General Cathcart. Brown's injuries had not improved his temper and a week after Inkerman he was writing to Airey complaining of General Codrington:

He is an odd fellow that Codrington, for not only have I not had a line from him Official or otherwise since I left the Camp but he has not even had the grace to send to enquire for my health! I wish you had detached him from me instead of George Buller, but there can be no doubt you have selected the best man.

Codrington was unapologetic, writing to his wife on 27 November:

Did I tell you that Sir G.B., having mentioned in a note to Sullivan that he had not heard a word of any sort from me, I took the opportunity of telling him by note that, little as I wished to be deficient towards him either privately or publicly, yet so much of my personal and written communications with him had ended in expressions and terms towards me which were painful and unpleasant, that I had purposely avoided putting myself in the way of either.

In the situation that the British army found itself after Inkerman, with even General Sir George De Lacy Evans urging on Raglan the abandonment of the expedition, such squabbles were decidedly unhelpful.

6

WINTER

Although Inkerman was a heavy defeat for the Russians, it had served its purpose as a 'spoiler': the Allies could no longer contemplate assaulting Sevastopol before the full onset of winter. For the British, who were now more over-stretched than ever, the prospect of spending the coming months on the bleak Chersonese uplands was a daunting one. Trench duty told heavily on the troops. The army was critically short of fuel. On 11 November Staff Surgeon Chilley Pine of the 4th Division noted in his journal:

> I find that the men are without camp-kettles, and that each is cooking for himself in his mess tin: frequently he is too tired to cook at all, & therefore some eat their meat in a raw state. I have brought the matter to the attention of the Brigadier. Heavy rain continues. All doctoring is out of the question, under the present state of affairs.

Raglan wrote to the Duke of Newcastle: 'To speak frankly, we want every man you can send us. Fresh Battalions, in addition of drafts, are most desirable, and warm clothing of every description.' On 12 November he wrote again to Newcastle, having just waved off A. H. Layard. In light of what his guest had already written home, and what he would later say in the House of Commons, Raglan's words of commendation were ill-judged: 'Should he go home, he would be able to give most valuable and accurate information as to the state of things here ... and his ability and powers of observation will enable him at once to put before you, what our Troops have undergone.'

Raglan did not yet see coming the political storm which was to engulf him in the months ahead. A storm of a different type, however, was altogether more imminent. Early in the morning of 14 November the weather finally broke – and it did so with a vengeance: there was a hurricane. The resulting scene of devastation in the British encampment was described by Lieutenant-Colonel Charles Lygon Cocks of the Coldstream Guards in a letter to his brother:

You will see long accounts of the fearful storm which we were visited on Tuesday last. I had luckily got up as the rain was pouring into the tent & the wind blowing up underneath & was trying to make the best of a bad bargain & smoke a pipe when Squall No. 1 came, sent my tent one way, the whole of my wardrobe, bed etc (wh[ich] I had got the night before from Eupatoria), another, & left me in a very singular, to say the least of it, costume in the rain. The scene was most ridiculous, the tents being all down & discovering everyone, some in bed, some like myself in Illustrated shirts *et pictorio nihil*, all being soaked through & bellowing loudly for their servants. The wind was most awful & we could only keep our tents from going to Sebastopol by lying like spread eagles on the top of them. The storm lulled a little so we took the opportunity of pitching our tents with many splices & braces & try to get something to eat. The fires of course were all out, so Shepherd & I breakfasted on biscuits & cheese, one holding the tent while the other ate. While we were engaged in the juicy repast crash went the tent pole breaking my shins & Shepherd's head & down came every tent in the camp with the wind & rain increasing every moment; one could not stand up for a few moments, it beat every wind I ever felt at Brighton. We had nothing for it but to be on our tents with our property underneath & with the course of events, towards evening it moderated & we rigged up jury poles & after another visit to the biscuits & cheese, I went to bed, *clothes & all* for fear of any more accidents.

However bad it was for the troops ashore, it was a matter of life and death for those aboard the shipping crowded outside Balaklava harbour. No fewer than twenty-one vessels foundered, including the mighty steamship the *Prince*, crammed full of winter clothing. Also lost was the *Resolute* and its cargo of ten million Minié rounds. The Duke of Cambridge, recuperating aboard the warship *Retribution*, was severely unnerved by the experience, as he admitted to Raglan the day after:

By a merciful interposition of providence we have been saved from a watery grave, and nothing but a miracle saved us. . . . It was a fearful gale & we had a more dreadful 24 hours of it than we ever spent. It carried away two anchors & our rudder; [we] had to throw over all our upper deck guns & then we had to hold on by one anchor 200 yards from the Rocks which by a merciful providence held us on. In short it was fearful . . . I find myself so completely knocked up & shattered in health by this & former exposure to cold & fatigue that I hope you will not object to my going for a short time to Constantinople, Gibson [his doctor] being of opinion that if I were at this moment to return to Camp in this dreadful weather I should only have to take to my bed.

The Duke of Cambridge left the theatre of war, never to return.

Although the flattened tents could be re-erected, fresh supplies took time to arrive from England. Some losses, the Commissary-General warned, were especially critical: 'Mr Filder's great fear is the want of forage for the horses', Raglan told Newcastle. 'We lost twenty days hay by the tempest. As it is the cold of the nights kills a vast number of the animals employed for the conveyance of ammunition'. Ten days later, on 28 November, Raglan reinforced the message: 'Our horses are dying fast; but until we are sure that we can feed them, I could not recommend that they should receive any addition here.' The planks that Raglan had sent for from Sinope to build huts had arrived, but with the army's transport wasting away there was no means of conveying them from Balaklava to the Chersonese uplands. 'Our Artillery horses are suffering much from exposure, and hard work, as well as want of food. We must try to find some cover for them,' Raglan concluded.

Morale among the army's officers was suffering as well. Paymaster Mosley of the 20th Regiment observed how: 'Lots of fellows are selling out, they say they would not stay the winter here for anything. How I wish I could do the same, the only two friends I have in this regiment are going, what I shall do then I really do not know.' But the authorities were unaccommodating. Nigel Kingscote described the response from Headquarters:

After the Inkerman some 30 resignations were sent in on account of urgent private affairs, the answer to one and all was a reference home, the answer from home was that they would be accepted as soon as other officers could replace them out here, but as every Regiment was to be augmented they could not say when that would be, upon which a large proportion found that their affairs were not so pressing and have begged to withdraw their papers. Lord George Paget was the only one who was allowed to go home as everyone knew he was on the point of going when his Regiment was ordered out. He had been in 3 actions and only a remnant of his Regiment [was] left with a good Major, so [as] there was no reason to keep him he went.

Lieutenant-Colonel Anthony Sterling had only limited sympathy for those who had been thwarted: 'The Officers are all tired of it; many want to sell out, losing ever so much on their Commissions; and these men are the more to be pitied, because after they have acknowledged their want of endurance, of patriotism, &c., they cannot go.'

In spite of the embargo placed on officers' retirements, many regiments remained in dire need of replacements. Of them, the 7th Royal Fusiliers Regiment was worst off. Its commanding officer, Colonel Lacy Yea, issued the Adjutant-General in London, General Wetherall, a warning on 1 December:

I have just heard that Honble. Lieutenant Crofton of my Regt. has managed to get off from Scutari to England with invalids, he having been very behindhand in returning to his Regiment when well. I have endeavoured over and over again to get the likes of him back, but Major Sillery appears to avoid the unpopularity of sending back unwilling young gents. Mr. Thomas has slipped off also, who had never landed in the Crimea or seen a shot fired. If he is too unhealthy to do his duty he ought to sell out. May I implore you to send Mr. Crofton back *instantly* as (between ourselves) he is a bit of a shuffler in duty. I am now reduced to Capt. Mills, Lt. Appleyard and Ensign Waller (Lt. and acting Adjt Cooper already failing, but kept up by pluck alone) and I leave to your judgment whether with 250 recruits who have not had a drill with the Regt. and with 19 Serjeants away wounded at Scutari and elsewhere, there is the slightest chance of my being able to do a Regiment's duty with such assistance. I foretell a catastrophe if we are brought in contact with the enemy, as I have had experience at Alma that *recruits* will not advance unless driven on by officers and supernumerary N[on] C[ommissioned] Officers . . . The weather is so dreadful that six of my draft died from cold and exposure the first night in the trenches; the 50 men by 'Ottawa' steamer arrived two days ago, and two have died already (alas! *no officer* with this draft). I am afraid to say what my anticipations are of the upshot of this affair. Climate, weather & exposure will beat anybody, but if I never write again I must *implore* you to *send me officers* (and Mr. Crofton & Mr. Thomas in particular).

Three weeks later Lacy Yea was reduced to a complement of three subalterns. 'What I want are Captains – I have *none*', he beseeched Wetherall. 'Where is Pack, and Capt. Brown, also Capt. Turner? Oh, pray send them.'

Major William Forrest of the 4th Dragoon Guards was similarly unimpressed with the claims of fellow officers in his regiment for medical leave. He wrote home on 5 January 1855:

I am glad to hear that the people in England look coldly upon Lord G Paget and others who go home without good reason. Our impression here is that neither Morgan nor Webb should have gone home. Pine says that Morgan ought not even to have gone to Scutari.

For those officers who remained, the priority was securing adequate shelter. Tents were too much at the mercy of the elements. Without planking, huts could only be improvised. On 22 November Captain William Radcliffe of the 20th Regiment informed his parents of his own solution:

My Hut is progressing steadily, I hope to be 'underground' by the end of the week. The first operation was to dig a pit, 3 feet 6 deep, 8 feet wide, & 13 long. An upright post is then placed in the centre of each end, & a cross-piece put on the top of these, & secured by rope, nails, or anything you can get; Poles or whatever Wood you can beg, borrow, or steal, are then placed from the earth to the cross-piece, & secured in the same way; the Gable ends are filled up with stones, mud & earth, & this forms the roof, or rather frame of the roof. The Walls are the sides of the pit, & we make the roof a sufficient height, for a man to stand up in. Now comes the covering of the Roof, this is generally made by twining brushwood between the Poles, & then throwing mud & earth over it, but I mean to improve on it, & am covering mine by degrees, with the skins of horses and bullocks (the former dying in great numbers) & so hope to make it water-proof beyond a doubt. This takes longer doing, for the hides have to be cured, 'in a way'. McNeil & I are hutting together, I have already named it 'Hide Abbey'. He is now making the fire-place, a hole cut in one side of the Wall, & the chimney made . . . of tin pots & clay. Oh! how I am looking forward to sitting by it. Now comes our great triumph. The other day we managed to pick up at Balaklava a small window, about 18 inches square, & this will be fitted in one gable end, the door in the other. This I assure you was got at, at a great risk, for 'Pillaging' is punished severely. If this window had not been procured, a small hole, to be filled up when the wind or rain was in that direction, would have done the duty. All our spare time is fully taken up in building this mansion, & it is a great amusement, as well as most necessary. I picked up a sailor the other day, who by good luck, happened to be a Carpenter, & he has been of the greatest assistance.

But in his next letter, Radcliffe explained the increasing difficulties that he had encountered.

After a week's almost constant rain, & certainly without an hour's sunshine, my hut building has been sadly delayed, both on account of the weather & the want of wood to complete the roof, so I determined on that day to ride to Balaklava, & see if by *any* means, I could make up the deficiency. It was very dark & gloomy when I started, & before I got there was raining steadily. The scene in that miserable little village was indescribable, there are only two 'lanes' in it, I can't call them 'streets', so narrow that if you want to turn a cart even, you must go to the end of it to do so. Well, these are so crammed & jammed, with Artillery wagons, Commissariat Arabas [carriages], Mule Carts, Camels, Bullocks, Pack & Ammunition Horses & Dragoons, not forgetting a crowd of Infantry Men, that it appears an inextricable mass of confusion, & it is no easy matter at times to cross from one side to the other. The mud & filth are over your ankles, & many an unseen hole *much deeper*. The little Harbour crowded with ships, & the *remains*, I am sorry to say of *what were*, magnificent ships & their cargos. But the swaggering cavalry (when at home) are the most pitiable objects of the whole, *out here*, Horse Artillery, Hussars & Dragoons, are in the same plight, it is a toss up, which have most mud on them, the Men or Horses: they all appear very much 'down on their luck' & assume quite a different [appearance] in the streets of Balaklava, to what they do in Dublin, or the Phoenix Park. The Infantry Man, as I have told you before, is by no means clean or smart, but he is certainly less an object of ridicule than the Dragoon.

After some time I managed to get the wood I required, without infringing the stringent orders of the Provost Marshals, & with the letters in my Holsters, for I found that the mail had arrived, I started for Camp, in a *perfect deluge* of rain, I speak within bounds. Nevertheless I was very cheery, I had on a MacIntosh with a hood to it, (an admirable contrivance, & for which I am indebted to some unknown French Officer, whose Kit I picked up, on the line of march from the Belbec, & who I doubt not, is deploring the loss to this day), I had secured my wood, & *more than all*, I had my *letters to read* ... The Roads are now so bad, it is with the *greatest difficulty*, the provisions for the troops can be brought to camp, & now & then, we don't get the full ration from that cause, the Horses would be starved, if we did not send for the forage ourselves, & that at present is so bad, that hunger alone compels them to eat it, poor things, the hay being that which was picked up out of the water, after the vessels were wrecked. The road was strewn with all manner of things, Guns stuck fast in the mud, Arabas with wheels off, & their loads scattered about.

Radcliffe had taken the precaution of conducting his business in Balaklava himself. Major George Mundy of the 33rd Regiment had occasion to rue not doing the same. He wrote to his mother on 27 November:

My Adjutant (Barrett) and self are just going to dine (3 PM) upon *salt* pork & rice (how I hate salt) & I will now tell you a piece of our luck. Yesterday we sent my Batman with my second charger to Balaclava to get *Goodies!* such as potted meat, potatoes, sardines, potted fish, pickles & flour. *He* came back at 8 o'clock at night *beastly* drunk, having lost the saddle bags and contents, made away with £4 (lucky it was not more) & all he brought was ½ a sack of potatoes. It was very provoking, as we were cleared out. *He* will be tried by a Court Martial tomorrow and most likely (almost certainly) will receive corporal punishment. I am *always* sorry to do this, but examples must be made when such unsoldierlike acts are committed. There is *no* other mode of punishment here, I am sorry to say, for the *Cat* is an implement that ought to be made as little use of as possible; besides few men have now strength enough to stand it. An officer's servant here has in comparison *nothing* to do, no pickets or trenches, no fatigues and a night's rest *always,* and they ought to be grateful, but I fear gratitude in a soldier is by no means a common occurrence.

Meanwhile, in response to Raglan's appeals, the army in the Crimea was being reinforced. Radcliffe again:

The 46th, 62nd & 97th Regts [the 62nd (The Wiltshire) Regiment; 97th (The Earl of Ulster's) Regiment] have arrived, *such a contrast* to the men that have been here for some time; they look as clean as new pins, & are easily recognised by their white belts & blankets & at a considerable distance, whilst we are more like the soldiers that returned from the Spanish Legion,* which you may remember to have seen: Belts guiltless of pipe clay for the last 5 months, black trousers mended with a bit of red cloth, or as is more often the case not mended at all. Coats the same; dress caps converted into chimneys, I saw these yesterday, one inside the other, piled over a few stones, & a goodly amount of smoke, ascending through them, whilst two or three grim unshaven fellows, were cooking their rations of tough beef, over a small fire of *green twigs.* The only things we pay attention to, are the Firelocks & Pouch belts, & they are in good order.

The new arrivals were horrified by the conditions that they encountered. Hospital Sergeant Frederick Newman of the 97th Regiment wrote home on 29 November:

We are now about 3 miles from Sebastopol and under canvas tents, the rain pouring in torrents and all around miserable. Cholera has broke out amongst the poor fellows who are exposed in the Trenches day and night with nothing but their big coats to shelter them from the rain or cold . . . .

We get biscuits Salt Pork or Beef and one gill of Rum with some Sugar Rice and unroasted Coffee. Just like our government, the idea of sending coffee here not roasted. We manage it somehow, by grinding it in a broken bomb shell with a round shot to crush it. Water is very scarce and extremely muddy. I have not washed my face nor yet shaved since I landed here on the 20th inst being satisfied with enough to drink without washing my face and as for a clean shirt I think when I can find it convenient to wash one then I will

---

* The British Auxiliary Legion, which fought in the Carlist Wars, 1835–37.

put one on. So I am washerwoman and cook and everything else at the same time. . . . This terrible Cholera . . . has made fearful ravages here. I have just commenced to write again and there are now six poor fellows lying dead. I am rather loose in my bowels, but take as much care of myself as possible.

He continued his letter on 2nd December.

It is a cold, windy morning and my feet feel like ice. We have lost 25 men by Cholera and we have now 18 in Hospital with this disease and 25 with Diarrhea. I must say we are fearfully situated and any man who lives to go to England from this ought to be a good man all his life after.

Within the month Newman too was dead.

Private Thomas Hagger, who arrived with a draft for the 23rd Regiment, was equally forthright in his condemnation of what he discovered. He wrote home on 1 December:

I have been at this place a forghtnight next Wensday. My dear parents this is a most Aurful place we are about 2 miles from Sebastopol. There is about 70000 of us hear at least as high as I can gues. You would be surprised if you could but see our camp & the French & Turkish together as far as the eye can reach you would see nothing but tents. The one that I am in there is 4 of us in it we have nothing but the bare ground to lie upon & the blankit to cover us with. I am sorry to say that the men that was out before I came have not had so much as a clean shirt on for 2 Mounths the people at home think that the troops out hear are well provided for I am sorry to say that they are treated worse then dogs are at home I can tell the inhabitants of old England that if the solders that are out hear could but get home again they would not get them out so easy it is not the fear of fighting it is the worse treatment that we receive.

John Fisher of the 1st Battalion Rifle Brigade was full of compassion for the replacements who arrived for his own regiment.

We now began to get draughts from England, poor men. The first 50 that arrived was soon taken off by disease & other causes. It was shocking to see the men walking about the camp in the last stages of dissentry, eyes sunken, cheeks all gone, mere skeletons; some actually doing duty when allowed, because they would not be thought schemers, a term that was in no wise rellished by any of us. But trench duty being so heavy about this time on account of the few men able to contend with it, caused this word to be used frequently; the men doing the duty being unwell thought those in camp on the sick list or a great number of them ought to be there as well.

The great problem faced by the new arrivals in the Crimea was that they were unacclimatized. At the beginning of December the 9th (The East Norfolk) Regiment arrived from Corfu, having previously been stationed on Malta. It had been recognized that sending the regiment directly to a Crimean winter was risky, but Raglan's need for replacements could brook no delay. Captain Hopton Bassett Scott of the 9th explained the result.

When the Regt. arrived here a fortnight ago, it was just after that fearful storm, and it continued to rain incessantly for ten days. Cholera broke out, and we lost 75 men out of 480, besides upwards of 100 in hospital. It was most frightful; there were no hospital tents, not a grain of medicine of any kind, and they were left to die without the possibility of help, amongst their comrades. Between the moral effect produced by these sights, and the physical, by the fearful way they are worked in the trenches, 12 hours at a time out of 24, our regt. is a ruin most painful to the sight.

After the arrival of the 17th (The Leicestershire) and the 89th Regiments, Lord Raglan wrote the Duke of Newcastle an assessment of the accretion of strength to his army: 'You will see that the additional numbers amount to 7282, that of these 514 have died and 1003 were sick on the 12th December.' Raglan was also concerned about the calibre of his replacements:

I wish that we had older men than those sent out. Some of the drafts lately come out are little more than sixteen years of age and there is a boy with my guard who only enlisted nine weeks ago, and tho' professing to be sixteen looks I am told about fourteen.

Staff Surgeon Pine summed up the situation at the end of November from a medical perspective.

Round all the Hospitals. Such misery it is impossible to fancy: men with dysentery, and diarrhoea and fever & cholera lying in the mud with insufficient covering, food, & medicine. Medicine under such circumstances can be of no use. My function, excepting in relation to Surgery is quite gone.

Others were unwilling to remain silent about the army's suffering. Among the papers of Colonel George Bell is the draft of a letter to the editor of *The Times*, written on 28–29 November. Although the letter of his which *The Times* eventually published was less astringent, even that, Bell later considered, had been quite sufficient to blight what was left of his military career.

All the elements of destruction are against us, sickness & death, & nakedness, & uncertain ration of salt meat. Not a drop of Rum for two days, the only stand by to keep the soldier on his legs at all. If this fails we are done. The Communication to Balaklava impossible, knee deep all the way for 6 miles. Wheels can't move, & the poor wretched starved baggage animals have not strength to wade through the mud without a load. Horses – cavalry, artillery, officers' chargers & Baggage Animals die by the score every night at their peg, from cold & starvation. Worse than this, the men are dropping down fearfully. I saw *nine* men of 1st Batt[alion] Royal Regt lying *Dead in one Tent* to day, and 15 more dying! All cases of Cholera, amongst them was a little Drum boy (which made ten) who came out with a draft last week. These Boys are perfectly useless, they are not required for any purpose, they only consume a man's rations & they come here to die. The poor men's backs are never dry, their one suit of rags hang in tatters about them, they go down to the Trenches at night wet to the skin, ly there in water, mud, & slush till morning, come back with cramps, go to a crowded Hosp[ita]l Marquee tattered by the storm, ly down in a fetid atmosphere, quite enough of itself to breed contagion, & die there in agony. This is no romance, it is my duty as a C.O. to see & Endeavour to alleviate, the sufferings & privations of my humble but gallant comrades. I can't do it, I have no power. Everything almost is wanting in this Hosp[ita]l department, so badly put together from the start. No people complain so much of it as the Medical officers of Regts & many of the Staff Doctors too. The Surgeon of a Batt[alio]n. came to me yesterday with tears in his Eyes saying, 'My Dear ——— I fear we will lose all our men, the state of things now is more frightful than ever. The Ambulance can't move through the mud & I cannot send a man to Balaklava.

21 Deaths in the Brigade last night and *45* in the 3rd Division!' The
1st Royals, 38th & 50th are perhaps the most healthy Brigade in
the Army although these three Regts have been continually in the
Trenches for 45 days & nights as guards & working parties, but now
humanity can't contend against the privations they endure, & must
endure, until the whole Army is diminished to a low figure.

29th. A fearful storm of rain & wind, the country is again in a
swamp, our Camp ground almost impassable, not a drop of rum to
day as yet for the men 4 o'clock & fear it will not be got up (if there
is any at Ba---). We consider that the Soldier's life here depends on
this ration. They never get back rations. General & other officers
have to send to Balaklava for their forage, or want . . . I heard Sir R.
E[nglan]d say yesterday that he had not a bit of anything for Dinner!
Sir John Campbell who commands the 4th Division lives in a little
cave, by candle light! Col. Bell has a wall 4 feet high built round his
Tent, to break off the wind, other officers have mud walls around.
Some have sunk deep pits, covered them over, & intend to live
underground & so on, for here we must stay, live or die . . .

Private. The Ed Times. If you think these hasty lines worthy of a
place in your paper, they are at your service for publication. I fear
to state the real state of things here. G Bell Col[onel] Com[manding]
1st Brigade 3rd Division.

Five days later Bell had the opportunity to discuss the condition of
his men with the commander-in-chief himself. As so often, veterans
settled down to draw comparisons with the last conflict in which they
had served together – in this case the Peninsular War, forty years earlier.

I went down to day to see Lord R[aglan]. He asked me a great
deal about my people &c and seems alive to all our difficulties &
privations. . . . I thought his Lordship looked haggard & broken.
'It is terrible weather,' he said, 'I can't remember anything like it.'
'Yes, My Lord there is no disguising the fact,' I said. 'The privation
is frightful, I knew nothing like it excepting the Retreat from Burgos
in Spain.' [Raglan:] 'Yes, and at Bayonne.' O yes there it was very
bad but we had covering, we got into little villages & [were] not
exposed as we now are up to the ankles in mud, & passing our days
and nights in the trenches under the fire of a vigilant & determined
enemy. 'True true, that was the case. What's your sick?' 253 to day
my Lord in camp, that is, in my Brigade.

Major Forrest, encamped with the cavalry at Kadikoi outside Balak-lava, was aware of the difficulties faced by the army on the uplands.

The unfortunate Infantry, many of whom only get 3 nights in bed, or rather, in undisturbed sleep, out of 14 have had also to march down to Balaklava and carry up their own rations; however, this was found impracticable, and now the Heavy Brigade have to find 500 horses every day for the purpose of performing the Commissariat Duty: it comes hard upon our Men, Horses and saddles, but it is absolutely necessary in the inefficient state of our Commissariat.

It was a coincidence that 12 December, the very day A. H. Layard delivered a wide-ranging speech in Parliament attacking the Government's mismanagement of the war – and highlighting in particular how the absence of ambulances (since arrived) had delayed the pursuit of the Russians after the Battle of the Alma – saw a letter written to him by his brother Captain Arthur Layard imploring him to publicize the fact that the transport and medical services had now utterly broken down.

The lower road to Balaklava is now open, at least many people go by it, the Cossacks do not now approach quite so near. The con-tinuous rain we suffered from, up to three days ago, did us a great deal of mischief. In the first place it has completely destroyed our transport service. The road to Balaklava was in a dreadful state. The mules etc. were overworked and underfed, the consequence was they died, the Commissariat could not get our rations or our forage, the troops were and are all on short rations and the mounted officers, the Artillery and Cavalry up here are obliged to send in for their forage and I hear we shall have shortly to send in for our rations ourselves. Our wretched Ambulance establishment of course went to the back. And only yesterday, don't hide the fact from any one in England, the French volunteered and took down to Balaklava eleven hundred 1100 of our sick, 200 going down from this Division (the 2nd), an officer of the staff attached to it going down with them. The sick were conveyed in the litters etc on the mules and reached the ships safely. The mules appeared in excellent condition, just as fresh as when they first landed at Gallipoli. Our animals are all dead or the few that remain are but a bag of dying bones. There is not an officer in the Army that does not blush at our being obliged to go for help to our friends the French. Our Medical department is of course in its usual state of efficiency... Cannot Government be persuaded to send out or embody a more efficient Corps of Ambulances? The present is worse than useless. The old rascals destroy more harness, break more carts, and kill more animals than would keep up a proper and thoroughly serviced establishment. I have, or had, two carts, the proportion of mules for them, and 15 men, and they give more trouble than a whole regiment. Both carts are broken, but two mules alive, and all the men continuously drunk, sick or prisoners for misconduct.

Although a single horse could only carry a third of the load that the same horse pulling wheeled transport might manage, with the road to Balaklava impassable to carts or wagons, a single horse was better than nothing. It was imperative to keep them in good condition, but this was far from easy. Sergeant George Cruse of the 1st Dragoons wrote to his wife on 3 January 1855:

There was a large deep trench dug out by our men for a stable for the Horses but no means taken to put a roof on it as yet. The Major was very anxious to get the Horses into it for shelter from the wind so we put about forty into it, and this morning we had a great job to get them out of it as the heavy rain had put about four feet of water into it... There were about fifteen Horses fell dead as they were going up to the front to day and I fully expect that many in the Brigade will be dead before morning. I should indeed be sorry for you to behold the pitiable plight the poor animals are in. We have a sort of clothing for them, but after they have had a good roll in the mud and after that a good fall of snow, and then the whole to be frozen on to them, it is enough to kill any animal except one cast in bronze.

For the horses with the army on the heights matters were even worse. Hicks Withers was the veterinary surgeon with 'E' Battery of the Royal Artillery, attached to the Light Division. He wrote to his father on 12 January:

Our horses have been suffering very much from the cold & wet and scarcity of food. We are frequently 5 or 6 days without hay for them, which is a great neglect for the ration of barley is not enough this cold weather. We have about 45 from each battery stabled at Balaklava

& I believe are going to send more. In this battery we have now 30 on the sick list from various causes, sore backs & shoulders, injured feet & wounds in heels from getting over chains. These are very difficult to heal, indeed I can do very little for them. Often they get their shoes off & break away the wall of the foot & on cutting away I find a greater part of the sole with wet soaked in between the sensible & insensible sole so am obliged to cut away all the horn and put rags on which gives no end of trouble. We ought to have had stables built long ago. I have kept on about it & have dug holes for my sick & gone so far as offering to give £5 myself & getting the others to do the same to get French or English fatigue parties to dig holes & help make them, for the gunners have not time to do it, but I cannot get any further than that & the poor wretches must die. The worst of it is the sound have to bring up food for the sick a distance of 4 miles.

Major-General James Estcourt, the Adjutant-General, believed the artillery and cavalry horses to be dying off too quickly. In a letter of 8 January to General Wetherall, he accused officers and men of not doing their best for them, of falling prey to apathy when they saw their horses fetlock deep in the mire. Estcourt considered that there was a contributory factor to account for this, at least in the case of the Cavalry Division:

> To you I say this confidentially, that Lord Lucan has disgusted them. He meddles, I hear, in everything. The Brigadiers find themselves put on one side and are disgusted: the same is the case with the Commanding Officers; and the Staff are tired to death of him. I am writing freely for your own information. Do not attach more to what I say than my words express.

The other villain, in Estcourt's opinion, was the Commissary-General, William Filder, whose transport had failed to bring forward supplies from Balaklava.

> We have great difficulty in getting ... comforts up to the front. The men are so short a time out of the Trenches, and so much is consumed in scraping together fuel to cook. Filder again. We should be well off if Filder brought to our tents the good things and the necessary things which have been so amply provided by the good people at home.
>
> Now goodbye. Pray burn my letter. I hold no such language here

as I have written to you. I have written in confidence, and in the hope that you will absolutely destroy my letter. I hate to think of croaking; and therefore hold no such language here as I have used to you.

Private John Pine of the Rifle Brigade, after burying his brother at the Alma, had since been appointed a divisional clerk at an extra two shillings per day; but his lighter duties had not saved him from six weeks of dysentery and diarrhoea, as he informed his father in a letter of 8 January 1855.

I was recommended at the Hospital to eat nothing but bread and cheese for my complaint so I sent down to Balaklava for a dutch cheese and they charged me six shillings for it and they charge two shillings for a two pound loaf. We have been living on biscuit and salt rations the greater part of the time we have been in the field, now and then we get fresh beef and once or twice we have had mutton but it is wretched stuff not fit to throw to an English dog.

Miriam [his sister] tells me there is a lot of German Sausages coming out for the troops. I wish they would make haste and send them for I really think I could manage a couple of pound at the present minute. I really should like to get hold of something good for I have been literally starved this last 5 or six weeks, but however I will say no more about that for I know well it is too far to send anything out here. If my dear father you could manage to send me in the form of a letter a few anti-scorbutic powders I should be obliged to you for I am rather troubled with the scurvy and I will settle with you some other time please God spares me.

Pine's condition worsened and he was shipped to the base hospital at Kulali outside Constantinople. He died within the month, but such was the administrative chaos that official channels could find no record of his demise and his family only discovered the truth from one of Pine's comrades a year later.

Lieutenant Thomas Lynden Bell of the 28th (The North Gloucestershire) Regiment also wrote home on 8 January. He reminded his father that his regiment had left Liverpool 900 strong eleven months previously. Now, at a pinch, fifty effective men could be sent to man the trenches; the other day there had been but thirty.

The Hospital arrangements are bad. I believe I can safely state that there are very rarely more than two different medicines to be obtained in the Field Hospital, and I heard a man say the other day in the trenches, when complaining of being ill, 'Where's the use in goin' to the Doctor, shure if I broke me leg or had the Cramps, He'd give me the one thing' (viz a pill). Our Camp Hospital contains accomodation for 40 men, now there are 85 sick, besides the 40, and these 85 have to lie in their ordinary tents. There is also a great difficulty in conveying sick to Balaklava and the Authorities use the remnant of our Cavalry Horses for that purpose very frequently. When an Officer falls sick, there are so many forms, so many signatures, and applications and consequently so much delay before he can be sent on board ship that many die, who would have lived but for the abominable want of system. We have lost three officers in the Crimea. Two died in their tents, and one when he arrived at Scutari *too late*.

At the end of December Staff Surgeon Pine had been placed in charge of the medical arrangements of the 3rd Division. The series of entries in his journal dating from 3 January onwards reflect his feelings:

The day throughout has been thoroughly cruel, not to those who have been enabled to keep within their tents, but to the poor soldiers so much exposed to the elements. Rain, hail, snow, and sleet have alternated since morning, and it is now hailing. Such weather combined with insufficient food, clothing, and protection must kill us. My day has been taken up with divisional duty, overlooking returns, circulating directions, inspecting sick officers. etc. etc. This evening Lord Raglan rode up to my tent to make enquiries regarding the sick, & the French mules, expected to remove our sick in the morning. I trust in God, and hope for the best, but the Army is in a miserable plight. 4th. Continued snow and hail thro' the night, and it is still snowing heavily. Some inches of it lying on the ground. French mules came up, and took away a 100 sick from the Division. Eight went away also in the Flanders Waggon. The latter is in daily operation. Our difficulties are increasing daily. PM The Waggon stuck and the sick had to return suffering from exposure. The day has been truly miserable not to myself personally, but in thinking of the position of the men. 5th. I am far from well, and with difficulty keep ab[ou]t. The Division is rapidly deteriorating in physical power and health. An extremely cold night followed by a disagreeable day. Intense frost.

No fuel; no food. 6th. A sleepless night. Frost continues. Yesterday I addressed Sir Rich[ar]d England upon the state of the Division, requesting him to put my letter before Lord Raglan. He promised to do so. I am pestered to death with rabid surgeons justly complaining of their difficulties.

Things began to look up three days later.

9th. In the evening Lord Raglan called at my tent, & I had a long conversation with him upon the state of the Troops. He was not pleased. Afterwards I rode over to communicate with Dr Hall on the subject. 10th . . . A great stir about the sick, which perhaps may lead to good. Oh! that the war may soon be over.

In a letter to his mother, Major Forrest, with whom Pine (before his brief sojourn with the 4th Division) had served as regimental surgeon of the 4th Dragoon Guards, put flesh on the bones of the exchange between his friend and the commander-in-chief.

Our late Surgeon (Pine) who is now Staff Surgeon in charge of one of the Infantry Divisions, has through his firmness, I hope done a service to the army. I must give you the story in the shape of a Dialogue.

Ld Raglan (with the tone and manner of a Man who quite expected to receive some smooth and pleasing answer, such as he is probably accustomed to) 'How are you getting on with your sick in this Division, Mr Pine?' Answer: 'Nothing can possibly be worse my Lord.' 'What do you mean Sir?' Answer: 'I mean, my Lord, that it is merely a question of time, as to the existence of this Division; more men come into Hospital, than we can either accommodate, or find Medicines for: their sickness is occasioned, principally through exposure without sufficient clothing: many of the cases are such as should be either on board ship, or with a roof over them, and we have no means of transport for them.' 'Who do you mean to insinuate that blame rests with Sir for these alleged deficiencies?' Answer: 'Everybody, My Lord, all the heads of Departments. I have reported all these deficiencies and the injurious consequence arising from each, and have some time received no answer, in no case, any help.'

Ld Raglan by this time considerably nettled. 'How long have you been in medical charge of this Division, Sir, and what Regt did you come from? I rather think that you are an old Dragoon Surgeon?'

'I am lately appointed to this Division, my Lord, and I come from the 4th Dragoon Guards.'

'Well Sir, you have made most serious charges against the Heads of Departments, into the truth of which I shall cause enquiry to be made.'

Exit Lord Raglan.

His L[or]dship paid Pine another visit upon the following day, and commenced questioning Pine, in a more affable mood, and ended by desiring him to send in a written report of all the deficiencies which he conceived to exist. It is to be hoped that some good may arise from this; I cannot believe that Ld Raglan had previously been aware of the extent of the mismanagement, and consequent suffering which exists in this Army.

Raglan had in fact been well aware of the rapid diminution of his fighting strength. On 26 December he had told the Duke of Newcastle that the number of British infantry under arms had fallen from 18,000 to under 16,000 in just four days. Yet clearly the sheer inadequacy of the medical arrangements took him by surprise. General Estcourt, meanwhile, had been pondering the arithmetic, as he wrote to General Wetherall on 15 January:

Our sick list continues to increase in such a manner that we shall be non-existent in about 30 or 40 days, so calculates Dr. Pine of the 3rd Division, and upon my word I very much fear he is not very wrong. I have today seen a miserable spectacle. I was sent to inspect the 63rd Regiment. They mustered 48 men: the Colours in the centre, and 48 men to guard them. That regiment is gone. Gone in men and gone in spirit. It is absolutely done for. I believe Colonel Dalzell is not a good hand; but that is not all. The men I saw were mere boys, 7 months, 6 months, 9 months, 12 months in the service. Raw fellows and so cast down with disease and disgust at their fate, the hardships they have to bear, that they cannot stay here. . . . All this comes of hard work, a bad Commissariat Transport, and want of shelter and rest.

Captain William Radcliffe of the 20th had reached a similar conclusion about the army's rate of attrition.

The reinforcements barely fill up the casualties, & it is a common saying now amongst us, that we shall all be soon home, as there will be no men left. Many Officers no doubt are sick, but *nothing at all in Comparison with the Men*, & this goes far to shew, that had the poor fellows the same *few Necessaries*, that we have been able to get, (thanks to our nearest & dearest) many valuable lives would have been saved, & many more, that are now at Scutari, would be doing their duty. We never seem to get back any of the sick, that go there, & so of course the duty becomes harder for the few that are left. I spoke to a man yesterday that was carrying some sheepskin Coats on his back, & said what capital ones they were. He said, 'Yes Sir, it's a pity they didn't come before so many poor fellows were in their Graves'; I could not but agree with him. A few Huts are put up at Balaklava, but none on the Heights yet.

Major William Forrest too deplored the lack of system.

The sickness in the Army generally, continues, I fear as bad as ever, and the neglect of the sick is as disgraceful as ever, or very nearly so. The only means of transporting the poor fellows, from the Front, down to Balaklava, is upon Troop-Horses. One of our Officers went in charge of one of these Parties a few days since; the day was bitterly cold: when he arrived at the Division, to which he was ordered to go, he found that the Medical Officer had received no intimation of the intended removal of the sick, consequently there was great delay before the different cases could be selected for removal, and when they at last started, these poor Fellows had no extra clothing, beyond a blanket to wrap round them, and many of them had no shoes; they were altogether in a most pitiable state; many of these poor fellows actually crying; Men, who probably had fought at Inkerman, or at all events, were of the same stamp, as those who did. One Man was obliged to be left in another hospital, upon the road, and another was put into the Boat in a dying state.

Some of the troops manning the trenches were prepared to contemplate desperate measures in order to escape their ordeal, as Lieutenant-Colonel George Mundy of the 33rd Regiment admitted in a letter to his mother of 12 January:

Nearly all our horses are dead and our men dying like rotten sheep & what is worse deserting; one of the 18th Regt tried to desert from the trenches yesterday & was I am glad to say shot dead by his own men. 1 of ours deserted last night, & his double sentry tried to shoot him but unfortunately his gun missed fire & he got away clear off. Another of ours tried to do the same but luckily was stopped by a sentry of another picket and he is to be tried by a Gen[era]l C[our]t Martial & I trust will be shot. We have means of getting but few things at a time from Balaclava on account of the weakness of our men, 246! fit for duty, 174! on sick list. Such is my Regt.

It was evident by the middle of January that the condition of the army had begun to impact upon its operational effectiveness. Yet at the onset of the Crimean winter the British had still been capable of an exploit of great elan. When the Russians dug rifle pits in front of Chapman's Battery which enfiladed the French works, General Canrobert requested the British to capture them. Lieutenant Henry Tryon of the 1st Battalion Rifle Brigade was detailed to lead the assault. Tryon was a man of considerable reputation: 'the best shot in the Rifle Brigade', according to Lieutenant Thomas Lynden Bell of the 28th. 'He killed 60 Russians at Inkerman and had two men loading for him.' Among the 200 riflemen that he led to the attack on the evening of 20 November was John Fisher.

The Officers consisted of Lieut T[ryon] Lieut C[uninghame] & Lieut B[ourchier] the men being volunteers mostly from his own company and some from other companies. I formed one of the company. We paraded and our good Lieut told us just as we were about to march what we had to face, so on we went just as the s[h]ades of evening began to fall untill reaching the trenches. One man out of the party complained of some trifling thing and was sent back, our Lieut not liking the spirits of his men damped, or wishing any man to come who was not heart & soul in the work cut out for him. We proceeded cautiously to the extreem right of the paralell. It not being quite dark and a very dangerous part withall, we had to be doubly cautious not to arrouse the enimys suspicions. At last we gained the appointed spot, the pits of the enemy close in front of us [and] waited anxiously for darkness to set in. A small rain was falling and it began to get very foggy and at last we prepared for the encounter. We passed by twos out of the trench quietly forming line as we left, halting on the side of the hill which sloped here and on the other side of the pits towards the town. Now said Lieut T after we had all left the trench, proceed in file untill you get a little farther and I give the order front turn then advance at the charge, by the bye a thing we very seldom did, however we did on this occasion, and then shout with all your might say's the Lieut and charge the enemy for they are superior to you in numbers. Forward. Front turn. We advance up the hill. Now says Lieut T shout my lads and let them have it and we did shout, I was hoarse for 3 days after. We soon was in close contact with the Russians. I fought close by the side of Lieut T who was fighting with sword & revolver. The night was very dark and there must have been at least 300 of the enemy. We fought hand to hand sometimes. We could not tell who were Russians or who were English so that we kept together as much as possible. In the midst of the meele [melee] our brave officer received his death wound being shot through the head. We now had very tough work of it so we thought it best to get behind the Pits under cover. The enemy in the batteries had now caught the spark and soon brought their guns and more men to bear upon us. While all this lasted we had no reserve brought to us although we was to have had one in case of need, but we stuck to it like wax never the less, and soon they began to retire for a short time. This did not last long. The groans of my comrades now began to be heard around and about me one man especially who had been shot through the abdomen groaned awfully but there is no time to think here they come again stronger than ever. Our little band meets them manfully once more. The cannonading is now deafening mingled with the rattle of musketry and the groans of the dying. Once more they retire for a short time then they come on again but all to no purpose. The pits are ours, take them if you can. A working party has arrived, a trench commenced which was held untill the fall of Sebastopol.

General Canrobert was so impressed with the riflemen's feat that he issued a general order to the French army lauding their achievement. The Russians, nevertheless, made a further attempt to retake their lost position, as Captain the Honourable Edward Gage of the Royal Artillery explained in a letter of 2 December:

The Russians made an attempt in force this morn[ing] to regain the advanced parallel we took from [them] a few days ago. They succeeded at first in overcoming a Detach[men]t of the 50th who were not sufficiently on the alert, but providentially the Relief of the Rifles was at hand & drove them out again. Several of the 50th were bayonnetted asleep on the ground & this conduct on their part will probably lead to some severe animadversion from Ld R[aglan] as it is a place where peculiar watchfulness is enjoined & required, yet the British Soldiers will not believe in any danger & would rather run their chance of being surprised than have the bore of watching. They certainly fight well when it comes to that, but they have yet to learn to 'faire la Guerre'.

The watchfulness of the infantry guarding the trenches was undermined by tiredness, exposure and poor nourishment. Even for the officers, things were bad enough, as Lieutenant Maxwell Earle of the 57th Regiment noted in his journal on 26 November:

Returned from the trenches at 5¼ am. The waterproof I bought at poor ——'s sale kept my body dry, so I was only wet up to my middle, but very cold. Went to bed and finding that the snow drift had occupied my place between the blankets was obliged to lie down in my clothes. Slept until 7½ when I awoke and found that I had lost the feeling in my feet and my formerly damp hair had become a mass of icicles. Got up half frozen and by constant rubbing regained the use of my feet & called to my servant for firewood to make some coffee. There was neither one or the other! The commissariat had failed in their issue. I borrowed a little of the latter & cooked it on the fire of my neighbour. What luxury was this! My clothes were drying! My boots were thawing! My blanket drying! And I shall soon eat my cold pork and then to bed. As the last mouthful of my poor ration was disappearing a struggle at my tent door denoted that some one was there. 'If you please Mr ——'s gone sick and you are to take his place for the trenches immediately.' Horror! Visions of a warm bed changed into the certainty of a wet ditch! Oh that this too solid flesh would melt, thaw and ——. 'The Party's waiting Sir.' The night was a night of intense misery. Till then I never knew what misery was!

With the men on almost continual duty in the trenches, it was difficult to find the working parties necessary to maintain the siege. On 26 November a meeting was held at Headquarters with General Codrington, representing the Light Division, in attendance.

Sir J Burgoyne, and all the Division Generals were there to talk over the possibility of a reduction of the piquets, so as to have more

working parties to carry on works in advance of the right where the
2d. Div[isio]n are. We have 500 men every night and day here in this
division: it is a vulnerable point if they chose – and knew; and
therefore I cannot say I will abate one man, unless they settle I am
to do so: when Sir J.B., or higher authority says you *must* do with
less, well and good I shall consider it merely as a post of observation
not of defence, though it risks the possibility of their occupying a
commanding height in our front. And the peculiarity is that no
military assistance can be given from the right brow to us, or from
us to them without going back to camp: the ravine is very steep.*

For the time being the British continued to muddle through, until
another Russian attack was launched against their trenches on 21
December. Lieutenant Earle reported the outcome:

This morning at 2.30 A.M. we were turned out owing to the enemy
making a vigorous attack on our Green Hill trenches. The firing
which was sharp while it lasted (about half an hour) was chiefly in
the most advanced works and this morning we heard with deep
regret of the losses we suffered. The enemy attacked the 50th in their
front & the field officer, Major Möller, directed his *whole* force against
this point. The consequence was that the Russians entered our trenches by the rear and succeeded in taking two officers prisoners, killing
two officers & mortally wounding the Major besides 13 men killed,
13 wounded & 10 missing. This is the 2nd time the 50th have been
caught napping.

Lieutenant Henry James Alderson of the Royal Artillery, in a letter to
his mother, described the annoyance that he felt at being roused from his
sleep on this occasion.

There was a shindy last night or rather this morning about 3. The
Russians made an attack as usual upon our advanced trenches, and
one of the new regiments whose zeal was at its boiling point
sound[ed] the 'Wild Assembly'. By the by talking about that call it is
the most unpleasant one I ever heard. Fancy in the dead of night
when one is all jolly between the blankets hearing this shrill call
taken up on all sides as fast as 'winking'. And then just as you are

---

* The Vorontsov Ravine lay between the British Right (or Gordon's) attack on Frenchman's Hill and the Left (or Chapman's) Attack on Green Hill.

trying to collect your scattered senses in comes a sergeant saying 'Turn out is sounded Sir'. And you immediately begin to pull frantically on the wrong boot and put your arms into your trousers or some such luck and all for nothing as far as we are concerned for it was found out to be a mistake our having been turned out, as the gallant siege train weren't wanted, as in fact nobody was, the guard of the trenches having beaten back the sortie though 2 officers were taken prisoners, Frampton and Fyler of the 50th who I do not know. I have not been able to see the fun of knocking us up as we could be of no use cutting down there, as if we fired we should probably hit our own men.

Whereas for their men, active service during a Crimean winter was a question of survival, some officers were capable of registering other concerns. How would their careers be affected by a setback in the trenches? Lieutenant Thomas Lynden Bell expressed his feelings in a letter home on 8 January:

There is another great source of uneasiness to most men who think on the subject, viz that our trenches are not sufficiently guarded. There should be 5 times as many men. Look at the position of an Officer who is sent down to protect a certain portion of the trench at *one* man for every 10 yards. His honor perhaps depends on the issue of an *unequal* attack, for the Russians always attack in force. If they were *men of steel* with their muskets loaded *and fired by steam* they could not prevent the Russians spiking our guns, if they made a *determined* attack.

In a letter to a brother officer, Major Robert Campbell of the 90th (Perthshire Volunteers) Regiment (Light Infantry) stated his anxieties more explicitly:

The nights are most wearisome, at the same time most anxious, because an attack has been long expected in Force upon our Trenches and Batteries, and immediately behind the Advanced Trench which I always Command, is the 21 Gun Battery alias Gordon's Battery. On either flank is a Ravine which has been considered always a weak point of ours, and our numbers in the Trenches during the bad weather were so small at times, that no Creditable Defence against a Force was possible. It was hazarding your reputation everytime you went into the trenches for any Attack was certain to be in Force and our numbers were not sufficient to occupy the Lines; besides this the poor men were often 2 nights together in the Trenches or on Picket and they slept so soundly and were so knocked up that it was an impossibility to wake them ... I reported it officially to the General and even went so far as to say it was not fair to an Officer to place him and his reputation in such a position and we have now put more than double the number of men. Major Muller of [the] 50th was killed in one of these attacks.

The welcome ability of the British suddenly to place double the number of men in the trenches came about when the French finally agreed to take over more of the front line. Lord Raglan had for a long time pressed Canrobert to do so, and, as he informed the Duke of Newcastle on 15 January, the Frenchman had promised his cooperation as long ago as 6 November: 'He, however, has been in the habit of pleading, that the reinforcements which had reached him, were detachments and not complete military bodies, and that he was not then in a condition to fulfil, what I should be justified in calling, his engagement.'

It was only when Canrobert – whose army Raglan calculated to be now four times as numerous as his own – was presented with what amounted to an ultimatum that he finally agreed to assist the British. In a letter to his wife of 23 January, General Codrington explained the circumstances behind this volte-face.

One result of our diminished numbers was either that we must send men more often than they could bear into the trenches, or that we must send fewer men – and the latter has necessarily been the case, till instead of 800 for the guard of the Gordon battery, our numbers diminished to perhaps 300. Constantly did I write telling them of these things at H.Q. I suppose they shut their eyes – disliked the being written to about it – went on putting the same number in orders – thought people had no business to 'make difficulties' – that I believe is the proper official term generally used about anyone that says or writes anything 'unpleasant'. From what I know, the H.Q. have been trying the last six weeks to get the French to take some of our hard duty – and Airey said that he had told Canrobert a few days ago when Ld. R[aglan] had a conference with him, that if it could not be done, he must tell Ld. R. that the batteries in our front must be given up. Canrobert was horrified at this and I suppose at last felt the necessity of complying. But it would have been well for the army, at least this part of it, if it had been insisted on long ago.

Ironically, the French taking over more of the trenches did not provide the relief anticipated. All it meant was that the British, instead of having 300 men to guard Gordon's Battery, could now afford the requisite 800, which meant the men still endured trench duty quite as often as before. In his letter to the Duke of Newcastle of 29 January, Raglan acknowledged that ideally Canrobert would offer further assistance:

> We are endeavouring to prevail upon him to do more, and I hope we may succeed. This kind of negotiation however is a delicate and difficult matter, and if not managed adroitly may lead to irritation. Gen. Rose,* who since my last discussion with Gen: Canrobert, has at my request had several communications with him, tells me that he gets animated & irritated, and that the conversation is not always very pleasant. The point therefore must be gained step by step.

General Codrington had a shrewd idea why Canrobert was reluctant to do more: the British siegeworks were simply too exposed.

> It seems that the French do not like our batteries; that is, I believe they do not like being in places so far from support by their main bodies. . . . I imagine this is the real reason – this isolation of the batteries, that they don't like. And indeed it is awkward. There are in Gordon's battery for instance at night 840 men. And it is further from hence [the British camp] than it is from Sebastopol, and no camp [for] our troops between this and that, for nearer than this our camp would be under fire of the town.

Fortunately, January had been a relatively quiet month in the trenches and the under-strength British were not put to the test, although one death occurred in the siegeworks which was widely remarked upon. Lieutenant Henry Spalding of HMS *London* who, it will be recalled, the previous year had been one of those who saw the war against Russia in terms of a religious crusade, was visiting the Picket House Battery on the afternoon of 21 January. A British gun was firing at Sevastopol and some retaliatory Russian shot was at any moment expected. An informant explained to Spalding's family what happened next:

---

* The British liaison officer at French Headquarters.

He had been talking the instant before with the Engineer Officer, who told him to lower for *shot*, as is the habit, & he did so, as might have been supposed sufficiently, but the parapet was faulty, & the round shot passed thro' it, altho' it had 6 feet of thickness.

The Russian cannonball killed Spalding instantly. Major Mundy marked his passing:

Poor Lieut Spalding of the "London" was shot in the trenches today, his head carried off. He was only looking on. What very bad luck. *We* keep our heads as much out of the way of their incessant fire as possible. Where on earth they get all their powder from puzzles us.

In a way Mundy had already answered his own question. Sevastopol, as he earlier observed, was the Russian Woolwich, stuffed full of the munitions of war. It was moreover an uninvested fortress which the Russians could replenish at will. More and more it began to be remarked that this was turning into a latter-day siege of Troy.

7

RECRIMINATION

The British army that landed at Calamita Bay in September 1854 had been a sickly one. A thousand cholera cases were almost immediately sent back to Scutari. Within a week many hundreds of casualties from the Battle of the Alma were sailing to join them. Accompanying the shipment were another thousand cholera sufferers. The transport *Kangaroo*, with a capacity to hold 250 men, was crammed with over 1,200 sick and wounded; its voyage was a nightmare of overcrowding and neglect. Upon their arrival at Scutari the enfeebled soldiers discovered that the General Hospital was already full and they were taken instead to the Artillery Barracks. The so-called Barrack Hospital lacked facilities of any description. William Howard Russell, *The Times'* correspondent, in a series of dispatches published between 9 and 13 October described the twin horrors of minimal medical treatment and appalling hygiene endured by the patients sent there. The reaction was instantaneous. On 13 October Sir Robert Peel inaugurated *The Times'* Fund to help alleviate the suffering. Three days later Sidney Herbert wrote from the War Office to his friend Florence Nightingale, an expert on hospital administration, asking her to raise a contingent of nurses to take to Scutari. She did not dally and her party of thirty-eight nurses arrived at Constantinople on 3 November. The medical authorities at Scutari were reluctant at first to make use of Miss Nightingale's nurses, but the flood of casualties that arrived in the wake of the Battle of Inkerman rendered their assistance indispensable and they were speedily set to work.

Lord Raglan had responded to the Duke of Newcastle's expression of concern about the state of affairs at Scutari by pointing out that a large proportion of the army's surgeons had either died or been invalided home. He nonetheless decided to replace the military commandant at Scutari, Major Sillery, with Lord William Paulet, who left the Crimea to take up his new position on 23 November. But neither Paulet nor Miss Nightingale could work miracles immediately and when Private Joseph

Pring of the 95th Regiment wrote home to his brothers on 13 December from a hospital ship moored at Constantinople, he felt reason to be aggrieved.

> I have been very ill with the bowel complaint for which I was sent down from Sebastopol here about 10 weeks ago but am now but little better than when I came down . . . I should have [been] writing to one of you before but since I left Turkey for Sebastopol I have [h]add no pay and my knapsack is left with the Regiment with all my paper and pens &c so that I could not write till some paper was given us by some Gentlemen* that have come out from England on purpose to look after the Wounded and sick, which it wanted someone to do as we have not been half look[ed] after but since they and some Ladies [h]as come out it is a little better in the Hospital but still as bad here as we cannot get the least thing and we have to wash our own clothes &c ourselves and some of us can [h]ardly move. That you may think how bad we are off . . . we are all cut up with lice and flees since we landed in the Crimea and we cannot get rid of them, that with one thing and the other I am quite tired of seeing the awful work of war and the hardships we have to undergo besides the treatment we get when we are sick or wounded.

The condition in which men were arriving from the Crimea did not make the task of treating them at Scutari any easier. Florence Nightingale, in a letter of 29 December, initiated a correspondence with Lord Raglan by pointing out the shortcomings which needed remedy:

> I regret to say that the three last arrivals of men, in number about seven hundred and fifty, have come down in a wretched state of sickness. They complain (upon the passage) only of want of order-lies & of utensils, by which a great amount of avoidable stench resulted.
>
>   Having been informed that there is a quantity of warm clothing in Balaklava harbour, I nevertheless grieve to find that these men (all landed since the 19th) are more ragged & even destitute of clothing than any of the preceding. The number of frost bitten cases might,

---

* The Reverend and Honourable Sidney Godolphin Osborne, a friend of Sidney Herbert's, and Augustus Stafford MP.

it appears to me, have been diminished by an examination of the state of the men on their return from the trenches.

The majority of cases are those derived from Dysentery & exhaustion, sometimes both.

These have suffered by the length of the time on board, ten days.

The usual arrangements for landing the sick have certainly not been so prompt as they might have been. The authorities do not seem to perceive the importance of this for the saving of life.

The truth of Miss Nightingale's observations received corroboration in the private journal of a newly qualified assistant surgeon called Henry Walter Bellew, who arrived at Constantinople on 2 January 1855. Although destined for the East India Company, he could not take up his post until he became twenty-one, and so he had offered his services to the Army Medical Department. Installed at the Hyder Pasha Hospital two miles from Scutari, he was immediately overwhelmed by the influx of 120 patients who had been landed at the quayside a few hours before. Their condition – several were more or less severely wounded and others completely prostrated by fever and dysentery – was heart-rending. Moreover, the stores with which they could be treated were almost totally lacking. The peacetime Army Medical Department had placed a premium on economy and even now was unable to adjust. This was where Florence Nightingale held the advantage. Whereas the medical authorities at Scutari had rebuffed the offer of aid tendered by The Times' Fund's local administrator (believing that acceptance would be tantamount to admitting their own deficiencies), Miss Nightingale was possessed of no such inhibitions. As a consequence, by the end of December she was acting as the chief purveyor of stores to the hospitals in the locality. Bellew, as he noted in his journal on 15 January, was a grateful recipient of her largesse:

Miss Nightingale & a small party visited this Hospital on the 10th inst. She drove down in a mule carriage & looked very sad. After inspecting the wards & kitchens &c she left 'carte blanche' orders upon her store at Barrack Hospital for beef jelly & other luxuries and sent us besides a most welcome supply of flannel shirts and stockings for the men.

Unfortunately, the scale of official inadequacy could not be entirely compensated for by private charity. Bellew was soon made forcibly aware of this, as the entry in his journal for 23 January testified:

> This morning twenty one sick and wounded men were brought in on stretchers from the landing wharf at Scutari by a party of Turkish soldiers told off for the duty. A large number of sick and wounded have been landed at the Scutari wharf today from transports just arrived from the Crimea. As fast as they were landed they were distributed over the several hospitals here. The condition of these poor fellows is truly deplorable. Many were landed dead, several died on the way to the hospitals, and the rest were all in a most pitiable condition; their clothes were begrimed with filth and alvine evacuations [alvine: of the abdomen], their hands & faces blackened with gunpowder & mud &c and their bodies literally alive with vermin. Of the batch we received at the Palace hospital most were more or less severely frost-bitten in the hands & feet & some in the ears as well. One poor fellow had lost both feet by frost bite: another had lost the fingers of both hands; they had been pulled off in the act of removing the gloves to which his mortified flesh had adhered. In all these cases the gangrene is far advanced and the whole air of the hospital is now tainted with a dreadful stench. The men bore all their sufferings with marvellous patience, indeed I may say indifference; they were nevertheless most grateful for our attentions, and truly we have worked hard in doing what lay in our power to alleviate or soothe their sufferings. All our stores are again found to be quite inadequate to the demand. There is no brandy nor wine in store here, nor are any clean shirts or sheets to be got. Requisitions are repeatedly sent in to the Commissariat office but they are repeatedly returned with the decisive 'None in store' written across the document. This is very disheartening. An example ought to be made of somebody for the neglect is inexcusable and under the circumstances criminal.

Lord Raglan had attempted to shake up the medical authorities at Balaklava by dismissing the Principal Medical Officer, Dr Lawson, who was held responsible for the sufferings of the sick aboard the transport *Avon* whilst it lay in harbour. Responding to this interference in the running of his department, Dr John Hall, Chief of Medical Staff of the British Expeditionary Army, appointed Lawson to Scutari instead. Henry Bellew encountered him at the end of January.

Our work continues very hard owing to no Assist. Surgeon having been appointed to supply the place of Simons who is now very seriously ill with a severe attack of continued fever. Dr Lawson P[rincipal] M[edical] O[fficer] General Hospital came down here in the afternoon on a tour of inspection. As neither Dr Menzies nor Barnett, who, by the way, was orderly officer for the day, were to be found at the moment of his arrival I had to go the rounds with him and came in for the full benefit of all his 'wiggings' and ill temper. The Hospital certainly is not as clean as it should be, but this is entirely the fault of the higher authorities, whose arrangements are, to say the least, most defective. Owing to the absence of a sufficient supply of cots more than half the men are still lying on the floor; hospital stewards and attendants are not to be got in anything like the required numbers; the dresser & dispenser are both ignorant of the duties they profess to perform and are besides idle & insubordinate boys; the Assist. Surgeons, now only Barnett and myself, are overworked: we are on orderly duty every alternate 24 hours and have upwards of a hundred men each to attend to; besides all this our stores of clothing, comforts, medicines &c are constantly running short from being in the first instance quite inadequate to the expenditure. Before he left Dr Lawson saw for himself that we were overworked here and that we had done our best under the circumstances; he softened down a little in consequence, gave us a few words by way of encouragement and promised to send us help.

When the hard-bitten Sir George Brown had passed through Scutari in December 1854, he had fallen under Florence Nightingale's spell, Lord Raglan reporting that 'Brown seems captivated with Miss Nightingale.' But by the time Sir John Burgoyne reached Constantinople at the end of March 1855, resentment amongst the medical authorities at the extent of her influence had reasserted itself, as Burgoyne informed Lord Raglan.

Since writing to your Lordship I have visited the great Hospitals in company with Lord William Paulet & Lady Strangford, & they certainly appear to me to be in excellent order, & without wants of any kind unprovided for; the Patients have generally that kind of countenance that indicates *amendment*, rather than *despondence*. There is however manifestly an under current of troubles & turmoils in the establishments. Miss Nightingale is decidedly not in favor with the authorities, & from the accounts I hear of her I can hardly wonder at it. Whatever Philanthropy she may have on a great scale, she does not appear to be amiable in ordinary intercourse with her equals or superiors. She likes to *govern*, & bestows all her tenderness upon those who *depend* upon her: for instance, she will not give an atom or a thought upon any *Officer* who may be in the most wretched state. She seems also to *court* popular applause, even unduly. If anything is wanted for the sick, she will *hurry* to provide it from her own funds & stock *for fear* it might be obtained in the regular course. She is considered also very hard, seems to delight in witnessing surgical operations, with arms folded, & where she can be of no use whatever, & is considered to be of that strong minded class of woman, that is indifferent on religion.

Although Florence Nightingale did much to alleviate the hardships of the sick, it was the work of the Sanitary Commission, which arrived from England in March and immediately set about purifying the water supply, that did most to reduce the mortality rate at Scutari from a catastrophic 42 per cent in February 1855 to 5.2 per cent by May. Least deserving of credit for the improvement was the Army Medical Department.

Russell and *The Times* had performed a great service by exposing the condition of the hospitals at Scutari and the press continued to have a voracious appetite for news of the Army of the East. But when a rash of letters sent from the Crimea began to appear in the newspapers this caused official concern, because almost invariably they highlighted the deplorable condition of the troops. There were rumours that the newspapers were paying for letters: Colonel George Bell (who had himself written to *The Times*) informed General Wetherall in London that one officer who had returned home 'told a friend of mine in confidence that his wife got a five pound note for his last Letter (from an Editor) which he flourished!!' Other letters appeared in the newspapers contrary to the writer's intention, as Captain Frederick Elton of the 55th Regiment complained in a letter to his father of 17 January 1855.

How disgusting it is that people will publish letters which were never meant for more than one's friends. Of course I allude to newspaper publicity. You will have seen that our Chaplain got himself rather into hot water by some kind friend having sent a perfectly private letter to the papers. I do not wish you at all to infer that I object in the least to your shewing any letters of mine to whoever you like but I should be very much annoyed if I saw any in a newspaper.

The previous month, Sergeant George Cruse of the 1st Dragoons had felt just as much alarm as annoyance when his wife informed him that he was now in print.

I never had such a shock in my life when I read in your letter that *that fool of a Brother* of mine had been so ridiculous as to send a letter of mine to the newspaper. It has quite upset me for the present and God only knows how it might effect my future prospects.

By 7 January, having escaped censure, Cruse felt happier.

My letter which Edward published in the 'Times' has been well circulated throughout the Camp, it having been copied into the 'News of the World.' The author of it was soon found out and it is said by everybody to be the best account published, and one of the best letters which has appeared in the papers.

Lord Lucan has been endeavouring to find out who wrote it. He has been questioning one of the Corporals about it, and when he failed in discovering the perpetrator he said, 'Well all I can say is that he has written a D—d lie.' . . . Lord Raglan issued an order the other night that Non C[ommissione]d Officers writing home to their friends were to caution them not to publish any letters in the public papers. So I suppose Dearest either my letter or some one's has been too near the knuckle for them.

At the outset, Raglan's main concern about disclosures in the press was not so much that they might undermine his command but rather that they would compromise the security of the army. As early as 13 November he had complained to the Duke of Newcastle about *The Times* publishing information useful to the enemy. The Deputy Judge Advocate, Romaine, had spoken to the newspaper correspondents in the Crimea; the Duke of Newcastle wrote to their editors in England. However, John Delane, the editor of *The Times*, felt little need for restraint. He considered Raglan incompetent and was not going to disguise the facts as he saw them. The increasingly condemnatory tone of Russell's dispatches went unsoftened. Raglan eventually felt compelled to protest. His private letter to the Duke of Newcastle of 4 January expressed his unease.

I deem it my duty to send you a copy of the Times newspaper of the 18th Dec., and to draw your attention to an article or rather a letter from its correspondent with this Army.

I pass over the fault the writer finds with every thing and every body, however calculated his strictures may be to excite discontent and encourage indiscipline, but I ask you to consider whether the paid agent of the Emperor of Russia could better serve his Master than does the correspondent of the paper that has the largest circulation in Europe.

I know something of the kind of information which the Commander of an Army requires of the state and condition of the Troops opposed to him, and I can safely say, that during the whole of the war in the Peninsula the Duke of Wellington was never supplied with such details as are to be found in the letter to which I am desirous of attracting your attention.

Some time ago the correspondent stated for general information, and practically for that of Prince Menshikoff, the Exact position in which the powder for our siege batteries was deposited, and he now suggests the ease with which the ships in Balaklava Harbour could be set on fire.

He moreover affords the Russian General the satisfaction of knowing that our Guns stick in the mud, and our horses die under their exertions. But as regards intelligence to the Enemy the mischievous parts are so obvious, that I will not further trouble you with a recapitulation of them. It will be sufficient that I mark the parts that strike me as the most obnoxious.

I am very doubtful, now that the Communications are so rapid, whether a British Army can long be maintained in presence of a powerful Enemy, that Enemy having at his command thro' the English press, and from London to his Head Quarters by telegraph every detail that can be required of the numbers, condition, and equipment of his opponent's force.

However, the Duke of Newcastle's concern was different to that of Raglan. He was feeling the political pressure. The letters reaching England from the Crimea alarmed him. When *The Times'* editorial of 23 December accused the army's high command of incompetency, lethargy, aristocratic hauteur and official indifference, he lost his composure. He wrote to Raglan attacking the Quartermaster- and Adjutant-Generals –

Airey and Estcourt – for their maladministration. Raglan leapt to their defence. 'It is with the deepest concern,' he wrote on 15 January,

> that I observe that upon the authority of private letters, you condemn Gen[eral]s Airey and Estcourt and the Staff generally, and this without reference to me, or the expression of a desire to have my opinion of their qualifications or imputed deficiencies.
>
> ... I can only regard your adoption of the imputations against these Officers, as an indirect reflection on myself, and an indication that you consider me incapable of judging of departmental Officers, the chief of whom receive their orders from me.
>
> I find that the attack upon the Staff has been so indiscriminate, as to extend to my personal staff, who are accused of aristocratic hauteur, incivility and God knows what besides. This indeed is a matter of surprize, more particularly as it has been frequently mentioned to me by Officers of the highest rank and consideration, that the general opinion was quite the other way. They are all perfect gentlemen, extremely intelligent, zealous beyond every thing, and most courteous to all.

Nigel Kingscote, in a letter to his father of the same date, was equally indignant.

> To begin with the lies that are written home are past all belief and where they originate I cannot conceive. As regards the letter you enclosed I distinctly deny for myself and the rest of my Lord's staff that there 'has been not enough sympathy from Head Quarters with the Troops' unless people expect us to go into everyone's tent out of which we should probably get kicked as a tent is as much an Englishman's home out here as his Castle in England but I know that we are always riding about the Camp and talk to officers we know and sometimes to those we do not and I am certain that because we have better quarters than the rest of the army that we do not the less sympathise or pity those who are obliged to be out. Not only from you but from other sources we have heard of our 'aristocratic hauteur' and our 'contempt of regimental officers' and the papers, at least the Times, are lavish in their abuse of both Lord R[aglan] and us, but one's consciences are easy and it is rather a subject of amusement than annoyance to us.

Not all agreed with Raglan's claim that his staff showed unfailing courtesy. On 9 February Captain Arthur Layard informed his brother A. H. Layard MP of his experience.

> There is a snobbish idea about the ADCs at HQ's that you are the author of all those articles in the 'Times' against Ld R and the heads of Depart[ment]s. I, a poor devil like myself, am looked at with suspicion by many of them & they don't wish me well. But I have little or nothing to do with them, so they may think what they like, I care not for them or their rude speeches.

Others were incensed to a still greater degree by the attitude of Raglan's staff. Colonel Charles William Ridley of the Grenadier Guards described to a relative the antipathy that he felt towards Raglan's military secretary, Lieutenant-Colonel T. M. Steele,

> who declared that I was the authority for so much abuse of the staff, that he had it from the best authority that my wife read my letters publicly and he added with the greatest coolness and impertinence *he had written to get extracts.* I never gave myself credit before, for being good-tempered or rather having a bad temper under command but since that day, I have never looked on Steele as a friend or a man I can have any respect or feeling for. If he was in earnest in his last remark it was ungentlemanlike, if he was not it was an impertinent staff swagger, for he threatened what he could not execute.

The professional competence of staff officers was coming increasingly under the spotlight. The time-honoured practice of generals appointing relatives to their personal staff was a subject of particular comment. Kingscote was dismissive.

> The Times beats everything again! . . . I have not had time to read the papers but the Times makes out my Lord's staff are all nearly related and therefore the fate of Europe hangs on a family party. I had no idea we were of so much importance.

Captain Maxwell Earle of the 57th Regiment was more reflective in his assessment. According to him, staff officers needed ability, a knowledge of business and the education of a gentleman, coupled with good sense.

> Let us endeavour to find men possessing such qualities. Throw aside all partiality, favour and affection. Let it not be said that our staff is composed of men of good family because they *are* men of good

family. Let it no longer be said (as I heard it said by a Major General not long ago) 'My nephew is useless to me on my staff, but I must keep him for my sister's sake.' Generals ought to choose men who are of use to them, if their relations so much the better. But if that relation is useless, throw him off the staff.

Writing home on 17 February, Nigel Kingscote showed that he was not prepared to let drop the subject of the iniquities of *The Times.*

Officers write more absurd and rascally letters than ever or else the Times concocts them for them, anyhow it is very bad and unsoldier-like of them. I still maintain that the soldier is very cheerful and they always seem in good spirits. The officers I do not see much of but I observe one thing and that is that the more aristocratic blood there is in the veins the less they grumble, in spite of the assertions of the Times.

Kingscote's opinion that the men were less complaining than their officers ('their letters are more cheerful and the general tone ... is that though subject to all privations they must go through with them') is difficult to substantiate: so few letters written by private soldiers survive. One that does, sent home on 24 February by Private Alexander Hood of the 42nd Regiment to his cousin, tends to corroborate Kingscote's belief:

You are right enough about us not being so badly off as those up in front of Sebastopol but we were bad enough. But I see that some soldiers send home false statements or at best gross exaggerations of the life we live. He is no true soldier who tries to make things look worse than they really are. I also see that some people are running down Lord Raglan. They do not know what they are talking about. We out here know better and can tell a different story than that he never appears among us. He even comes down to Balaclava to see how we are getting on and even when he is not present we derive benefit from his judicious arrangements. But there are discontented men in all classes of men and the Army is no exception to the rule.

Nevertheless, as Hood admitted, he was stationed with Sir Colin Campbell's Highland Brigade at Balaklava, and things were never so bad there as for the soldiers on the heights before Sevastopol. For another soldier, E. Griffiths,* writing home on 31 January to his friends from the camp before Sevastopol, Lord Raglan was culpable.

i am very thankful to hear that you and your father and tha famley are quit well wich i am sorry to say is not tha cace with [me]. i am very ill and have been so for tha last week or moor in fact i am scerche able to walk about i cannot eat and in a short time i shall soon bee in my grave if i do not get better. Well we have an horspitl hear but a man must bee all but gon before he goes ther so that i must walk about as long as i can and then when i can walk about no longer drop into my grave such is tha usag of your british armey in the crimea such is what tha think good a nof for them that are gaining laurels and victouries it is enough to brak a mans hart and i think that is what tha are try to do. . . . what use lord Ragland is out hear that is tha man that can sit down and wright [h]is dispatch home and talk about tha position of the armey when on the 5th of november at inkerman he was not never among it to see them onley [knowing] what he was toald. such cowardic i never saw in a generl officer for i had tha chance of seeing him from wher i was so i tell you the truth the man is old and foolish not fit for this servies but he answers lord aberdeen very well. if the Duak of Camberage had camanded us at inkirman Sebastopel would have been ours and tha whoule of tha eneney put to tha rout insted of anoying us in the way thay are.

At the turn of the year the Duke of Newcastle made explicit his wish that Generals Airey and Estcourt be dismissed. The scandal surrounding the army in the Crimea was threatening the Government. As he told Raglan:

I shall, of course, be the first victim to popular vengeance; and the papers, assisted by the Tory and Radical parties, have pretty well settled my fate already . . . But more victims will be required. You and I will come first, but those who are most to blame in these matters will not escape.

* Although it is impossible to positively identify E. Griffiths, his unusual enthusiasm for the generalship of the Duke of Cambridge suggests that he was a Guardsman, in which case he was perhaps Evan Griffiths of the Scots Fusilier Guards, killed before Sevastopol on 10 August 1855.

Raglan nevertheless refused to sacrifice Airey and Estcourt and, in his response dated 23 January, adroitly switched the point at issue. The army's problems stemmed from the difficulties it found in bringing supplies forward from Balaklava.

Neither Gen. Estcourt nor Gen. Airey have anything to do with the transport of the Army, nor with the issue of provisions. All these depend upon the Com[missary] General, and the Officers under him.

Mr Filder is an able Man, and devotes himself to his duty, but his department, so far as I am able to judge of it, has never been in an efficient state, and the Men whom he has had to take charge of his packhorses, he has always seen reason to complain of.

I did not after the storm attempt to get fresh horses, for the Com[missary] General did not encourage me to hope that he could feed them, and there was no use in buying horses, and letting them die of starvation, and want of due care.

I got some from Eupatoria for the Commissariat; and they, like the snow, have melted away, and I now have sent for some to Constantinople, but they may share the same fate, if the forage which should have been sent from England does not arrive.

Six days later, Raglan reinforced the message that there was fault to be found at home: 'Mr Filder complains sadly of the non-arrival of the supplies of hay, which he was led to expect he should receive from England periodically.'

General Estcourt received the news that the Government wanted him dismissed from his post with equanimity, telling General Wetherall on 10 February:

I have been called upon to answer a charge of the Duke of Newcastle, contained in a letter to Ld. Raglan, in which the Duke imputes our difficulties and distresses to negligence or inefficiency in our two Departments, Airey's and mine; and in fact he wishes us to be removed. If for inefficiency I have nothing to say; but to fall back into private life perhaps better suited to my tried want of capacity. But if for negligence I shall chafe under an unjust imputation, which I do not think Ld. Raglan would support. But the Duke has been listening to people who are not authorised sources of information.

The irony of what he had written then suddenly occurred to Estcourt.

Had he himself not whispered against Filder and Lucan a month previously? And as he understood it from Wetherall, the blow was about to
fall against Lord Lucan.

> Pray let me beg of you to permit no change to be made, as you have
> hinted to be likely, in consequence of my private letter to you. Get
> your information from '*authorised sources*', which mine is not.

Estcourt tried also to temper his earlier criticism of Filder and Lucan.

> I do not like the idea of undermining any man's reputation. I have
> written quite openly to you; but I beg of you to obtain the sanction
> for anything you may think it right to do from Lord Raglan. . . . I
> have a high opinion of Filder, for instance, though I don't think he
> is capable of forming an establishment of Transport for the Army.
> I have a high opinion of Ld. Lucan too; but I think him not judge-
> matical in many things. He is a soldier, though. He is sticking to *the
> collar*, up hill as it is for the Cavalry and others. There is no flinching
> on his part. I don't think he commands well, however. He interferes
> too much in detail.

Lord Lucan received notification of his recall on 12 February, but the
effect of this was immediately overshadowed by far more momentous
news. The Government had fallen! On 29 January two-thirds of the
House of Commons had voted for a motion of the Radical MP John
Arthur Roebuck calling for the appointment of a select committee to
investigate the condition of the army before Sevastopol, and the conduct
of the Government departments responsible for supporting it. The Prime
Minister Lord Aberdeen had resigned the next day to be replaced by
Lord Palmerston. Lord Panmure succeeded the Duke of Newcastle as
Secretary of State for War. General Estcourt, an erstwhile parliamentarian
himself, evinced pleasant surprise at the change – with one exception.
'The new Ministry appears to have been well formed,' he told Wetherall.

> I rather like the idea of Lord Panmure. I remember him in the House
> of Commons, where he always stood up manfully for the Army
> against his radical friends. The appointment I think exceptional,
> I mean *discreditable* is that of Mr. Layard. It is a sop to the *Times*,
> a mean pandering to the Public Press. A conceited, ignorant, mis-
> chievous man, who ought never to be placed in a position of trust,
> or where he may lead any one.

Nigel Kingscote was equally disgusted by Layard's projected appointment as Under-Secretary for War. He had already heard quite enough about him of late.

> Lord Panmure's a good appointment but why go and spoil the whole thing by appointing such a man as Mr Layard, notoriously unfit for business and not a gentleman into the bargain. What provokes me more than anything is that they should telegraph all he does as if he had never been in the Trenches or to Balaklava before. It really is childish and they will telegraph when he blows his nose next!

The fact that Layard did not in the end take up his appointment was no doubt a relief to both Estcourt and Kingscote. Yet their plaudits for Lord Panmure were short-lived. On 12 February he wrote a stinging dispatch to Lord Raglan calling, as had his predecessor, for the supersession of Airey and Estcourt. Major-General James Simpson was to be sent out as Chief of Staff to report on the efficiency of Raglan's headquarters. Woundingly, Raglan was himself criticized for not visiting the troops often enough. Nigel Kingscote attempted to refute the charge.

> One accusation against my Lord is that they [the troops] never see him. For a time after Inkerman he had a really over powering quantity of writing work and was not out much but for the last three weeks hardly a day has passed that he has not been in some camp or other and spoken as much to the private soldier as to the general officer.

Responding to Panmure's strictures, Raglan's chief aim, as before, was to defend his subordinates. Their position was saved in the end by the favourable report which Simpson delivered upon them in April. However, not all were convinced that they deserved vindication. Captain Maxwell Earle, writing on 18 February after news of the change in Government reached the Crimea, pointed the finger of blame at the Quartermaster-General, Airey.

> It has always been my humble opinion that the fault does not lie at home with the Duke of N[ewcastle] but in the Crimea between Balaklava & the camp. *There*, indeed lives a man who may be charged with *indolence* added to *incompetence*. I am not alluding to the Commander in Chief, but the head of the Quarter Master General's department. I myself can positively assert that long ago letters have been written, hints have been thrown out as to measures calculated

for the improvement of the state of Balaklava, all of which were laid aside in contempt, and only *now* adopted. . . . Every one could plainly see that when clothing, food, hutting and a thousand etceteras were daily being disembarked at Balaklava, some place, some store, would be required wherein to deposit them, & that for this purpose the houses of the town would be eminently useful; for the business of transporting them to their several depots a clear space & uncrowded streets would be necessary, and last but not by any means the least important requisite, a clear, authoritative and business like Head would be absolutely indispensable. Instead of which we permit Turks, sutlers, paymasters, quartermasters, & all the followers of the army to occupy the best houses, we permit the Zouaves to tear the old ones to pieces, to permit every description of cart & horse, man & beast to block up the streets and retard business. We build no quay, whereon articles could be speedily disembarked even had masters of vessels the option or orders to do so, or wherefrom we might embark our sick, wounded or dying soldiers, and lastly to crown all, we place an old worn out Colonel at the head of the Babel, for the simple reason that he *is* an old Colonel and is unfit for regimental duty. It is true that when this old dotard was found wholly incompetent for the task, he was removed and replaced by one of the most active men in the army who was young but at the same time had gained knowledge by experience, I mean Lt Col Haines 21st. But when they installed him, he was thought so young that he was to have no direct power of his own but only to act on the orders he might receive from the nest of noodles at Head Quarters. The consequence was that the Invalid Battalion instead of being comfortably housed in the town, was exposed to all the miseries of a tent life in the winter. The sick were heaped in marquees, instead of the largest buildings the place afforded. And to save enumerating them, all the evils named in the part of Mr Stafford's speech concerning Balaklava, arose from the thickheadedness (if I may use the expression) of the Quarter Master General and his immediate inferior the late Prime Minister's son.*

By the second half of February, warm clothing and improved supply meant that the army could once again contemplate offensive action.

---

* Colonel the Honourable Alexander Gordon, described by Lacy Yea as 'a red tapist of the worst description'.

An Anglo-French operation against the Russian forces in the vicinity of Balaklava was set in train on 20 February. Alexander Hood of the 42nd Regiment was among the troops mobilized.

On the 20th instant we suddenly got orders at 9 o'clock at night to cook our next days provisions and be ready to march against the enemy. It began to snow at a fearfull rate, but we had got the order and out we went floundering through the snow in the dark for about 4 miles when we heard several shots fired in front. The snow fell so thick that we could not see 10 yards in front. Hurrah's my heros we all shouted we shall get warm at last. We fully expected that we had fallen in with the Russian Army, but to our disappointment it turned out to be only a party of Cossacks. When they found out who we were they gallopped of[f]. We took two of them. We then continued our march until daylight when we found that we were close in under Kutar McKenzie. We sent out parties who scoured the hills and valleys roundabout, and with the exception of some parties of Cossacks we found that the whole Russian Army had left the Valley of Balaklava. All that we got by our march was a great many of our ears frost bitten, [and] some of [the] Grenadiers got a Bullet or two through their Bonnets. Our Brave old General Sir Colin Campbell was evidently on nettles, eager for a row. He had a fine little army under his command 3 Regiments of Highlanders, 3 Regiments of French Zouaves, Gallant Fellows, 3 Batteries of Horse Artillery and all the Cavalry, so you see that we would have given the Russians a surprise had we fallen in with them.

A recently promoted Sergeant-Major George Cruse of the 1st Dragoons was among the composite cavalry squadrons created for the expedition, as he informed his wife.

The weather took a sudden change and the rain came down in torrents. I was not so well clad as I could have wished, having put on very slim Regimental boots the day previous having been so fine. But I was not [at] all prepared for what was to follow. It was about ten o'clock when we moved off, and although it was only about one mile to Kadikoi (that is the small village attached to Balaklava) it took us nearly three hours to pass that place, the night being so extremely dark. And to crown our comforts? The most severe frost set in which ever fell to my lot to experience. I am not going to tell a pityful story about it, but merely a few facts Dearest. According to the rumours I heard, we ought to have been six miles out by daylight, and so have surprised an army of about ten thousand Russians and either killed or taken them all prisoners. It was just daylight as we passed a small (destroyed) village about one mile beyond Kamara and where we halted. Two or three of our Highland Regts were there crowning the heights and the French were beginning to arrive in great force.

The junction with the French had been anticipated earlier, as Major William Forrest, who was also part of the expedition, explained: 'The French division who were to have accompanied us were too wise and were countermanded, but the officer who was to have countermanded us lost his way. The French hearing that we had gone came out in the morning.'

The rigours of what the British underwent that night – and which the French had spared themselves – were described in detail for his wife's benefit by Cruse.

We tried to dismount, but it was rather a difficult thing to accomplish as we were litterally frozen to our saddles. The snow came down very thick accompanied by the keenest north wind I ever felt in my life, and I am not going beyond the truth when I say we were solid masses of ice from head to foot. I managed to get a bottle into the corner of my mouth and took a good swig of grog (a thing I am never without) but I tried a long time to eat a bit of bread; my mustache and beard were so frozen together that it was an impossibility. I was quite jolly all the time and was highly amused at seeing the Major as he dismounted. Having on some waterproof things they had frozen to his shape as he sat in the saddle, but when he dismounted he looked exactly like the figure of the old woman who had her petticoats cut off up to her knees. We got back about eleven o'clock in the morning and dearest perhaps you might think it rather strange but it took Weaver and Clements more than half an hour to get my frozen things off me and I had to hold my head for more than that time over a charcoal fire before I could get my Helmet thawed from my head. It was rather a painful operation to get the collar of my pea coat disentangled from my beard and whiskers.

Among some, the events of that night had perhaps caused a measure of disenchantment with the French. If so, it was as nothing compared with what was to come. Until the beginning of February 1855 the French had prosecuted the bulk of their siege operations against the Flagstaff Bastion, at the south-western tip of Sevastopol's defences. Much of the French activity had consisted of mining but the Russian engineer, Todleben, proved their master at underground warfare. First, he exploded a camouflet to wreck the French tunnels; and second, when they attempted to create a fourth parallel by blowing a crater between themselves and the Flagstaff Bastion, he ensured that his men were sufficiently alert to be able to occupy it before the French. The French turned their attention instead to the Malakhov, which stood opposite the trenches recently taken over by them from the British. Sir John Burgoyne had always held that the Malakhov, crowning a hilltop overlooking Sevastopol, was the key to the town and would have liked the French to release the British to assault it. General Canrobert, however, had insisted that the French take the ground on the right of the line adjacent to the Inkerman Heights, which had left the British sandwiched between the French Left and Right Attacks with only the Redan in front of them. When Todleben saw the Allies creating new batteries with which to bombard the Malakhov, he guessed what was intended and on the night of 21/22 February sent seven battalions of infantry to dig fresh batteries on Mount Inkerman. The *Ouvrages Blancs*, as they were termed (because of the newly exposed white limestone), commanded the approaches to the Malakhov, particularly the high ground known as the 'Mamelon' which the French would need to occupy. On the night of 23/24 February the French attacked the *Ouvrages Blancs*. The Zouaves led by Colonel Cler, lacking support, were beaten back. Lieutenant Charles Gordon of the Royal Engineers, who would achieve fame thirty years later as Gordon of Khartoum, reported these occurrences to his brother Henry in a letter dated 28 February:

> In spite of my weekly letters, I still get wiggings, it is too bad. I cannot write oftener and as [to] news out of the trenches, I cannot get hold of any. The French as I told you attacked a battery the Russians had made on the open ground 600 yds from their works near the Malakoff Tower. They attacked in three columns but found the *Rus* well prepared. The Zouaves carried the battery but the *Rus* Reserve coming up they were driven back. Their own reserves, a battn of Marines having declined coming to the scratch. They suffered

greatly and own to 200 killed. One thing is positive, the battery must be taken, as it will never do to let the *Rus* make batteries where they like, at that distance from their works. The French Imp[eria]l Guard went over that way today, so that I think they are going to try it again: if they will not do it, we must. The *Rus* had an hour's armistice yesterday to bury the dead of the above conflict, & all round our trenches, the *Rus* came out of their Rifle Pits which are marked on the [enclosed] sketch, and called out for tobacco. They have 50 in the top and 20 in the lower one. One of the latter as near as possible did for me, the bullet was fired not 180 yds off & passed an inch about my nut into a bank I was passing. They are very good marksmen.

It was obvious that the Mamelon would be the next target of the Russians. Canrobert rejected the advice of his chief engineer, General Bizot, to seize it first, believing that the Mamelon could be captured at will. On 10 March the Russians occupied the strategic feature. British artillery was directed to fire at the new target. General Codrington was in a mortar battery on 12 March:

While waiting there till the working party arrived, I saw the artilleryman rasping the wooden fuze for the 10 inch, or 13 inch shells which were to be fired on the Mamelon: they did not fit the shells, and wonderful to state they were as old as, some of them *1801*, and most of *1805!*

Codrington remained to watch the covering party go up to the advanced work. The mortars then opened fire.

A sudden flash and report told me of the shell going to its destination, its path marked by its twinkling light. Up it went, turned its corner, descending threatening towards its point. A sudden flash and report alas! it had burst in the air. Well I thought the next fuze will be left longer. Some little afterwards away it went – no better luck. The next succeeded apparently well – but most of the others were true to 1801 and thought they ought to have been off long ago. One went as soon as he could from the muzzle, the others mostly burst in the air! Thus a shell, rather a heavy, costly article with 6 or 8 pounds of powder in it, and brought to the battery with great labour is allowed to fail from I suppose, 'using up old stores', or taking them like wine the 'first that was bottled'.

Of more general concern to the British was the realization that the French were not going to risk assaulting the Mamelon but were sapping up to it. Nigel Kingscote, writing on 20 March, expressed his disgust:

I shall be very glad of peace if it is only to free us from our friends, and I vote that next time we go to war we go entirely on our own footing. This opinion I am afraid is getting too prevalent in the army and tho' I feel it very strongly myself I *hold* differently if I can out here for fear the soldiers should get hold of it and cry 'no bono Frances' as they did to the Turks, for our men are getting very savage with them for not taking the Rifle Pits in front of their advance trench opposite the Mamelon and tho' a ravine is between us and them still, the Riflemen (Russians) can reach our advance trench and consequently there are some casualties. The French did try to take them on Saturday night but could not hold them, why I cannot conceive, and before morning the Russians had flung up some new Rifle works. The French are frightened to death and are actually sapping up to these Rifle pits!! My firm belief is that a Co[mpany] of our men would take them and hold them and we are longing to do it, in fact when all the Division were turned out by the immense peals of musketry on Saturday our men were quite disgusted when turned in again saying 'if they cannot take it let us have a shy and we will show them how to do it'. This is the dangerous feeling and I hope will not spread.

Captain Nathaniel Steevens of the 88th Regiment, like many others, could not but agree: 'I am beginning to think that the French are *all talk and do but little.*'

The French sap nevertheless alarmed the Russians sufficiently to provoke them into making a mass sortie on the night of 22/23 March. It was mainly directed against the French works, but no fewer than four separate columns attacked the British trenches on the Vorontsov Ridge. The defenders had to meet these attacks in turn and were stretched first one way then another; Colonel Kelly of the 34th (The Cumberland) Regiment and Captain Montagu of the Royal Engineers were both captured. The fiercest fight was in the mortar battery, as General Codrington recorded:

An Albanian with a sharp wavy sword – a kilt, fine dress and 32 pounds on him, shot Capn. Browne of the 7th who was doing his duty in fighting up the battery, and the Albanian was himself killed. I saw him lying there with 3 Russians – a coarse reprobate looking fellow – he had a pistol loaded with a curious pair of balls like this and joined by a brass spiral wire.

The defence of the mortar battery was the turning point and the Russians retired. During that night's fighting the British suffered 70 casualties, the French 600 and the Russians 1,300. On 24 March a truce was agreed to clear the dead and wounded. Nathaniel Steevens witnessed the scene.

Here we saw a crowd of English Officers & Men mingled with some Russian Officers & escort, who had brought out the Flag of Truce; this was the most curious sight of all; the Officers chatted together as freely & gaily as if the warmest friends, and as for the Soldiers, those who 5 minutes before had been firing away at each other, might now be seen smoking together, sharing tobacco and drinking Rum, exchanging the usual compliments of 'bono Ingles' &c; the Russian Officers were very gentlemanly looking men, spoke French and one English; at length on reference to watches it was found 'time was nearly up' so both Parties gradually receded from each others sight to their respective works, not however without our men *shaking hands* with the Russian soldiers & some one calling out, 'Au revoir'.

Captain Earle, in contrast, took the opportunity to assess the lie of the land, as he explained in a letter home dated 26 March.

The day before yesterday I went with a flag of truce to bury the dead killed in the trenches the previous night. On the left most of the bodies had been removed so we had a good opportunity of reconnoitering in front of our trenches. It was not until then that I knew how indefatigable the Russians were in building small walls and pits for their riflemen, who perhaps might wait a week before they got a shot and a month before they killed a man, which would sufficiently recompense them for their stubborn perseverance. In some of these 'pits' we found mutilated limbs which proved that they also had their share of wounds from our riflemen, ten times worse than any they could inflict on our men as come what may they could not be removed in any case until dark.

By the onset of spring the situation before Sevastopol was not altogether satisfactory and even the diplomatic Lord Raglan, in a letter to Lord Panmure of 27 March, had to acknowledge that the methods of the French left something to be desired.

> The failure of the French to keep the Russians off the ground they endeavoured to drive them from on the 24th Feb. has checked their disposition to lay violent hands upon the Enemy's ambuscades, and the Russians still occupy some of those in the immediate front of their advanced parallel, contiguous to our extreme right, and the French are content to proceed towards the Mamelon by sap. Gen. Rose is somewhat uneasy upon this point, and will I believe write confidentially upon it to Lord Clarendon [the Foreign Secretary]. I earnestly recommend that the subject should be considered confidential in the strictest sense of the word. Our allies are extremely sensitive.

The British high command had weathered the political storm which had buffeted it over the winter. Now it had to try and ensure that the military alliance with the French did not fall apart under the strain.

8

ASSAULT ON THE REDAN I

At the beginning of March 1855 a familiar face had returned to the Crimea to take command of the Light Division. Sir George Brown had recovered from the wound sustained at the Battle of Inkerman. Even while he had been absent, the state of the army in the Crimea continued to cause him concern. Lord Raglan had received a letter from him condemning the troops for throwing away their hated stocks and Albert shakos: 'The rogues ought to be reminded that they are making away with what does not belong to them!' The Adjutant-General, Wetherall, was forcibly informed of Brown's view of the men's appearance:

> If there is any one circumstance more than another that has tended to increase their discomfort & augment their inefficiency it has been the light Marching Order dodge, against which I have all along so strenuously set my face! With a view to their marching light, the men were ordered to leave their knapsacks behind, and to land with only a blanket and a great coat. The consequence was that nobody had the means of cleaning himself or his appointments; and from that time to the 5th November, when I left them, no man in the army had *ever cleaned his belts*, and very few had even washed their persons. The consequence was that all the men and many of the officers were covered with vermin and in such a state of filth and discomfort as can scarcely be conceived.
>
> All this time the French troops who had carried with them their usual load, *which is larger than ours* appeared cleanly and in comparative comfort.
>
> Another cause of the dirty and ruffianly appearance of the troops has been from 'Whisker and Moustache Pish'. Lord Raglan having been against the introduction of that foreign fancy, the measure having been introduced against his recommendation, was determined not to interfere in any measure whatever with their hair and beards. The consequence is that any officer and man is allowed to exercise

his own fancy, and as there are no looking-glasses in the camp, no one has the least idea how villainously ill he looks. With all this, and when you consider that worked as they are it is impossible to attempt anything like a Parade, you may easily conceive what a *nice set of fellows we are.*

Brown returned to the army in an uncompromising mood. His previous bad relations with General Codrington, who had reverted to his command of the Light Division's 1st Brigade on Brown's return, soon resurfaced, as Codrington informed his wife in a letter of 14 March.

I have just returned from the top of the hill to see if I could cool myself, and my feelings of annoyance and almost indignation: for it seemed pretty nearly the crisis of an intercourse as disagreeable – indeed more so – than I have ever had with any man, private or official. I refer to an interview with Sir G. Brown, . . . all about Campbell having two batmen to take care of his horses! He sent direct without anything to me to the Off[ice]r. Com[man]d[in]g. 23d. that Campbell's 2d. batman was to be 'forthwith withdrawn'. Lysons of course showed me this, and I desired him to leave the answer to me which was official to Sir G.B. that as he was allowed 3 Chargers and 1 baggage horse by the Queen's regulations, and had them, I did not think the duty could be properly done unless he was permitted to have two soldiers to look after the 4 horses – particularly as we had to fetch our own forage and fuel from Balaklava. . . . As I got into the room of his hut, he began by saying that he was just answering a letter I had written him about young Campbell's having two batmen. And then he flew out into violence indeed . . . 'Damn it, Codrington do you mean to think young Campbell's services are of value enough that the Queen should find him 2 servants.' . . . He said that it was a 'dodge'. I contradicted him flatly and said, 'It is not a dodge, it is no such thing, and it is not my duty to remain and have such terms used towards me', and I got up to go away. He then entered into my manner, having always been so very improper towards him that even the D. of Cambridge had remarked it to him. Of course I said I did not see what the D. of Cambridge's opinion had to do with the matter. In short a tissue of offensivenesses. . . . I had said I should wish to refer this question of the number of batmen to Head Quarters; 'I shall allow no such thing, except through myself.' Of course not, Sir – and with my own remarks upon it – Of course, Sir. After many such offensive recurrences to my manner and my conduct, tolerably personal but official, I standing up grinding inwardly, and as this seemed to be going on for ever I went to the door, with 'any further orders?' and came away in indignation! And I hope this will cool me more than the warm air on the hill seems to have done. There is nothing of the real gentleman in that quarter: and I am not Sir George Brown's slave, or a schoolboy to be made the scapegoat of his ill-temper and most overbearing manner and expressions.

Codrington wrote another letter to his wife the following day.

I hear from several that in his visits yesterday to the regiments of this brigade, Sir G.B. was most offensive in his language and manner. I am not surprised at it; and it is enough to disgust anyone. Yea of the 7th who has been working most successfully for his men through this arduous winter, for arduous it has been, and who has had to share personally all the Trench work as well is thoroughly disgusted, and won't stay a day longer than he can avoid when his 30 yrs. are complete. To Col. Kelly of the 34th he said, 'Who are you Sir, the Major?' No Sir, the Com[mandin]g Off[ice]r; and seeing a man cleaner than the rest, he said how is it the men are not all as clean, and on his [Kelly] beginning his answer by saying 'I fancy' (as if he was going to say he was a Serg[ean]t or someone who had not the same work) 'I'll have none of y[ou]r damned fancies.' In short as coarse and as browbeating as any 'gentleman' could be.

Brown was soon issuing orders in an attempt to get regularity in the men's uniforms again. Codrington was unimpressed, as he wrote on 17 March.

To-day has been cold enough to make people forget pipeclay and stocks, I should think: and now the insisting on the men having the wings those nonsensical shoulder things, put on their coats, they will not be able to get fur coats over them.

The nadir of Codrington's relationship with Sir George Brown came on 3 April during an inspection of his brigade.

I heard yesterday evening of something coarse said to a C.O. and in the hearing of others, connected with me. I find on enquiry that this was heard [as] 'Damn Gen. Codrington', or 'Gen. Codrington be damned': this with regard to an order I had given to have the [percussion] cap pouches put on the waistbelt. Now though this was not said *to* me, it was said of me to officers under my command, and by what I can make out, in the hearing of his staff, and must have been in the hearing even of the men of the company: and I mean to go to Head Quarters presently on the subject, for it as well to have this sort of thing stopped before it is said *to* me personally, which will be the next thing. But I must tell you a funny and not unpleasing comment upon the find fault coarseness of expressions which had been heard by some of the men. An officer heard one of the privates say quietly to his neighbour, after I had come and passed by the company which Sir G.B. had been *at*, 'well, there goes the bully, and here comes the gentleman.' How amused I was when I heard this just now.

On the 5 April Codrington took action.

I have sent in Campbell with a private note to Steele, whom I did not see yesterday on the subject of the gentlemanlike expressions of Sir G.B.. I have written it privately – but that Ld. R[aglan] should know of it, and my wish that Sir G.B. should know I had mentioned it.

Colonel Steele, Lord Raglan's military secretary, acknowledged Codrington's note and discussed it with him on the 7 April. 'He said something about Ld. R. being willing to make it better for me by moving me to another brigade – but I begged him not to think of it'. One of Brown's staff officers attempted to persuade Codrington that the words in question had not been uttered, but he refused to be mollified, and on 11 April Lord Raglan's intervention had its effect: 'Yesterday Sir G.B. came to my tent and shook hands and we had a conversation that one w[oul]d fancy was between the best friends,' Codrington reported with satisfaction.

It was as well that this matter had been resolved when it was: two days earlier the siege of Sevastopol entered its latest phase. After the Russian sortie of 22 March, it had been agreed that an assault could not be launched against the town until a further bombardment had taken place. Five hundred British and French guns opened fire on 9 April. Three days later, John Fisher of the 1st Battalion Rifle Brigade was sent into the rifle pits to protect No. 7 Battery from the attentions of Russian sharpshooters.

One fine morning I remember going on trench duty when a circumstance occurred that froze my blood in its veines almost. We were all in good spirits and had been in the trench about an hour popping away at the Russians when we caught sight of one or two close together. Now for a volley, there they are boys. There were five of us to fire having taken cover under a part of the trench or the embankment higher than the rest [which] formed a better cover, the Russians having battered some parts level to the ground. No sooner said than we all took aim; whether we did any execution or not it is hard for me to say. All I know is that we had no sooner fired than whack! came a shot from a Great gun knocking the bank away, smashing two of my comrades all to a mortar, laying two others prostrate on the earth one of them loosing an arm, the other very much bruised and smothered in dirt, myself only left standing out of five. I stood rooted to the spot, nor could I lend any help to extricate my poor bruised comrade. However he was soon got up [and] sent home. The other poor fellow still laid there for a short time. I shall never forget this poor man. I will not mention his name but the poor fellow turned quite black in the face, stared at me some time and said Ah! F[isher] if it had not been for the adjut[ant] this would not have happened. It appears that he had had some presentiment of evil before leaving camp and asked the Adjut. to let him stay in camp, but he was not allowed to do so, hence the result, the loss of an arm. The Adjut. was on duty in the trench the same morning, and when poor H* was carried along on a stretcher he espied him and used the same words as above, which, when the Adjut saw him, caused the tears to start into his eyes. The poor fellow died at Scutari, they say.

The same day a further casualty occurred. Captain Gustavus Crofton of the Royal Engineers wrote to his brother, William.

I was on duty in the battery today and the fire was heavy. I thank God I did my duty. This note will seem queer, but I cannot write straight. The fact is I am lying on my back wounded. The papers will perhaps frighten you, so I write and only tell you what is the matter. My left leg is broken, and in ½ an hour I must suffer amputation. I know not what may be the result, but I am in the hands of God. Think nothing about it. Remember I have met a

---

*   The casualty returns identify him as Private Thomas Holland.

Soldier's fate. Write to our dearest Mother. I *may* perhaps write again.
I feel this support that to the best of my ability I have served my
Country and my Queen. Best love to all as if named, & believe me
ever your very affectionate brother.

Captain Crofton died three days later.

The British bombardment did not have it all its own way. As in
October, the rocky ground opposite the Redan made it difficult to arm
batteries within effective range. Batteries number 7 and 8, of sandbag
construction and sited within 700 yards of the Russian defences, were
still not ready when the bombardment commenced. Captain Oldershaw
of the Royal Artillery brought No. 7 Battery into action on 13 April.
Captain Maxwell Earle reported the mixed fortunes of that day's firing
against Sevastopol:

> Capt Peel (Leander) told me today that he believes the place to be
> doomed! He declares that from the batteries he saw the Russians
> return *5 times* to their guns! Our fire is so severe that it quite swamps
> the enemy. However by concentrating his fire on our advanced battery
> of 4 guns he completely swept it away & Oldershaw RA tells me that
> as many as 10, 68 pr shot came through the parapet simultaneously.
> He lost 9 men out of 22.

The Russians, as it emerged later, were suffering the effect of a
temporary ammunition shortage. Captain the Hon. Edward Gage,
writing home the same evening, could tell that something was amiss.

> The Defence, as regards long Balls, is as obstinate as the impetuosity
> of the Attack, and every thing that genius & bravery can accomplish
> is conspicuous in the Russians. However it cannot but be perceived
> that their fire is comparatively weak tho' the effects is very distressing
> to our Gunners. We have had more casualties than during the last
> siege, but we have had more Men & Batteries engaged. Lt Luce has
> been killed & Lts Sinclair & L'Estrange wounded, 43 Gunners killed &
> wounded. An advanced Battery of ours was almost demolished to
> day, but luckily the Guns are not materially injured, & will be repaired
> to night & be ready to open fire with a sister Battery in the Morn[in]g.
> I do not suppose the Fire will last much more than a day longer,
> for the Men are completely beat, having been in the Trenches every
> 12 hours since the Fire opened & human flesh & blood cannot stand

this much longer. A new 8 Gun Advanced Battery of ours opened today with great effect, almost every shell burst in one of the embrasures. The French have demolished the advanced Russian works at Inkerman & the Mamelon hardly fires at all. The Bastion Du Mât only fires a Gun now & then.

Although the Russian fire had been largely subdued, once again no assault followed. General Canrobert vacillated: his chief engineer, Bizot, had been mortally wounded and succeeded by General Niel, who had secret instructions from Paris to allow no move to be made against Sevastopol until the Emperor Napoleon III arrived in the Crimea to take command in person. The British, unable to act alone, confined them-selves to clearing the Russians from some rifle pits forty-five yards in front of their Right Attack. Captain Nathaniel Steevens of the 88th Regiment described the preparations that were made on the night of 19/20 April: 'The numbers of the Covering-Party were considerably increased, and I had 224 men & 4 Officers under my command; when I started I fancied *we* were to take these pits, but the 77th were appointed to do so.'

The 77th Regiment was commanded by the giant Colonel Thomas Egerton, six foot eight inches tall. He was seconded by the twenty-year-old Captain Audley Lemprière who, judging by his coatee, now in the collections of the National Army Museum, stood well under five foot. The attack, launched at 8 p.m., succeeded in capturing the rifle pits. Russian counter-attacks were successfully beaten off. But, as Captain Steevens remarked, victory came at a cost:

> Our loss was *severe* 60 men killed & wounded, & *seven Officers*, of whom Col. Egerton (a tall powerful man) & Capt Lempriere 77th were *killed*; the latter was very young, had just got his company and was about the *smallest* officer in the Army, a great *pet* of the Colonel's and termed by him his *child*; he was killed, poor fellow at the first attack in the rifle pit, the Colonel, *tho' wounded*, snatched him up in his arms & carried him off declaring 'they shall never take my child'; the Colonel then returned and in the second attack was killed.

The nearer of the two rifle pits captured was immediately connected to the British trench system. The one further away was supposedly rendered useless, but this did not stop the Russians re-occupying it, as General Codrington acknowledged in a letter to his wife:

> Col. Yea had written up to me about some hand grenades which would have been very useful – these are small shells thrown by hand. And the rifle pit to which some Russians had returned was only 8 or 10 yards from our new trench, and therefore it was an object to be able to throw something destructive into it. But there were no hand grenades.

Some tried their hand at improvisation.

> Young Millett had made a soda water bottle into a shell, by filling it with powder, and stones and a mortar fuse, to throw into the Russian pit – but it was sent short: they were throwing stones at each other, and talking to each other.

The Russians made one final attempt to recover their lost ground, as Captain Mark Walker of the 30th Regiment noted in his journal on 21 April.

> The Russians advanced to the Rifle pit taken the night before but on being fired upon and our men cheering they retreated. A tremendous fire was opened on us and there were several casualties. About 3 am I volunteered and took a party of about 20 men to attack the remaining pit. To the astonishment of every one on our reaching it it was empty. A volunteer working party came up and destroyed it. Through the mercy of God again have I escaped.

For the present, this was as much as the British could accomplish. On 24 April Raglan wrote to Lord Panmure: 'We must prevail upon Gen. Canrobert to take the Mamelon, otherwise we cannot move forward with any prospect of success or safety.' In the current state of suspense, and with the British and Russian forces in such close proximity, Raglan was glad for reinforcements in the shape of the 1st Regiment* and the 48th (The Northamptonshire) Regiment: 'Their arrival is most seasonable for it has been found necessary to increase the night Guard of the Trenches by 600 men.'

---

* The 2nd Battalion of the 1st (or Royal) Regiment arrived to join the 1st Battalion, already present in the Crimea.

The Quarries on the morning of the 8th of June.

36. The aftermath of the desperate fight for the Quarries, drawn by Lieutenant H. D. Radcliffe.

37. Captain Mark Walker reading general orders, 1 May 1855.

38. Standing side by side in the doorway, Lord Raglan (left) and General Pélissier.

THE LATE COLONEL YEA.

39. Lacy Yea, pugnacious to the end.

40. A soldier of the 28th (The North Gloucestershire) Regiment, part of Eyre's brigade.

41. View from Sevastopol looking across the Russian Strand Battery towards the Vorontsov Ravine. The buildings occupied by Eyre's brigade on 18 June 1855 are in the distance, right of picture.

42. Officers of the 18th (Royal Irish) Regiment. Colonel Clement Edwards is seated, cap on knee, towards the right.

43. The British encampment before Sevastopol.

44. Admiral Lyons, Sir Colin Campbell, and Generals Scarlett, Eyre, Airey and Bentinck stand in line to receive the Order of the Bath, 27 August 1855. Painted by Cadogan.

45. The view from the Mamelon of French approach trenches snaking towards the Malakhov.

46. The Redan from the curtain wall of the Malakhov. On 8 September 1855, the British had to attack across 280 yards of open ground, top left.

47. The assault on the Redan as drawn by Lieutenant H. D. Radcliffe, 23rd Royal Welsh Fusiliers, who was among the resulting casualties.

48. The interior of the Redan, looking towards the salient angle. This was the view of the Russian defenders, massed behind the barricade at the rear.

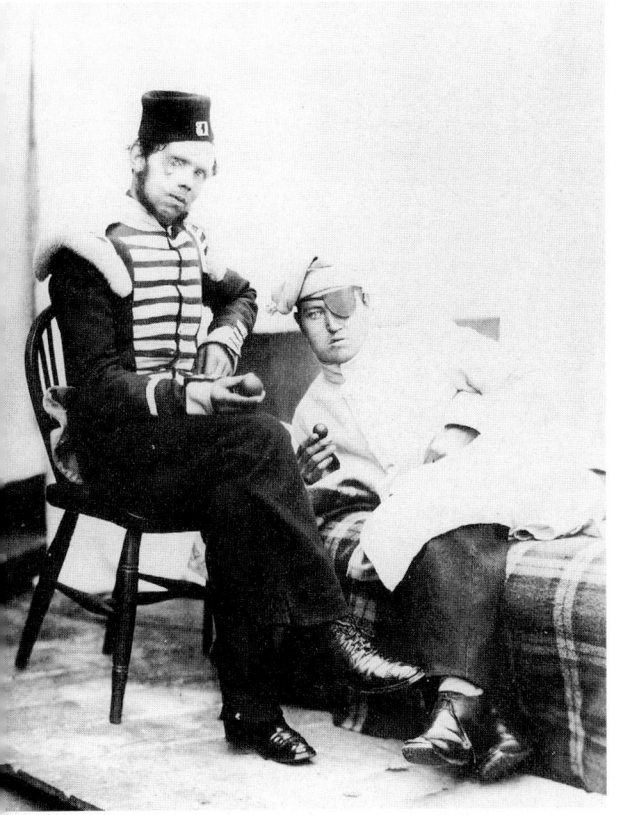

Above, left.
49. Brigadier-General Charles
Ridley, drawn by Cadogan.

Above, right.
50. Lieutenant William Stirling,
Royal Horse Artillery.

Left.
51. Private Jesse Lockhurst,
31st (The Huntingdonshire)
Regiment, and Private O'Brien,
1st (The Royal) Regiment,
holding the grape shot which
disabled them.

52. The dry docks at Sevastopol before . . .

53. . . . and after demolition, January 1856.

In the trenches, alerts were commonplace. Lieutenant-Colonel Clement Edwards of the 18th (Royal Irish) Regiment, part of Major-General William Eyre's 2nd Brigade of the 3rd Division, was on duty on the night of Saturday 5 May.

About dusk I was out in front posting the sentries and giving my instructions about them for the night when the General Officer of the day sent for me. I had not left the front a second when the enemy fired at one of the parties who were throwing out sentries and that party retired. Capt Arnold fell, saying 'Oh my God' from which we suppose he must have been wounded, as he was missing from that time; he must (if alive) be a prisoner in the hands of the Russians. The result of this was to cause the General to become very violent and wrongfully he put a brother Officer of Captain Arnold's in arrest, implying that he shewed a want of spirit. There has been a Court of Enquiry on the subject, my evidence and that of another officer (a stranger to me) was so much against the General that the Officer was immediately released by an Order from Head Quarters, and told that there was no implication against his character or blame of any kind attached to him. The General has received a very severe censure from Head Quarters but we shall never know the wording of it. Unluckily he commands the Brigade to which the Regiment is attached, and I believe him to be a very vindictive man. We must only be the more guarded.

The officer who escaped General Eyre's wrath was Captain Cocks of the 4th (The King's Own) Regiment. General Codrington, as he revealed in a letter to his wife, knew slightly more about the affair than Colonel Edwards.

A Court of Enquiry, Gen. Pennefather, Col. Spencer of 44th and another, justified Capn. Cocks. Gen. Eyre therefore sent in his resignation, oh! bang, slap dash – I believe not only to resign his brigade but his commission 'if he was not supported' &c. In short, in all from the beginning, lost his temper and his discretion. However, was induced or allowed to withdraw his letter and now has found a quarrel with Estcourt for visiting Capn. Cocks whilst under arrest (his wife's nephew): Estcourt being Adjt. Genl., which quarrel seems a funny one.

Frustrated in his attempt to get Canrobert to commit himself to a direct attack on Sevastopol, Raglan persuaded his ally instead to sanction an expedition against the port of Kerch. Situated 120 miles away at the eastern end of the Crimean Peninsula, Kerch commanded the straits leading to the Sea of Azov; its capture promised to interrupt the Russian line of supply to Sevastopol. The British would contribute 3,000 troops, mostly from the Highland Brigade, the French 7,000 more. Sir George Brown had overall command. On the afternoon of 3 May the expedition sailed. Almost immediately, however, Canrobert informed Raglan of the arrival of a telegram from Paris (sent via the new submarine cable which had been laid just the week before between Varna and the Crimea) instructing him to bring up the French Army of the Reserve from Constantinople. For this purpose all available French shipping would be required. The Kerch expedition must be recalled. Raglan attempted to dissuade Canrobert but the arrival of a second telegram decided the matter. The expedition returned when already within sight of Kerch.

The reaction in the army to this ignominious episode was a wry acceptance, tempered with humour. General Codrington commented: 'Kertch is the place from whence Caesar wrote his celebrated letter "veni vidi vici". We must say 'veni, vidi, redivi'. 'All kinds of jokes are afloat about Sir G Brown's share in the affair', added Captain Earle. 'Some say that he forgot his razor and stock and was forced to return for them.' The humiliation was too much for General Canrobert. 'Bob Can't', as the British soldiers called him, resigned his command. He reverted to the command of a division, at his own request, and was succeeded by General Aimable Pélissier, a squat, brutal-looking sixty-year-old. Pélissier's reputation was that of a man who would secure his objective regardless of the cost in human life. Nigel Kingscote, writing home on 19 May, gave qualified approval to the change.

Well, we have got rid of a real bad one and sincerely hope we have now got something better but cannot say that his appearance is in his favour, altho' his countenance shows great determination more than that, savagery. It is curious that we have had two French Generals since we have been out here, two very different men. Poor Marshal St. Arnaud being of the two the greatest man and best General I think. He was much cleverer than Gen. Canrobert, more intriguing, a great actor and did not scruple to tell a lie to serve his purpose. His temper would not brook delay and had he been here we should have been in Sevastopol ere this. Gen. C. was a much more vulgar man, promises were never performed by him, lies predominated and though not wanting in personal bravery had no moral courage and funked responsibility to a degree.

Pélissier was determined to prosecute the siege of Sevastopol and studiedly ignored the views of the Emperor Napoleon III emanating from Paris. He also agreed to a renewal of the expedition to Kerch, which Sir George Brown would once again command. Brown reported the progress of the enterprise to Lord Raglan in a dispatch dated 28 May.

As we approached Kertch on the 25th, we were met by a numerous deputation of the principal inhabitants, including the Consuls of Austria & Naples imploring protection & begging that a Garrison might be left in the town for the protection of the lives & property of the inhabitants, seeing that all the Russians had flown & that there was no longer any authority in the place to protect them from the Tartars who threatened to come in in great numbers from the Country!

This I positively declined to do, stating that I was not Governor of the Country, that they had no Claims on my protection further than as regarded the Conduct of the Troops under my Command, for whom I had other employment, & I recommended that they should proceed in the absence of the Russian Authorities to establish some sort of Municipal Council to secure the police of the town.

A second deputation composed of nearly the same persons came to me next morning at this place to represent that the place was in a state of anarchy & that the Tartars were plundering & distroying every thing. I could only give them the same answer they received the previous day, & all the additional security I could be induced to promise was to request of the Admiral to send a steamer into the Bay, which he has done.

As I stated in my former letter not a single thing was touched during the passage of the Troops but since then I fear some of our boats crews as well as those of the French have been getting drunk & doing even more mischief than the Tartars. I have therefore determined to send the 79th with 20 Hussars into the Quarantine Station tomorrow, there to remain for the present with orders to detach frequent patrolles into the town & if possible to restore order by giving continuous protection to such provisional authority as may have been appointed. I however have this moment had a Communication from Captain Loaring who in the 'Furious' is in the bay representing that the uproar is worse than ever, & calling for immediate assistance to repress what would appear almost to amount to a revolt of the Tartar inhabitants.

I have ordered 20 Hussars to mount & to see what is the matter, but I dont mean to have a 'finger in the pie' further than to give protection to the weak from outrage, for after all, if the Tartar peoples really are disposed, as I believe them to be, to take a part in this war, it will only be so much the better for us.

This, if a happy, is not a particularly well behaved *family* that I am at the head of; I said nothing about it in my last letter which I concluded you might think it necessary to publish verbatim, but our allies on the march here & after leaving Kertch spread themselves for miles over the Country & amused themselves with shooting Pigs, Sheep, Ducks, & Geese, to the no small danger of those who took no part in this discription of sport.

Had this been all it might have passed over & been forgotten, but unhappily on their arrival here they broke away in their old style, & most of the inhabitants having flown, broke open the houses & not only completely gutted the town but finished by setting it on fire in two places!!

I grieve to say that some of my Countrymen were not slow to follow their example & if not so deeply implicated as our allies their conduct was very far from blameless.

With us however there is this difference, that the Officers are always ready to maintain & to restore order, whereas on the part of the French they appear to be utterly powerless to stop if they dont sometimes approve of such proceedings. I am quite sure they have not authority sufficient to put a stop to such excesses after they have fairly commenced, for it is pitiable to see the faces they put on when men appeal to them.

Nevertheless,

... They seem to think that they themselves are alone entitled to plunder with impunity, for nothing can exceed the zeal with which they apprehend the Turks when they find them employed in that way, & there is scarcely an hour in the day that they do not bring me some unhappy culprit who has been stopped at their outposts loaded in the same way as they themselves probably were the day previous!

But by the following day Brown had decided that the Turks deserved little sympathy.

I have a great deal of trouble with these confounded Turks who straggle over the Country & commit all sorts of excesses in spite of all I can do to prevent it.

Yesterday one of them I understand deliberately knocked out the brains of a Child in Kertch & having resisted the Guard in their attempt [to] apprehend him was shot dead on the spot ... I have [an]other two worthies in confinement for rapes committed on mere children. You will not therefore be surprised that I have no desire to have any more of them.

Henry Ridley James, an officer of the merchant navy serving aboard the steamship *Colombo*, revealed how a genteel looter went about his business. He sent an extract from his journal home to his mother.

Sunday 27th May. Went ashore at 7 and got to Kertch a little past 8. Went up to the Museum of which you have no doubt heard, for it is celebrated for valuable collections from the Ancient Roman times here. From a little behind the town you ascend a gracefull flight of steps until you come to a level with the Museum which is a large white building in the Ionic style ... I found a Tartar who I made come in with me & carry my things. The entrance is open and the interior is a large plain room white washed and fitted with glass cupboards in which are arranged or rather *were* arranged the relicts of the Times. I found a box 2 ft long and then I commenced to pick & choose. The place was covered with broken relicts & glass panes smashed, tables overturned and all [the] signs of war. I filled my box with lachrymal casts, bits of old brass coffins; my companion found 2 rings, one with a stone in it and the other with a finger bone in it. The gold had gone to decay & looked very like old iron ... I made my Tartar friend take my box down to the boat, & from there we took a stroll along the sea side popping into any house that was not inhabited, the inhabitants having fled. I found a few trifles which I did not much care about except a picture (sacred) ... We then went up to the other part or evidently aristocratic part. I opened a door & went into a house because I saw a fellow that was a soldier, but he was provided with a French pass & so, was a very gentlemanly man that came forward & spoke to me in French. I told him very politely that I would be much obliged if he would show me his house which he did, introduced me to his family and asked us if we would have anything. I spoke to him about the war & expressed a wish that the nations were united &c &c. After him, we went to cruise & a vagabond jew an ill looking hound, came & said that there was a Russian house & so I barged away at the door until it was opened. There was a lot of poor Russian women in the house and 2 men. All the jew wanted was for me to let him pillage so I kicked him and six more like him out of the yard, locked the door and proceeded to examine. The houses here have a large yard or compound behind and all one side are the servants houses and in front was the master's house, which was pretty well cleared by the owners. So we said good by, & went to look at the local church, but it was locked up. Several very pretty women were walking about. We then saw a good & evidently a crack house. The back door was open and in we went. We went to the servants quarters and there saw a very fine picture which I bought for my friend for 5/- as perhaps it belonged to the poor servants. I then went up to the Great man's house and a splendid one it was. I found a very fine picture of Jesus Christ in a regular frame, which I took. The house had been deserted very quickly, every thing was as they had left it [and] evidently [had] not been visited by a marauder. In the ladies chamber was a very fine down bed & large square pillows covered with scarlet satin, a very comfortable pair of fur boots which just fit me so I took them, a large piece of pale silk enough for a dress for Fanny or you. There were lots of silk gowns &c &c and before the toilet glass was a lot of her hair and a large pair of scissors. She had evidently been cropped before she left. I have a bunch of her hair & some side curls. From her room I went to the next, I suppose a school room. Some of the leaf work for dresses was under weigh on the table. A nice sofa but nothing for me except a penknife & a silk purse just begun. I then . . . found out the M[aster]'s room. He was a naval man. I took 2 sets of Epaulettes, a shako, a naval cloak but it was too heavy so I left it, and two or 3 trifles. In the drawing room was a very good piano open & music all ready. I expect they indulged in a little music before they left. We left Kertch at 3.30.

28th. Several of the men and officers went ashore but English & French patrols prevented anything being brought off.

Strategically the expedition to Kerch was a great success. Allied steam vessels gained access to the Sea of Azov and systematically cleared it of Russian shipping. Landing parties destroyed stores at Taganrog and other Russian ports. A supply route to Sevastopol had been cut. While the looting and wanton damage inflicted upon Kerch attracted international condemnation, in the British camp there was pleasure felt at a job well done. Lieutenant-Colonel Charles Lygon Cocks of the Coldstream Guards wrote home from Balaklava extolling the success.

I am glad that the Highlanders have at last done something as the army were beginning to throw stones at them for doing nothing, as from having been here at Balaclava they have nearly escaped the trenches and were not present at Inkerman so that all they have done was at Alma and the 93rd receiving a Charge at Balaclava, though according to the newspapers and common report in England, they have been everywhere & done everything . . .

Captain Hopton Bassett Scott of the 9th (The East Norfolk) Regiment, in a letter of 28 May, informed his father how Major-General Eyre's brigade of the 3rd Division received the news of the capture of Kerch.

A most absurd scene occurred at the termination of the reading of the General Order announcing this: we were ordered to give them three cheers, and the Brigade had been previously formed in three sides of a square. At the first yell and flourish of caps, out of the open side of the square bolted Staff Field Officer &c headed by Genl. Eyre, their astonished quadrupeds kicking, plunging, rearing and galloping wildly in every direction, the ground strewn with cocked hats, chacos & caps. Shouts of laughter had the field all to themselves, cheering being nowhere.

With General Pélissier as determined as Lord Raglan to take Sevastopol by assault, the Allies concentrated on softening up the town's defences. In an attempt to set fire to Sevastopol heavy shells called 'carcasses' – a primitive form of incendiary bomb – were lobbed at the town. Lieutenant-Colonel George Mundy wrote to his mother on 4 June.

Yesterday I was in command of 1200 men in our advance works. At about 9 am our batteries commenced firing carcases at the town. About 7 out of every 10 instead of going to the enemy, burst over our advance works. So serious did this become that I thought it my duty to inform the General of the trenches & to request that a stop might be put to it. Whilst I was talking to the Gen[e]r[a]l (Yea 7th) at about 10 am, another carcase burst. I rushed under a parapet, but unfortunately a little too late; a piece of shell about the size of a cheese plate, struck me on my left shoulder. Luckily I had a thick rolled gold shoulder knot on my shell jacket, it just struck the corner of this, striking me from the shoulder to the elbow and throwing me with great force at the Genrl's foot. I soon got up and attempted to walk to the 1st parallel but after a short time I fainted and found myself being doctored in the 21 gun battery. My shell jacket was torn up in the sleeve & a large black mark where the shell struck, my shirt also cut through but a very slight cut in the arm, nothing but what is called 'severe contusion'. Finding that there were several very much worse cases than mine waiting to be attended to (all shot by *our own* artillery) I sent back the men with the stretcher I was on, and with the aid of two jolly tars I managed to walk down to the French hospital in the ravine.

Mundy did not think it necessary to conceal from his mother the extent of his good fortune.

Was it not a providential escape? One ½ inch nearer and my left arm w[oul]d have been carried clean off at the shoulder, and 2 inches shorter my head would have been smashed to atoms, it just passed the end of my nose.

General Codrington, having long considered Mundy 'an arrant humbug' who did not look after his men properly, had scant sympathy.

He made a great fuss about it, came up on a stretcher, another officer went to relieve him: I saw him, he was in high talk, and Pretyman tells me scarcely a mark on his arm then. However, it *is* now black and blue and it is just exactly the thing for him – sufficient to delight him by being called wounded, not sufficient to do more in the way of damage than keep him in camp pleasantly for some little time. But it is too bad about these carcasses: a gross failure, and showing the Russians that it [is] so, besides damaging our own people. They were made they say in 1808 or so: and the composition must have changed its nature from a mere burning composition to an explosive one. We continued to throw shells instead.

Before the French and British could launch their decisive assault against the Malakhov and Redan respectively, the outworks of these two fortifications – the Mamelon before the Malakhov and the entrenchments in front of the Redan known as the Quarries – had to be captured. Lieutenant-Colonel John St George of the Royal Artillery described the events witnessed by him in a letter home dated 9 June.

On the 6th the Bombardment opened, and was kept up all night and next day. I knew an assault was intended on the 7th so I spent my day on the lookout. The French were to assault the Mamelon and the works they call the 'Ouvrages blanches', while the English are to assault some works called the Quarries in front of the Redan. Unfortunately from no position could I have seen *both* operations so I selected the French. At half past 6 o'clock [p.m.], the hour privately fixed, Pellisier rode up to the spot I had chosen, and sent a rocket into the town. Another followed in ten seconds, and then a third. As the last was in the air up jumped thousands of Zouaves &c who had been crouching in the trenches, jumped over the parapet, and ran straight at the Russian lines. The Russ did not stop for them but bolted like smoked out vermin, and ran back into the Mamelon, closely followed by the French. All went pell mell into the work together and were lost to view for a few seconds, when to my surprise I saw all, Russ and French tear out on *the other* side, and rush on against the Malakoff. Then such a fire opened from the Malakoff tower as never was seen before I am sure: sheets of flame, with their explosion, followed each other in the rapidest succession. The Russians worked the guns wonderfully well, (and as it is my trade I am a judge) and fired like fiends upon the multitudes of poor little Zouaves, whose pluck had carried them to the edge of a ditch they had no means of crossing, & who stood in hesitation till they were knocked over. It was too much for them, and they wavered and retreated into the Mamelon; and even this became too hot for them, and they had to retire into their trenches again. Reinforcements came in strength. Again they dashed into the Mamelon, (whose guns they had already spiked) and killed its defenders, and again (foolishly I think) went through to try the Malakoff. They failed a second time and had to retire, but this time no farther than the Mamelon, which they are holding still, having won it with admirable courage, and left between 2 and 3 thousand killed and wounded on the field. All this I saw for I was close enough to have to keep bobbing from big shot & shells that passed by me, and killed a man near, who was, like me, indulging curiosity. The French carried 2 of the ouvrages blanches also.

As soon as the Mamelon had fallen – for the first time at least – the British attacked the Quarries. In order to minimize casualties during the Allied bombardment, the Russians had limited the number of men that they committed to their forward trenches, trusting to counter-attacks to regain any position lost. Consequently, as General Codrington admitted: 'There were not above 40 Russians, who ran immediately – principally down the trench – and the Quarries themselves and immediate neighbourhood were easily taken.' Working parties were sent forward with gabions to turn the defences round. Codrington continued:

The Redan tried to throw grape, but could scarcely depress its guns enough, and the troops lining the parapet of the Redan with difficulty fired so low. About ½ p[ast]. 11 the Russians came out from the flank of the Redan in force, it was dark – no moon – ... and then there was hard fighting – hand to hand – firing at 30 yards – beat back and regaining the same ground, across the trenches several times – one officer I know who shot 4 Russians, and had to run his sword through a 5th! Bodies of our men and Russians lying thick. Again at ½ p[ast]. 1 or 2 in the morning, a similar heavy attack – the same sort of desperate fighting: but we held our own and the Russians, carrying off many dead in the night, left heaps, more than 300. Whilst I was at the look out, at dusk, I got a telegraph message from Shirley 'They are too strong for us, we must have assistance'. I went immediately to the camp, fell in the troops and sent down 600 from the division under Major Welsford.

Among a party of troops which had already been fed into action was Captain Frederick Elton of the 55th Regiment:

Just after writing this much of my letter I was ordered for a working party to follow a party which was to storm some fortified quarries between our works and theirs while the French attacked the 'Mamelon' and I finished off my letter thinking it very probable that

I should not come back again. The French attacked the Mamelon in great force . . . On our side the storming party attacked the quarries very well and carried them but very soon found that they had not men enough to hold them. The support was then ordered up but it was not enough so we were ordered to throw down our tools and form a support instead of a working party which we did and shortly afterwards advanced to where the others were fighting and joined them. We had some hard fighting and soon drove them back and followed them down a hill – this was about 7 P.M. as the attack had begun about 5½ or 6 P.M. We were soon obliged to retire to the quarries and after some very hard fighting quite close to each other we drove them back and began to fortify ourselves as well as we could which considering we had neither tools nor working party was not very well. About 2 a.m. a large column came on and attacked us but they were soon repulsed and did not make another regular attack though they kept on annoying us all the time we stayed there. The 55th were sent home about 5½ a.m. which you may imagine pleased us very much. One of our officers who was quite a child and the pet of the whole Regt. was killed. You cannot imagine how sorry we all are for the little fellow who was one of the best that ever lived.

The truth was that the British army in the Crimea was filling up with young officers. There were few experienced ones left. Taking and holding the Quarries had cost the British another forty officers killed and wounded, as well as over 600 men. Colonel Lacy Yea of the 7th Royal Fusiliers revisited a familiar theme of his when he wrote to General Wetherall in London.

We want *Captains* – we are pretty well off for *boys* and some young Clippers there are among them. The two Jones', Waller & Lord R. Browne are not to be surpassed. That young Waller is the merest child to look at, with the heart of a lion. In the repulse of the night attack on the Quarries he, with three or four men, actually followed the Column in its retreat, *driving them* before him, by his shouting a long way beyond our lines; and if light had enabled the Muscovites to have seen what they were running from, they would have seen a little boy, *followed* by a few men – which boy any one of them could have held up in one hand.

Not all the officers who arrived to take up duty with the Royal

Fusiliers gave Yea such satisfaction. Lieutenant the Hon. Edward Crofton, that 'shuffler' as Yea had previously styled him, had finally been sent out to the Crimea from England. Yea continued his letter to Wetherall:

> Mr. Crofton (thanks to you) rejoined three days ago, & has been riding ... about the Camp every day. Last night he was for the trenches, and he marched down there; but as soon as [he got] there he reported himself sick and came home. It turns out to be Gonorrhea with an incipient bubo, which he has brought on by riding in the state he was.

For Captain Elton of the 55th Regiment the fight for the Quarries – even though he emerged unscathed – left a sour taste, as he wrote to his father the following month.

> We are awfully disgusted at Lord Raglan's despatch about the Quarries. Our party was not only there but was so desperately engaged that we lost 1 Officer and 27 men killed and 28 wounded and yet the number of the Regiment is not even mentioned while in every other instance or nearly so, every single officer is mentioned as having greatly distinguished themselves while they were most of them not nearly so forward as we were nor were they in nearly so much danger. It is enough to disgust one of ever going to the front again if it can be avoided and I should not be surprised if it had that effect on the men for of course they look out for being mentioned as a body in the papers just as much as we do.

The irony was that when the Victoria Cross was instituted in 1857 as the foremost award for gallantry, Elton would be one of its first recipients, largely for this night's work in the Quarries. However, another man destined to be awarded one of the first Victoria Crosses, in this case for his heroism during the Battle of Inkerman, was rather less fortunate than Elton in the immediate aftermath of the capture of the Quarries. A week before, Captain Mark Walker had transferred from the 30th Regiment to the 3rd (The East Kent) Regiment (The Buffs). The entry in his journal for 10 June was as follows:

> Last night I went on with the reserve, just as I got into our approach which joins the trench on the right heavy firing commenced at the Mamelon. While I was in the act of hurrying the men up a howitzer shell dropped beside me and exploded. A peice struck me on the

right elbow and smashed it. I immediately tied a large handkerchief above the fracture and walked to the rear untill I met some of the 55th who put me on a stretcher and carried me to Camp. I received great kindness from my new brother officers. After some time I was carried to a hut at the General Hospital where I now am. I was put under chloroform and on coming to consciousness I found my arm taken off above the elbow during the night and today I suffered a good deal of pain. The loss I have experienced is very great but I am very thankful that my life has been spared. The hut has been filled with sympathising visitors particularly my old comrades of the 30th.

Walker's handwriting changes abruptly as he learns to use his left hand.

As the British worked to consolidate their hold on the Quarries and connect them with Egerton's Pits – the rifle pits that they had captured the previous April – there was a novel hazard to be guarded against. Fougasses were a primitive form of landmine. General Codrington explained how they worked in a letter to his wife of 14 June.

The Russians have buried powder boxes all along their front – one was trod on and hurt two men: it is by a small copper tube and acid communicating fire to a buried box, on being trod upon and broke. This little bit of copper and glass tube cannot be seen. Several of these have been found – and taken up safely: so fancy my having seen two Artillery men surrounded by a dozen soldiers, hammering at one with a stone! to break it open. I could scarcely get them to leave off except by a positive order: the d—-d fools. I do not think this quite a fair mode of warfare; a mine blown up is all fair – but to have things left behind them when the ground is not in their possession, that explode in this way is scarcely fair: it would justify the marching Russian prisoners over the ground in our own possession to find out where they are.

Preparations for the final assault on Sevastopol were fixed for 18 June, the fortieth anniversary of the Battle of Waterloo. The anticipated triumph would provide an alternative anniversary with which to commemorate Anglo-French unity. But in the days before the attack General Pélissier began to make some serious misjudgements. He decided not to attack the Flagstaff Bastion, which the Russians considered the most vulnerable to assault, confining himself instead to an attack on the Malakhov. Next, the experienced General Bosquet, having disagreed with

Pélissier's tactics, was removed from his command of the siegeworks opposite the Malakhov. Finally, the evening before the assault, he decided to dispense with the following morning's preliminary bombardment. This had been scheduled to last two hours in order to disable any guns which the Russians might have succeeded in bringing back into action after the punishing Allied bombardment of the previous day. The Russians, moreover, were fully aware of the intended assault and brought forward their reserves. It was believed that they had been warned by a deserter from the 28th (The North Gloucestershire) Regiment. 'But there was another intimation', wrote Lieutenant-Colonel Sir James Alexander of the 14th (The Buckinghamshire) Regiment: 'The men, being excited, did not go to sleep but remained up till we were directed to fall in at midnight. Our Camp looked like a fair, lighted up, with a buzz of voices everywhere. The Russians must have remarked this.'

Worse was to follow. The right hand of the three French assaults was launched an hour prematurely at 2 a.m. when its commander mistook a shell trailing light from its fuse as the rocket intended to signal an advance. Pélissier, in an attempt to coordinate his assault, let off the genuine signal rockets, but his two other generals were not ready. The disjointed French assault was a bloody fiasco. Dawn revealed to Raglan the scene. Only one French column, to the left of the Malakhov, had managed to break into the suburbs of Sevastopol. Its supports, however, were being decimated by flanking fire from the Redan. Raglan felt that he had to act to try and subdue the Redan's fire. 'I always guarded myself from being tied down to attack at the same moment as the French,' he informed Lord Panmure,

> & I felt that I ought to have some hope of their success before I committed our troops; but when I saw how stoutly they were opposed I considered it was my duty to assist them by attacking myself and both Sir George Brown and General Jones who were by my side concurred with me in thinking that we should not delay to move forward. Of this I am quite certain that if the troops had remained in our trenches, the French would have attributed their non-success to our refusal to participate in the operation.

Sir George Brown had been given operational control of the British assault on the Redan. The left column of attack, led by Major-General Sir John Campbell, comprised units taken from the 4th Division. Men of his own command, the Light Division, composed the right column. Brown made an official report on the Light Division's preparations, which mirrored those of the 4th Division.

> The troops for the attack were formed in the Quarries, & in the trenches in front & to the right of them while those of the 4th Division formed in the works to the left of them. The covering party was composed of 100 Men of the 2nd Battalion Rifle Brigade, & the same Corps furnished 50 men to carry wool bags [to fill the ditch] & 60 for scaling ladders in addition to the seamen similarly employed. The assaulting or attacking party was composed exclusively of Officers & men of the 34th Regiment under Captain Smith. The immediate support to the attacking party was formed in the two Boyaux leading out of the 3rd Parallel & consisted of the 7th, 33rd & 23rd Regiments under Lt. Colonel Lysons of the latter Corps, while the Working Party of 400 detailed in the orders of the day consisted of the remainder of the 2nd Batt. Rifle Brigade under Major Wood-cock [r. Woodford]. The rest of the 1st Brigade & the portion of the 2nd not required to take part in the Guard of the Trenches were placed in Reserve in the 1st Parallel. Colonel Yea who commanded the 1st Brigade placed himself at the head of the Assaulting party in the Quarries, & Major General Codrington stationed himself in the Left Boyau to superintend & direct the whole.

The attack began at 5.30 a.m. It soon became apparent that it was a hopeless undertaking. 'The enemy during the night had replaced all the guns which had been silenced at the close of the firing on the previous evening', commented Brown, '& the troops no sooner began to show themselves beyond the Parapet of the Trenches than they were assailed by the most murderous fire of grape that ever was witnessed.' Lord Raglan agreed: 'I never had a conception before of such showers of grape as they poured upon us from the Russian works. Some of the grape must have been thrown from very heavy guns.' General Codrington explained the effect of the barrage on men attempting to struggle over 400 yards of open ground towards the Redan:

> The moment they showed themselves, fire of grape was opened upon them – it ploughed the ground – it knocked over many, the dust blinded them, and I saw many swerve away to the trenches on their left. The officers told me afterwards they were blinded by the dust

thrown up by grape; and one told me he was quite blown – out of breath – before he got halfway.

Lieutenant-Colonel Mundy of the 33rd Regiment, who, after his previous wounding, had only come off the sick list the day before, was once again a casualty:

> I was bowled over by a minié ball striking me (passing right thro' only a flesh wound) about an inch below my right hip; I was in the open & on my way to the redan & I had to remain pretty quiet for fully two hours as every time I moved minié and grape came in hundreds at me, however I could stand the heat no longer & besides I thought the Russe w[oul]d follow us when repulsed so I dragged myself on my belly for about 150 yds & managed to get safe into the old advance work.

Major Arthur John Pack of the 7th Royal Fusiliers, who had come out to the Crimea as a replacement the previous February, was left stunned by the fusillade: 'All an inexperienced person like myself can say is that I assure you the shots knocked up the dust & were as plentiful as drops of rain on a Pond on a Wet Day,' he informed General Wetherall. Among those shot dead was Colonel Lacy Yea, hot-temperedly courageous to the death. What causes for chagrin might have occupied his thoughts at the end? Pack had an idea: 'I am doubtful whether poor Yea wrote to you about Crofton,' Pack's letter to Wetherall continued, 'I half fancy he did, as one Post day he was anxious to know how to spell Gonorrhea.'*

The attack of the 4th Division's left column fared no better. Among its ranks, nervously awaiting the signal to advance, were a higher number of new recruits than ever before, including Private Henry Clayton of the 17th Regiment. He wrote to his father on 1 August:

> You will read of all the Particulars of the Battle on the 18th of June. It was an a[w]ful day it being the first General Action I was in. I can[n]ot Describe the sensations I felt Peculiar to young Soldiers on being formed up to front an enemy for the first time. When we were waiting behind the trench and got the order to fix Bayonets and cap

---

* In his posthumously published memoirs, Pack (then Reydell-Pack) wrote that Yea had a premonition of death.

our firelocks I began thinking and Wondering what you would be Doing at home. I was sure [you] were all in Bed at that time of the morning 2 O'Clock and I began to feel as if I would like to be at home.

He was at least able to reassure his family about the publication of his name in the casualty list.

PS If our Mother mentions about my name being in the paper it was only correct but a mistake in the number of the regt. It was only a spent Bullet in the arm from a revolver by a Russian Officer. I was only 3 days in hospital with it [and it] does not show the mark now.

Major-General Sir John Campbell told Lord West of the 21st Regiment to command the left column's reserve – consisting of the 17th Regiment and part of the 21st – and provide support to him and the 57th. 'The different Parties had great Difficulty in finding their way to their respective Places in the Quarries & the Approaches adjoining', West commented, 'and Daylight had fairly broke before anything like order could be attained.' He continued:

When the pre-concerted signal of a Flag hoisted in No 8 Battery was given, Sir John, after some little Delay, proceeded to move the 57th Regt. round the Corner where the Parapet in the advanced Trench breaks off; which at once brought those who passed it, under a smashing Fire of grape & Rifles from the Russian Right Face of the Redan, not far from the salient angle. The Naval Bag Carriers & Ladder Carriers had previously moved out, as also the covering Party of 100 Rifles, but these several Parties were speedily dispersed by the murderous Fire to which they were exposed. These Parties moved through a Breach knocked down in the Parapet & had a wider opening been made in it, & had the 57th moved through it instead of filing to their left, & turning the Corner of it, more might perhaps have been accomplished.

Sir John Campbell was killed almost as soon as he left the trench. The next senior officer, Colonel Shadforth of the 57th Regiment, fell almost immediately after. It was left to Lieutenant-Colonel Henry Warre of the 57th to explain in his subsequent report why the left column had found it so difficult to leave their trenches:

The Lieut. General will not fail to observe how much above the average is the loss of officers and Non Commissioned Officers to that of the Men: & I trust I shall not be called upon to particularise Regiments when I attribute this loss to the very irregular manner in which the Troops, not only of the Supports, but from other Divisions, crowded in upon our men: so that it was impossible for them to get out of the Trench to follow their Officers to the attack.

Having blamed others for his regiment's failings, Warre proceeded to accentuate the positive.

I trust I may be permitted to call the attention of the L[ieutenan]t General to the gallant conduct of the Men of the Rifle Brigade, who led the advance; these men formed with some of my own Regiment & some Men from other Corps. They accompanied Major Inglis 57 Regt & myself to within 20 or 30 yards of the two gun Battery below the Redan, which inflicted so much loss by its heavy fire of Grape upon the attacking Parties: I sent Major Inglis back for reinforcements, the men lying down & keeping up a heavy fire upon the Embrasures of this Battery. Major Inglis being unable to obtain reinforcements we were reluctantly obliged to retire, & so steadily did the Men behave that we effected this object with the loss of three men only.

The attack on the Redan was a disaster. No fewer than 62 officers and 717 other ranks were killed or wounded. General Codrington analysed the reasons for the plan of attack's failure in a letter to his wife four days later.

Many were the defects of this plan: the trenches were so narrow and so few of them that there was no proper room to stow the men; the supports had consequently to be placed much too far off, and would have to cross open ground and under fire for 800 yards. But above all the main defect of the plan was, an Engineering mistake in fancying that the fire of the guns was sufficiently overcome, that the works were in a fit state for assault, not knowing any single thing of the breadth or depth of the [Redan's] ditch, being some 200 yards from the abbatis – between which and the ditch the distance is about 30 yards.

Yet the assault on the Redan was not the hardest fighting encountered

by the British on 18 June. Major-General Eyre's brigade of the 3rd
Division had been held in readiness in the British Left Attack to approach
Sevastopol down the Piquet House Ravine. His command was 2,000
strong. His instruction was to occupy some Russian rifle pits, and if the
success of the main attack against the Redan on the right allowed it, to
push ahead further. In a letter to his daughter, Lieutenant-Colonel
Clement Edwards of the 18th Regiment described their advance.

> We got under arms a little after one o'clock on the morning of the
> 18th and marched down to the ground in front of the 9th's Camp.
> There was a leading party of 30 men from each of the five Regiments
> of the Brigade in front. Then came the Regiments as follows: 18th
> (Royal Irish), 44th Regt [the 44th (The East Essex) Regiment], 38th
> Regt, 28th Regt, 9th Regt. At about three o'clock we got down into
> the valley and when the ravine opened sufficiently we formed in the
> same order, in a mass of columns. It was then nearly daylight. M[ajor]
> General Eyre told the Regiment they would have a good place, only
> to be steady. He knew they would prove themselves brave. Up to this
> time the enemy had not noticed us. We again moved on and halted
> in the open ready for action. Just here the first round shot danced
> amongst us and as the advanced party had extended and were under
> such cover as they could find we met the intruder. That peculiar cry
> (once heard never forgotten) of a man shot shewed that the round
> shot had told but we were compelled to wait a little longer. After
> this the Grenadier Company moved off in skirmishing order, soon
> followed by Nos 1 & 2 Companies.

Captain Hopton Bassett Scott of the 9th Regiment was less tolerant
of General Eyre's eagerness for combat.

> Meantime old Eyre, who is the most impetuous old fellow, did not
> wait to see what success we met with on the right but pushed on
> our Brigade. We drove the Russians out of the Cemetery at the mouth
> of the Work Yard Ravine, and took possession of a number of houses
> and about 200 yards of ground between the Cemetery and the Strand
> 21 gun Batt[ery] when the attack on the Right having failed we
> found ourselves in a cul-de-sac, we could neither advance or retire,
> and had to hold our ground from 4 A.M. to 9 P.M., 17 hours under
> a tremendous fire of shot, shell, grape, canister, & hundreds of their
> sharp shooters, our only cover being the houses which crumbled

about us at every discharge. The Col. Borton, Elmhirst, 8 other officers and myself with about 40 men [were] lying down under one house. At first they fired round shot at us, and as every shot came through both walls one half of the house had crumbled down after a couple of hours. Had they continued it hardly one of us could have escaped; but fortunately they could not see the damage they were doing, or known the number collected there, for they gave that up, and took to shelling us. Fortune still befriended us, for the ground behind the house where we lay was a vineyard, and soft enough to bury the shells so far that the splinters all flew up and none of them horizontally; so though we were treated to a great number, some of them falling within ten yards, not a man was touched.

Colonel Edwards was still with the Brigade reserve.

The remainder of the Regiment advanced and took up a position of support to the advance in a narrow lane. The enemy soon found the range of our position, and the men commenced falling fast. The General had given me orders to stand there, but the casualties were then so great that I put the men behind the houses and walls, which saved them much. I did not see the General again – he was wounded across the head. All this time the men were coming back from the front, hopping or crawling according to the nature of the wound, amongst them my friend Captain Hayman supported by two men, shot through the knee but with a cheerful smile on his face. Seeing that the advance was much weakened I supported them with another two companies sending Major Kennedy to the front. He was shortly after slightly hit on the side of the head but not compelled to return. The enemy knew well the position of the houses we were in and threw the shell amongst us. Fancy one of these visitors falling within ten feet of you. Down you must lie, and close too, and wait for its bursting. When you are fortunate you have nothing worse than dust to complain of. They not only gave us shells but rifle balls and grape and many a poor fellow, who went out to help a wounded comrade, was obliged in his turn to be carried in, desperately wounded. Again, the front calls out for ammunition and more men. Up my boys, catch hold of that barrel of ammunition and rush through the whizzing balls, the tearing grape; away they go, with a cheer. About 12 o'clock the last company but one went out and the companies returning, but dreadfully thinned, formed the support.

Lieutenant-Colonel Sir James Alexander of the 14th Regiment, also of the 3rd Division but whose unit remained uncommitted to the fight, heard reports of the conduct of the 18th Regiment which Colonel Edwards neglected to mention.

General Eyre led his Brigade down the left Ravine towards the Admiralty creek and cemetery. Some say that this was a feint until the Malakoff, Redan and Barrack Battery fell (the last was to have been our portion); but the 18th Royal Irish rushed on into part of Sevastopol, got among houses with women in them, pictures, mahogany, furniture & pianos; got also among some strong wine! . . . Some of the Irish boys dressed themselves up as women and so fought; some of them brought back looking glasses, tables & a gooseberry bush with the berries on it!

By the time Edwards himself reached the front his men's initial dissipation had exhausted itself. He saw only the aftermath.

Shortly after one [p.m.], more men were wanted. I sent out the last company and went out myself. Away we hop, from stone to stone or bush. Ping ping passes the rifle bullet; crashing around you, you feel the grape; never mind as you must go [on]. I found the advanced party in a row of houses under the battery. Regularly enclosed by a screen of missiles you could only creep about. In the morning these houses had been original. By the time I got there every thing was broken, glass in pieces, the piano torn open (or as a man called it, the music box), chairs, tables, beds, wardrobes in jumbles of masses. The enemy did not like us being there nor did they like that the houses gave us cover, they therefore set fire to them with shells.

Captain Scott had already had to endure the Russian bombardment most of the morning.

The day passed as such days do, every minute an hour. The sun was fearfully hot, and the cries of the wounded and dying men for water were most painful, as we had no way of alleviating their tortures, as leaving the cover was almost certain death, and therefore was useless. Once a round shot came through and carried off a man's head in the midst of us. How Borton and two others who were in the same line escaped we cannot tell, for we were all lying down. This man had been previously wounded and had his head on the ground. We imagine the shot ricochetted, just taking his head and bouncing off over the others. Before night we had three dead men and twelve wounded, two mortally, amongst us. We were covered with dust and blood, suffering fearfully from the heat and thirst. Part of the house fell on Elmhirst, Gaynor and a man of the 38th. The two former escaped with a few bruises; the man was buried in the ruins but he was just dead before from a rifle ball through his chest. At dusk we got our wounded away and then retired. The casualties in our Brigade amount to nearly a third the men engaged. The 9th lost Capt. Smith killed by a grape shot two officers wounded & 57 men. The 44th had 3 Capts. killed and one seriously wounded. Genl. Eyre was wounded in the head by a stone, but did not leave the ground.

Colonel Edwards too had to wait until dusk before he could escape the Russians' attentions.

About 3 o'clock I received an order to retire which I could not comply with, as there were eighteen wounded men to bring away, which could not be done till dark. Every moment our small party was decreasing. What weary hours they seemed from 3 to 8 o'clock. And just before it was time to move, the enemy brought field pieces to bear upon the houses, and they commenced knocking them down about our heads. At last I heard with joy 'The last wounded man has been carried off Sir'. Well then go away by twos and threes. Keep up a warm fire. When across the open, bugler sound the Regimental Call and the retire. The work is done, but out of 669 men who left the Camp 250 of the Royal Irish had suffered more or less. We did not get home until 10 o'clock, wearied and exhausted.

Although General Eyre was criticized within the army for incurring so many casualties for so little result, it was the closest thing to a British success that miserable day and so his standing with the public at home increased. For the failure overall, various culprits were identified. Captain Maxwell Earle, who was himself wounded during the attack on the Redan, blamed its planner: 'We are prepared to try it again provided Sir G Brown has nothing to do with it.' Lieutenant Lynden Bell of the 28th Regiment aimed higher:

The failure was entirely owing to a want of agreement between Ld Raglan and Gen Pelissier. Ld Raglan should at once be recalled and then tried by a court Martial and shot, before he can murder any more of us.

Raglan, writing to Lord Panmure, blamed Pélissier. Changing the hour of the assault on the Malakhov at short notice had been unhelpful, but Pélissier's decision not to attack the Flagstaff Bastion at the same time as the Malakhov was the crucial error.

The greatest mistake is the partial attack of Sevastopol. If the attack had been general the enemy's troops must have been scattered and there would have been no great mass anywhere and if confusion on their parts had ensued total defeat would have been the consequence.

The explanation advanced by Raglan for Pélissier's determination to attack on the narrowest possible front betrayed his doubts about French discipline:

My impression is that he is in great apprehension lest his Army should run riot in the event of the successful assault of the Town & should in consequence get into disorder and expose itself to defeat. This is not unlikely, but it is rather late in the operation to be governed by such an objection.

Raglan wrote his letter to Panmure on 19 June, the day after the Allies' repulse. On the 20 June he toured the camp, the convalescent Mark Walker being among those visited by Lord Raglan in hospital. The following day General Estcourt was taken sick with cholera. He died on 24 June. Raglan was grief-stricken. He was already unwell but continued conducting business until 26 June, when he took to his bed. Two days later he died, a worn-out old man. Dr Fowle Smith, General Estcourt's physician, who had been among the medical staff attending on Raglan at the end, had no doubt as to the cause of death. As he wrote in a letter to the historian Kinglake in 1877, the cause – contrary to rumours in camp at the time – was neither diarrhoea nor cholera but depression.

The last sorrow which broke the heart of Lord Raglan, was General Estcourt's death. General Estcourt loved Lord Raglan, as one Brother loves another, and I have every reason to know that, that love was reciprocated. It is probable that if on the morning of the 24th June, Lord Raglan had heard that General Estcourt was better & likely to recover, the attack of depression with painless diarrhoea would not have come on, or would have passed off without any outward symptom . . . His disease may therefore be described as a case of acute mental anguish, producing first great depression, and subsequently complete exhaustion of the heart's action.

General Airey, writing to General Wetherall on 4 July, had his own explanation for Raglan's death. He could not forgive the persecution of Lord Raglan by two successive Secretaries of State for War.

To me Lord Raglan had always been all that confidence and affection could picture! He died of a broken Heart. Altho' he kept *it hid*, to me his mind was opened, and at night he spoke of nothing, our rooms communicating with each other, but the shameful treatment he had experienced . . . The tone of both [the] Duke of Newcastle and Ld. Panmure, but most especially the latter, was not to be borne.

Raglan might not have been a dynamic commander but he was the most urbane of generals; and the respect engendered by his long experience enabled the British in the Crimea – even when the relative strength of their contingent had been so diminished – to maintain a certain parity in dealings with the French. The skills of the diplomatist, rather than those of the general, were to be those most missed with the passing of Lord Raglan.

9

ASSAULT ON THE REDAN II

Since the army's second in command, Sir George Brown, was under medical orders to return home, the Government appointed Lieutenant-General James Simpson, the chief of staff, to succeed Lord Raglan as commander-in-chief. He inherited a demoralized force. Captain Maxwell Earle wrote home on 26 July:

> I have not known any period during the siege when people so openly complain of their being heartily tired of it. There is nothing going forward at present, and we can look forward to nothing. Before the attack of the 18th of June when there was a hope of terminating the siege I took an interest in watching the operations of the Enemy. Now whole days pass sometimes without my ever going 20 yards to look at the town. Cathcart's Hill used to be a rendezvous for everyone. Now no one comes up here.

Nor was there much expectation that a renewed assault would accomplish anything. Charles Ridley, commander of the 2nd Brigade of the 1st Division, admitted as much to his cousin:

> I do not believe (but please Maggy don't quote me) our next assault will succeed, unless by some wonderful *fluke*. Appearances just now are against us. The 18th showed them their weak points and they are three times as strong now as they ever were.

Lieutenant-Colonel Anthony Sterling agreed that the Russian fortifications appeared more formidable than ever. As he noted, even the pugnacious Sir Colin Campbell felt disquiet:

> C, who is by no means of a desponding mood, shakes his head, and hopes we shall not have another 18th of June. He thinks we ought to go on sapping till we get right into the ditch. I doubt that being the plan intended, as it would take so much time; but it is the only sure way.

The need to sap up to the Redan, reducing thereby the extent of the exposed ground over which an assaulting column must advance, was an obvious lesson to draw from the debacle of 18 June. It was a policy adopted by the French with regard to the Malakhov, Pélissier having recognized that General Bosquet had been right to urge this course of action earlier and reinstating him in his command in order to pursue it. But the French could afford to lose one hundred men a night in this dangerous work; the British could not spare a tenth of that number. Assessing the progress of the siege, Captain Earle commented:

> I have worn the subject threadbare and our engineers do not afford us an opportunity of commenting on their work, for they do none. About a week ago they commenced what is called a 'flying sap' from the Quarries straight up to the Redan. During the 1st night they lost 11 men filling 40 gabions and the 2nd night they lost 8 men filling 4 gabions.

The high rate of attrition gave General Codrington cause for concern.

> Our casualties are many daily – no doubt we inflict loss perhaps more on our enemy: but I think our Engineers put our people in places, and to work in places by day, into which they ought not to be put. And so I have said – but it is difficult to make an engineer believe that a gabion is not of more importance than a man – except a sapper.

The rate of loss, taken together with the difficulty of working the rocky ground, led to the abandonment of the sap. But the engineers continued to be criticized. In a letter, Captain Nathaniel Steevens registered his disgust:

> This war is and has been rife with numerous blunders, and I will now tell you what our *bright* Engineers did a few days ago; they determined upon constructing an 8 Gun Batt[er]y far in advance; the ground was selected, the Battery commenced when it was found to be *placed too low*, and *fired into a bank*, so they were obliged to convert it into a Mortar Batt[er]y; this is however only one of the numerous blunders committed by that educated portion of the service* throughout this Siege.

* The Royal Engineers received a thorough technical training at the Royal Military Academy, Woolwich.

As had been the case the previous winter, demoralization among officers of the army was reflected in their increased incidence of sickness. Doubt was cast on many of the applications for sick leave, Captain Earle reflecting on the instance of a young friend in the Rifle Brigade:

> Kit is gone to Scutari on sick leave. What we call sapping up to England by parallels. There are a great many shirks of this nature in the army. L[ieutenan]t Colonel Cole 17th [Regiment] who married one of the Hattons, made a flying sap & is home by this time.

General Codrington too passed comment on the phenomenon: 'The fashionable complaint is *all overishness*; and jokes are made as to small illness to Scutari being the "first parallel" towards England.' General Airey, however, was altogether more caustic: 'This army is full of Skulkers and Malingerers, and something ought to be done to force officers to rejoin,' he complained to General Wetherall.

One officer who felt that he had performed more than his due was Lieutenant-Colonel Mundy of the 33rd Regiment. 'I have fully made up my mind to come home some how', he told his mother. 'I *can*not and *will* not stand another winter. I know if I did, I should be a useless decrepid old man in a year and I w[oul]d rather be a live jackass than a dead lion.' Three weeks later he returned to his theme:

> A nice staff appointment either in England or abroad would be very pleasant after ruffing it out here. I have no wish to command a regiment, particularly since such alot of dirty Irish blackguards have enlisted. There is no pleasure or pride in comm[andin]g a Reg[imen]t now.

On 4 August he reported: 'I am just going to H[ea]d Q[uar]t[e]rs and intend trying to get on the soft side of Genl Simpson about leave &c'. A week later General Codrington, who had once again taken command of the Light Division following Brown's departure, became aware of Mundy's intention. 'Colonel Mundy of 33d has begun a manoeuvre to get home', he told his wife.

> I saw him trying to catch me or General Simpson as we were coming down the hill from the piquet house – he came to me, and told me it was of the greatest consequence to him to go home immediately on private affairs – that he wanted to change to 'substantive rank' having the likelihood of some staff appointment elsewhere, and he

might miss all this &c. As he almost joined me when I was riding with Simpson, I stopped and did something to my horse's head for a time – and then said, that for private affairs to be urgent and to be certified by me, I must know something about them – that I could not make out that and that it had better be put on its true footing – indulgence: – after some conversation we got on again towards Simpson – I knew his object was to do this and get from us together some favourable answer, so when he began to Simpson, and saying he had been talking to me, I said – oh yes, and I will talk to you about it whenever you wish to come to my hut, and put an end to his manoeuvring for the time. A gentleman not to be trusted as to truth.

When the private soldier found a way of returning to England, the justification was apparent to all. Brigadier-General Charles Ridley confirmed as much when writing to his cousin, Maria, on 11 August:

Some of our wounded go home tomorrow, 3 with one arm the other one leg. The rest are not yet well enough to be moved. I think I have 10 other cases of amputations. Others have died & I fear one man won't last that I am anxious about. He is very patient, shows great pluck and begged I would write to his Brother to say he was getting quite well. Poor fellow, he varies from day to day & half an hour ago I thought badly of him. One man, Weston, with one leg, has grown into a good looking man. An *old* soldier alas & one I can ill spare. But his illness has *fined down* his features – he really looks well bred and I never saw a better patient from the very first. Another man going with him lost his arm and part of the shoulder-blade, a man of fretful irritable temper. But in a few days he came round and I saw him often under intense suffering, without more than a gentle groan to be heard and he has done so well; looks as healthy in the face as any man. All are *cheerful*, you may depend upon it at the thoughts of getting home. I believe many a man would gladly lose an arm to get off these heights & this siege.

A listless army was not set a good example by its commander. As General Codrington observed after a conference of the army's generals, General Simpson was a reluctant leader of men:

The meeting which we had at H.Q. a few days ago, did not show us much decision, or originality or determination on the part of our

Chief. I do not think he would be sorry to be away; indeed after Lord Raglan's death it is well known he wrote to say he did not wish to remain; this was by the letter post. In meantime on hearing of Lord R's death, it was telegraphed to him that he was to be Com[-man]d[er] in chief. Then shortly came his letter – but in the meantime Barnard had been ordered to be published as Chief of Staff; and Gov[ernmen]t had praised up Simpson in the House as the proper man. So that when his letter of doubt came home they telegraphed him to suspend appointment. But it was too late – Barnard had been in orders, and Govt. could not say the contrary of what they had already said viz: that he Simpson was the best man to succeed Lord R.. He is very kind, very gentlemanlike and I believe was a very good officer in India with Sir C[harles] Napier. But I cannot say he seems to me to have the energy of feeling and mind to enter into this business, which has plenty of difficulties now and to come. Then again he is not much of a Frenchman in language.

With no leadership provided from the top, there was dissension among Simpson's generals as they jockeyed for position. Major-General Sir Colin Campbell had earlier in the year received his own divisional command, the Highland Brigade having been separated from the Guards Brigade to which it had previously been yoked. He shared the resentment felt by many in the army towards 'the Guards', whose officers tended to monopolize the highest ranks because of the accelerated promotion given them by their system of 'double ranks'. Of this General Codrington, a Guardsman himself, was aware. In a letter to his wife of 4 August he described an unpleasant incident between Campbell and the new chief of staff, Major-General Henry Barnard, yet another Guardsman.

I met Sir C. Campbell, and had a shake hands and congratulation about his G.C.B.. I found that he afterwards went in to Barnard and was very offensive in his conversation to him – almost personally so – about his division being broke up, or not completed when he found others had not their divisions changed. Violent remarks against 'the Guards' and what the feeling of the army was about it, and how a note B. had written to him, detailing the temporary arrangements made till more Highlanders came out was unfair and improper towards him: that he was an old officer and was 'no courtier' and brought up in camps and no business to be treated in this way &c

&c. So much so that Barnard had to say to him he was only sorry that he was in a position that any officer thought it in his power to speak to him in such a manner. I certainly saw nothing offensive in Barnard's note.

Meanwhile Lord Rokeby, who commanded the Brigade of Guards, was agitating for a division of his own. 'Rokeby also was most disagreeable both to Simpson and Barnard', added Codrington. Shortly afterwards, the news arrived in the Crimea that to accommodate these truculent generals, six infantry divisions were to be created from the existing five. 'Thus, I see, that making a row and being disagreeable, is the way to carry a point,' Codrington concluded.

The Royal Artillery was not immune to the current spate of personnel change. After Colonel Edward Warde had returned home, command of the siege artillery devolved on Lieutenant-Colonel John St George. He wrote to a friend, Charlotte, with whom he maintained a flirtatious relationship, on 12 August:

I have been spending hitherto a comparatively idle life at Kardvic [sic], and had only to keep 500 men in order and idleness. I was however on the 1st appointed to the command of the Siege Train, and here I am a great swell, with some 4000 men under my Command, and the direction of every British shot or shell that is fired day or night into Sebastopol. I think you will acknowledge that the right man is in the right place at last, and expect when the Czar hears who has got the management of affairs, he will give in at once. I have 2 Lieut Colonels of Artillery appointed to serve under me, and I have a Brigade Major attached to me. But I have made a representation of the inadequacy of my rank, and asked to be made a Brigadier General, and to have a commensurate Staff. I don't know what the answer will be.

St George continued by describing his new domestic surroundings.

I have changed my home in front of the Siege works, and am most comfortable. I have besides 2 bed rooms and a sitting room, a kitchen, pantry, hall, hen roost & stable. You may imagine that my work is no trifle. I have some 40 or 50 letters a day to reply to, and I have to be continually present at the Siege directing the armament of Batteries, the supply of ammunition, and the objects to be fired at.

I have always thought it absurd to leave the splendid buildings of Sebastopol untouched; and therefore since the reins have been in my hand, I have not let them rest. I have ordered all the mortars that will bear upon them, some 40 or 50, to keep firing at these buildings &c day and night steadily and determinedly, and I expect in a few days we shall see some ruins. I have set one building on fire, which burnt for 30 hours.

St George's tactics had provoked a reaction.

The Russians don't like their *town* being bombarded, and have been retaliating by throwing an occasional shot into the Camps. However it is a bad game for them to play & a losing one. He can only throw one or 2 a day, and I think we shall be able to manage as many as *1600*, or more.

From the commencement of the siege, it had been necessary for the British to site their encampment up to two miles distant from Sevastopol if they wished to avoid the possibility that the Russians might reach it with gunfire. This had been a serious inconvenience during the winter: it left the undermanned British trenches further away from the camp and the hope of reinforcement than was safe. A powerful Russian sortie could have easily captured the British siegeworks and wrought severe damage before help arrived. Yet, despite the precautions taken by the British with their encampment, the Russians could on occasion still reach it with their artillery. In a letter of 23 August, Lieutenant-Colonel Sir James Alexander described the result:

The long range guns have been sending hissing balls over our tents & dumping among us for the last 10 days. One Artillery man was struck at night whilst asleep among 9 others, and his leg carried off with a 40 lb shot – a fearful awakening. Another man, a servant (68th), boiling coffee at his master's tent at 7 a.m. had his leg carried off. Both men died.

For the Russians to achieve this took some ingenuity. The technique was eventually copied by the British, as Captain Nathaniel Steevens noted in a letter of 27 August.

I was at our lookout yesterday, and saw some long shots made at the shipping in the Harbour from our Batteries; the shots fell beyond and in rear of the vessels; we have adopted the Russian contrivance of what is called *sinking a gun in the ground*, digging a hole and lowering the breech, so as to obtain great elevation, thus [Steevens encloses a drawing]: this is generally done with disabled guns, which can no longer be fixed on carriages; the 'Range' of these is enormous, and the Russians in this way frequently send shot into the Camp.

During August the British were losing sixty men a day strengthening and improving their advanced works before Sevastopol. Brigadier-General Ridley was anxious not to add to the total. In a letter to a relative he explained that between the British right and the left of the French Right Attack ran the precipitously sided Dockyard Ravine. Within it was a ruin unoccupied by either the Russians or Allies, although the enemy maintained a picket nearby once darkness fell.

One night when I was General of the Trenches, that ass Walker spread a report that I intended to take it that night. It was over our encampment in an hour. Had I ever thought of doing it, I certainly should have said nothing till the moment came. But the instant it spread here I had 150 men at least volunteering, & then the 1st Company got angry, & said it was their *right* to take it. However they had a little excitement so the shave was worth something.

One officer came up very quietly to ask whether it was really true. I told him, if any one could prove to me, who knew the ground *well* that we could *keep* it when we got it, I would try it on. But I did not believe we could keep it, neither was it worth the lives it would cost. I know the ground well now and it is of no value to us. We could not keep it without a large daily loss. They would always be *shelling* us as if we were so many peas & thus turning us out of our skins. But in this ravine the bears are always skulking about. So we have sentries on the top on one side and the French on the other, the bears growling between us, a curious position, is it not? They can't bring any body of men down without being instantly discovered and a few straggling sneaks don't signify.

Ridley's determination not to occupy an exposed position for the sake of it was not echoed by the practice on the other British flank. Here the cemetery captured by Eyre's brigade on 18 June was retained as evidence of the success of the assault. Captain Hopton Bassett Scott of the 9th Regiment, who endured seventeen hours of shellfire as the price of success at the time, was unamused. He wrote home on 10 August:

> I spent the night in the Cemetery, which supplied Eyre with such a crop of laurels. The papers made such a good story out of it that I wonder he was not created Baron Tombstones or some other appropriate title. I should suggest two ghastly headless privates as supporters for the Eyre arms. This said cemetery is not a pleasant post, as being in front of and almost between some of the enemy's batteries, they each have a pound at the unfortunate occupiers, and vary the amusements as much as is in their power. One moment a shower of hand grenades, just as the last has burst and parties are congratulating themselves on their various narrow escapes, a hissing noise is heard, followed by a pattering which has much the effect of the first heavy drops of a thunder storm on a tent. If this iron shower is well pitched the stillness of the night is broken by the groans or screams of one or two unfortunates who are rudely waked from a half slumber by such a wound as may be caused by the blow of an iron ball weighing upwards of a 1lb falling from a height of 2 or 300 feet; for besides the usual method of distributing grape, the Ruskies fire it out of mortars, and so make a vertical fire of it. However, it frightens more than it hurts. The seconds of suspense everyone in its vicinity must suffer who has not a bomb-proof skull, between the time the descending shower is heard and their arrival, are very trying. Shells you can see coming and can avoid their lighting on you, though you may not be so fortunate afterwards in dodging splinters. Of course the usual supply of round shot, common grape, shells and rifle balls are served out to complete the entertainment.

All the time, more and more young officers were arriving to replace those veterans whose numbers continued to diminish. Seventeen-year-old Lieutenant Thomas Harvey of the 77th Regiment was among them. Because his father was Colonel of the 1st Royal Guernsey Militia, he had been given his commission without purchase. Harvey had not been long in the Crimea when he was temporarily transferred to the 34th Regiment, which had lost so many of its officers on 18 June during the attack on the Redan. His youthful self-confidence makes his letters home among the best from this period of the war. What he wrote at the end of June reflects the fact that cholera was once again stalking the British camp.

I caught a tearing-asunder Diarhea in the trenches last night. I went down there without anything at all, not even a greatcoat. All my things were with the 77th. The rule is also never to go down without a flask of sherry or brandy & water, not so much to drink as to take away any sudden attack of twinging inside. You take down *filtered* water to drink. My servant could not get any & so instead brought some liquid cholera morbus from the nearest water but[t]. . . . I asked the doctor for something for the Diarhea, he gave me a pill which has really done wonders. . . . There has been a sale here of one of the 34th officers effects; I have bought a canteen complete for 2£ that is nearly the full price. It is a large one, new & complete & I only wish I had bought it before . . . One unprepared night in the trenches has nearly given me the Cholera, within 2 shaves of it, last night I got up 12 times & nearly entirely from not having a *large* canteen.

Harvey went on to describe his food and drink.

The ration of bread & meat that they serve out is not good. We buy our bread regularly at the rate of 14d a loaf (6d in England), our meat except once a week we regularly buy. The other day we bought a live lamb, 18s. which we killed, sold one half to somebody & ate the remainder in three days. I can't find fault with the ration they give [of] tea, coffee, & sugar & rum (which latter thing I hate) limejuice if you prefer it (liquid cholera morbus). You must not drink water without some rectifier, so my dodge is to put some tea with a good supply of sugar into a kettle (which article my servant has stolen – foraging of course allowed) & boiling the concoction together, cork it away in a bottle & drinking it cold all day, it makes a wholesome refreshing drink very nice & minus the cholera. . . . I prefer bottling off my rum & doing wonders with it with the soldiers, some of whom I do believe would let you shoot them if you gave them a glass of rum beforehand. I am going to get my tent dug out by its able assistance.

Tom Harvey also took his duties seriously. In a letter to his family of 9 July he described his dealings with an ineffectual Guards officer, 'this guy' as he derisively termed him. Harvey then continued:

At about 11 o'clock at night the Russians set up a frantic yelling in Sebastopol & this Guy told me to stand to my arms tho' there were 2 trenches in advance. It showed me however what obedience I might have expected from the 34th in as much as a Sergeant came up to me & told me if there was an attack he would immediately lead the men to the assistance. Very brave very fine, in fact quite discarding my authority. I should have been cashiered if I had left my trench to go in advance, but a broad hint that in that case I would immediately send a bullet through him, quite astonished him, even more than his speech had astonished me. My orders were to protect the working party in case of sortie, & of course could not think of leaving without an express order to that effect, besides what use could it be me going to the assistance of a party much stronger than me, with another trench behind them.

Trench duty in the summer, although not as trying as that of the winter, had its own unique hazard, as Harvey explained in another letter.

The bright sunshine of the trenches, & also sleeping in the trenches with the sun blazing flat on your face has given to numbers of the soldiers a complaint called 'Moon-blindness'. They can't see in twilight, in dusk, or at any time after the sun is gone down.

The common factor between trench duty at whatever time of year was the tiredness of the men. Harvey went on:

These trenches are terrible. The harrassing responsibility during the night if you are the commanding Off[icer] is abominable. I defy you or anybody else to keep the men awake. Orpen takes off his sword & walking round the trenches with the scabbard on, digs it into their posteriors with all his force, about 20 times in the space of 2 seconds, the best plan I have met with yet. But still they will sleep & always will. And what's worse is that if the Gen[eral] comes round he blows you up like blue blazes. The consequence of which I immediately blow up the Serg[ean]ts which they pass on to the Corporals, who hand it down to the men.

Towards the end of August, with the prospect of a renewed assault on the Redan approaching, trench duty became even more dangerous. Harvey explained why in a letter to his family of 23 August.

The day before yesterday I was in the Trenches with orders as we were in the advance to keep up a continued fire the whole night, so as to prevent the damage done to the Redan being in the slightest degree repaired. We did so; the consequence was the Russian mortars were directed entirely for this Trench & we had 25 men killed & wounded. This was something too bad but the only wonder is that more were not killed as the shells were falling *into the Trenches*. I don't think we killed many with our musquetry but the object was gained in it being perfectly impossible for any working party to attempt coming out of the said place.

Three days later Harvey described in greater detail the heightened sense of alert.

I came out of those dirty trenches this morning & am going in again tomorrow night. I will describe last time from beginning to end. The day before yesterday we paraded for trenches at 6pm, [and] marched down to the Russian trench (it is now our rear). We got there about 8, [and] stuck up sentries. I was very sleepy but of course could not think of such a thing & walked about in order to keep awake. In a few minutes the musquetry began to fizz pop & glitter between the Malakoff & Mamelon, which soon spread into a general roll. The Russians were attacking *en masse*. All *our* batteries opened fire upon the Malakoff. The Mamelon opened fire upon the advancing Russians, the Redan peppered into the Mamelon, the Quarries peppered into the Redan & shindy was all the order of the day. A slight silence ensued only broken by the screams of the round shot, when a yell was heard from the Russians & the volley continued for nearly a quarter of an hour when everything ceased. We sat down made ourselves as cozy as possible & waited patiently till morning broke. As soon as the slightest dawn was seen I lay like a warrior taking his rest with his martial cloak around him & was off in a sound sleep in half a crack. I did not get up until my servant came down with my breakfast & two jolly letters, one from Grandmama & Aunts, the other from Loo. Didn't I read! I set up a sunshade, read the letters over again [and] read the paper. The sun was as hot as the night was cold. Then came an order to go & defend a working party [so] off we set. The place was already filled by another party sent for the same purpose so we had to walk back, which always puts everybody in a decided wax. When we came back the field officer said it was *his* mistake and I was sent to another working party. The Rifles were there as sharpshooters so I sent back the party, got one of the men's Rifles, a barrel of ammunition & caps & with Knowles we had some of the most first rate shooting imaginable. Between the Redan & Malakoff there is a Ravine where the Russians cut down for water. It is 800 yards. One fellow ran out & was walking down slowly not to be seen. I showed him to Knowles & we both fired; we went ten paces on each side of him. I saw another fellow walking down as cooly as possible the inner slope of the Redan. I was told it was out of shot so I determined to try a dodge. I rested the Rifle on the parapet, [and] laid the direction at about double the distance of the sight. We watched & saw the ground ploughed up about 10 paces beyond him. He immediately broke out into double time. But this place was getting far too dangerous so we walked down to another place & commenced peppering into the embrasures of the Malakoff to see who could fire best of us two. We continued this fun until I could not ram down the shot, the gun was so dirty. Maybe we did damage for a tearing round shot crashed through the parapet. Nobody was hit. So we recommenced and gave it to the embrasures that had fired. The result was another crasher which smashed gabions, parapet & all like glass. We thought it time to go.

In spite of how things may have appeared to the besiegers of Sevastopol, the Russians too were feeling their resources strained. The inspirational Todleben had been wounded and had left the town to convalesce. However high the daily total of British and French casualties rose, they were always exceeded by Russian losses: in July they averaged 250 a day. With the supply line through the Sea of Azov severed, the Russians made a last great attempt to break the siege. On 16 August an attack was launched by the Russian army outside Sevastopol against the French and Sardinian* positions on the River Chernaya. It was repulsed with heavy losses. The defenders of Sevastopol thereafter looked over their shoulder. They began to construct a pontoon bridge across Sevastopol Harbour. It could quite as easily facilitate retreat as reinforcement.

On 5 September the sixth bombardment of Sevastopol commenced. The day before, the Allies had agreed that the assault would take place on 8 September. Pélissier considered that the French could sap no closer to the Malakhov: they were already within fifteen yards of the fortification's ditch. Preparations were made in the British camp. General

---

* Sardinia had entered the war against Russia in January 1855, sending 15,000 troops to the Crimea.

Codrington had been given command of the attack. He made his dispositions and chose his men.

> Major Welsford of [the] 97th a fine gallant fellow had frequently said
> to me 'Now, General, I hope you will give me a chance if you can',
> and after all the positions and duties had been settled, I spoke to
> him in my hut, saying that his regiment, one not yet engaged here,
> was of course one I selected for storming and that I was very glad to
> put him in an independent command. He thanked me saying it was
> just what he had wanted.

The Russians anticipated that the Allies would attack either at dawn
or at dusk; such had been the pattern to date. So when the French
attacked the Malakhov at midday, it came as a complete surprise. The
garrison was in the process of being relieved. The relief had not yet
taken its place. French troops swarmed over the defences and within ten
minutes were in effective control. The British White Ensign was then
hoisted in the Mamelon. This was the signal for the British to attack the
Redan. Once again the Light Division, supported by the 2nd Division,
headed the assault. Captain Robert Grove was with the storming party
of the 90th Regiment.

> At a very few minutes past 12 o'clock, noon, yesterday it having been
> ascertained, beyond all doubt, that the 'Jack' was flying from the
> Mamelon, the word 'go' passed along the 5th parallel. Unfortunately
> instead of 'go' applying only to the 'covering party' (as was intended)
> it was caught up and accepted by portions of the storming parties,
> who were, with much difficulty, restrained at this particular juncture,
> by the fortunate presence of Lt. Genl Sir Edw[ar]d [sic] Codrington.

Ahead, in an unfinished trench 150 yards from the Redan, were the
ladder parties. They would enter the ditch and place their scaling ladders
against the face of the Redan. Captain Edmund Legh of the 97th Regiment made his report:

> I was one of the Ladder Party, furnished by the 97th Regt. under
> Major Welsford, at the Attack on the Redan yesterday. The men were
> told off in parties of eight to each ladder. On the signal being made,
> the whole moved to the front by the left of the Boyau, running
> with the Ladders to the Salient Angle of the Redan, where they, after
> some difficulty raised them & ran up together with the remaining

portion of the 97th, which had come from the 5th Parallel. The Russians made a strong resistance for some time, when a rush was made, and many got in at the Embrasures, or jumped down from the Parapet.

The first man through the embrasures of the Redan was Major Welsford of the 97th. The discharge of a Russian cannon killed him instantly, carrying away half his head.

Captain Grove led the storming party of the 90th Regiment in pursuit of Major Welsford. His report, essentially factual, hints that not all the British troops behaved well, seizing the excuse to take cover. Ladders too were left behind.

My two left companies under Captains Vaughan & Tinling did *not* cross the parapet *exactly* at the same place as the 97th did, but as they were in tolerable good order and *files well backed up* and *losing no ground* on the flank of the 97th, I passed the remaining Companies over the same place and when in the open, they followed on in the trail of the 97th. On quitting the 5th parallel I announced to the officer leading the storming party of the *2nd Division*, 'that all my men had gone', but he had yet some way to defile before he could bring out a Column of double Comp[anie]s. Some of the storming party of my left, seeing themselves in *advance* of *ladders*, took shelter awhile under the new sap, and my acting Major, (Capn Smith) begged for ladders to be brought & put down, but *ladders were left in the new sap and never were taken to the front*, excepting about 7 or 8 (and of this number *I* sent one chiefly with men of the 90th). At no time was there more than three ladders on the ennemy's side of the ditch. Captain Smith *here* experienced his first confusion. The most eager trying to pass others more orderly, and as the ladders could not accommodate all, a mixture of corps took place, scrambling became the order of the day and as we could offer no front to our ennemy (having no frontage of ladders) we fell an easy prey to the concentrated fires of the Russians.

Even when the British stormers broke into the Redan, they found it difficult to deploy. Captain Legh reported that the Russians ran behind some traverses 'from which they kept up so heavy a fire, that as the men advanced, of necessity, with a small front, they were picked off.'

The attack of the 2nd Division was led by Major-General Charles Ash Windham. The day afterwards he submitted his official report:

As soon as the rear of the Storming Column of the Light Division had cleared the 5th Parallel, the storming Column of the 2nd Division immediately advanced in open Column of Companies right in front . . . I placed myself with Lt. Col. Eman CB at the Head of the Grenadiers of the 41st commanded by Captn Rowlands, a fine and gallant young Soldier, whose wound I am happy to say is but slight.

We quickly came to the Ditch of the Redan and passed it, but owing to the heavy flanking fire, and the difficult parallel, we had to start from, not in such regular order as could be wished. The same may be said of the 62d Regt.

They however both advanced with courage & resolution, but on crowning the parapet of the Redan, got intermixed with the Regiments of the Light Division . . . Had the Regts. not become intermixed I believe we should have carried the Work.

General Codrington meanwhile was anxiously watching the progress of the attack from the 5th Parallel. He wrote to his wife afterwards:

All this time a considerable number of men were getting hit in the parallel. The large grape came bounding about, knocking up the dust and *whisking* about with its peculiar screaming noise: shells too most vicious and the part of the parallel I was in was that not exempted from the fire of both sides crossing; one or two well directed, and disagreeable horizontal shells were nearly giving me the 'good-bye' to this world. They came just hitting the lower part of the parapet of the trench, then jumped up slowly like a cricket ball, and bounded comfortably fizzing just over the trench; bang – smoke, dust and stones, a general crouch down for the time, the men half knocking me over, a poor fellow's leg gone close by me. On another similar occasion I saw a sad thing happen: a drummer on the banquette, and in the rush and confusion of the close explosion a man near him, with his firelock in the trench, it went off close to me and this poor drummer and shot him through the side! You may, or may not, be able to realize to yourself the confusion, the painful scenes to which eye, ear and heart could scarcely give head at the moment, the coming back over the parapet of many a poor fellow with a limping leg, or a broken hand, or a bloody side, just getting into the half shelter of such a place, and bandaging his wound: officers the same, I saw several brought in, or come in alone: but a recognition or squeeze of the hand was all that could be shown just then.

Captain Legh, in continuing his report, confirmed the impression of General Windham that units from the 2nd Division, coming up in support, became so intermixed with men of the Light Division that hopes of the attack's success were compromised.

Men of other Regts. principally 90th, 3rd & 41st then came to help us; & the parties got so mixed and jammed together that one could not get a formation for a rush. Just at this time, the enemy driven out of the Malakoff, took us in flank, and by keeping up a heavy fire killed a great number of men. They profited by this, made a charge, and by their superior numbers drove our men into the angle of the Redan, where from behind 2 Guns, they kept up a vigorous fire for nearly 2 hours, the men of different Regiments being closely packed on the extreme slope of the parapet, and firing over its crest; with a great many on the other side of the ditch who were trying to keep down the fire of the Flanking Batteries, which were causing great havoc amongst the supports, both with grape, and musquetry.

As Codrington was to learn, Windham had got into the Redan with his troops of the 2nd Division; except

he could not get them forward in a rush or mass. The first people, some of 97th and 90th had got inside, and past many of the side traverses, but by the time they got towards the more open part beyond, the Russians seem to have come up in force, and kept up a fire from a long low mound with a few gabions about it, which drove them back. And when once the check took place it gave time for what really happened as we now know it: viz. that the Russians sent back the columns which had been relieved from their night and morning guard at 11 a.m.; our attack, a little after the Malakoff, started them up again immediately and direct; more particularly as by losing the Redan they would lose the line of retreat of those falling back from the 'Little Redan' and Malakoff side. Poor Cap[tai]n Vaughan of the 90th who was wounded far in Redan, was dragged down at once, and described how in going down towards the rear the men of the columns brushed by his broken limb! He said they were very numerous.

Codrington went on to explain to his wife the deployment that he now made:

I had by this time ordered the reserve (the 1st brigade) to come up and take the place of those who had now been sent in advance. Straubenzee brought some of the 34th regt. over the open from parallel to parallel – some of the 7th and 33d. came along the trenches. The 34th were kept in the parallel; the 7th and 33d. seem to have been ordered out without communication from me for, seeing the mass of men remaining hanging at the crest and not advancing, I should not have sent more on to add to the crowd of wounded and separated men all over the ground, unless with a hope of a strong push in. I had no hope of this under that amount of flank fire from both sides.

As had been the case during the attack on the Redan the previous June, the inadequacy of the British trenches hampered their ability to bring reserves forward. Lieutenant-Colonel Arthur Goodenough of the 34th Regiment soon discovered this:

On entering the Zig zags opposite the General's Bunk I could get no further. Here I met General Straubenzee who said to me 'You have no chance of getting on this way, there is only one thing left for it, make a dash across the open, depend upon it you will lose less men that way than by the trench – and I will go with you'.

Goodenough therefore dashed over open ground to the 4th Parallel, and then again from there to the 5th Parallel. In doing so he suffered most of his casualties.

On reaching the 5th parallel I found it completely choked up, the 49th & 47th being in that part of the Trench that I reached. The 49th were endeavouring to move off to their left, but the Trench was quite blocked up, & all the wounded were being carried to the Rear.

Some of the wounded were taken past Tom Harvey, stationed with the Light Division's 2nd Brigade in the reserve trenches. He recounted what he witnessed in all its gruesome detail for the delectation of a young female relative, 'Em'.

As to the Redan I suppose you know by this time as much as I do. I saw a most amusing scene. A sailor walking away with two Russian prisoners on both arms, on his kissing one of them he got a punch in the eye from the Russian. Half in a rage he said '*Look to your front ye rascal*'. All this time when perhaps you are splitting with laughter at some joke the wounded are passing you groaning & the men carrying the stretchers are shot down. I know I suppose I rowed about a dozen soldiers one after the other for putting down the stretcher in order to take a drink. The wounded were carried away & if they had the ill luck to die on the road they were pitched out of the stretcher into the trench & the stretcher would go back for more. Now this is quite right as far as humanity goes but when a dead man with goggle eyes & grinning mouth is pitched down at your feet & left there until the next day you don't like it.

Lieutenant-Colonel Daniel Lysons of the 23rd Regiment, writing to General Wetherall two months later, was precise in his description of the unsuitability of the British trenches.

Our Trenches were not prepared for the reception of attacking columns. The 5th parallel was a narrow stoney uneven trench about 840 yards long in parts of which the cover was very indifferent ... The 4th Parallel was a good trench, but had only 2 approaches to the 5th parallel, one on the extreme right and one through the Quarries, which was narrow and very dangerous, being infiladed from the batteries on the opposite side of the ravine, and a regular shell trap. The profiles of the trenches about the Quarries were such as to render it impossible to get troops from one trench to the other over the open. The ladder parties were placed in the sap, the covering parties and storming parties in the 5th parallel; but there was only one place to get out at between H & K [two points marked on a plan] where some rickety boards were placed on barrels to enable the men to get over the parapet, so that one party had to go out, the next fill up into its place and then follow, and so on. The supports who were in the 4th parallel and approaches were obliged to thread through these long narrow trenches, up the 5th parallel or through the Quarries to replace the stormers, and follow in their turn. This process took so long that few Officers waited to form their men between H & K but jumped over and led their men on in long straggling strings, without any formation. The ladders were so

cumbrous and heavy that the men were glad of any excuse to drop
them and run on with their firelocks; consequently not half the
number required ever reached the ditch.

The storming parties on their way to the Redan had to pass the
end of the sap, which proved too tempting a refuge for some of
the young soldiers, whose only lesson in fighting had been skulking
and hiding behind parapets. All the advanced trenches soon became
choked up with dying, wounded, skulkers and stretcher-bearers consequently very difficult to pass through.

Lysons was, however, to hand when Codrington needed him. 'I got a
message from the Redan', Codrington wrote,

saying that a regiment in order, might succeed on the proper right
face of the Redan. Col. Lysons with his 23d. Fusiliers was in the 5th
parallel being part of the reserve. I told him to advance with a wing
of this regt. to do this.

With the storming parties already in the Redan crammed together in
its salient angle or apex, attacking the flank of the fortification – perhaps
even breaking in at the re-entrant angle at its base – held out the
possibility of being able to take the Russian defenders of the Redan in
their rear. It was the last throw of the dice. Lysons described his regiment's
attack.

The little part taken by my regiment on the 8th has never been heard
of because we are not in the habit of feasting Mr. Russell. The only
notice taken of us in the Times is *false*. We were in reserve. Seeing
that the advanced trenches were not filled up by the support as fast
as they ought to be, we went on through the Quarries to the 5th
parallel. General Codrington ordered me to try to attack the *flank* of
the Redan with a wing of my regiment. I formed up the 5 Companies
in line, got the rickety boards put straight, cautioned the men to be
ready, then gave the word 'line will advance – quick march'. The
moment we were out shot, grape and musketry came from the
batteries on our left the flank before us in storms. It was a beautiful
sight to see all the rosey faced boys of Officers leading on the men,
waving their swords in the air. The men came on splendidly. But
when we had passed the crowds clustering on the salient angle, the
Russians fired down on our shoulders from the long face. I was
knocked over and got into a large shell hole. When I looked round

Dyneley was close to me, and Drewe, Corporal Shields and about a dozen men. All the ground behind was covered with killed and wounded. I desired Drewe, if he could get men enough, to charge across the ditch; and after putting a tight bandage round my leg I crawled to the Salient angle. The rascals fired at me all the way, and shot off my shirt ornaments; but my posteriors escaped unhurt. I sat down there, and finding Wyndham [sic] had gone back to the trenches, I asked an officer of the 2nd Division, whose name I have never been able to find out, if possible to reinforce our men at the re-entering angle, and to try with Drewe to get in there. He did so; but the fire [was] too heavy for any thing to live in it. Some of our men were killed on the top of the parapet, where they were found next morning. Drewe crossed the ditch, when the rest of the men retreated the 23rd with Drewe were left out and very nearly cut off, not knowing they were alone. 16 Officers out of 18 were hit, and 200 men out of about 282.

As Lysons had discovered, Windham had returned to the 5th Parallel to confer with General Codrington. According to Codrington, their discussion was as follows:

Windham told me it was no use sending more troops unless they could be got there in some formation, and that he was quite ready to go on with a regiment if I thought it could be done – but that as an old friend he could tell me openly it was not to be done unless by some fresh troops keeping military order.

It was too late for a decision. The crisis in the Redan was at hand. Captain Legh described what happened to the troops struggling desperately to maintain their foothold:

Ammunition was failing those in front, we supplied them from men in the rear. The Russians also appeared running short of Ammunition. All of a sudden the enemy threw volleys of stones over the parapet, which caused our men at its crest to vacillate and fall back on those behind who were then forced into the ditch. The body of men on this side of it supposing the advanced party was driven back turned and ran in, the remainder following them under a very heavy fire of grape and musketry.

Captain Nathaniel Steevens of the 88th Regiment was one of those caught up in the sudden panic.

At length our ammunition began to get scarce, the enemy aware of this advanced, pelted us with *hand grenades, large stones, & firelocks*, we speedily retired, and shall I ever forget the scene that ensued? The dense mass of humanity which thronged the Redan was carried *headlong into the Ditch,* upon the *top of bayonets, ladders,* and *dead & dying, writhing in their agony under the crush of us all*; I was carried headlong into the Ditch among bayonets &c, and found myself *jammed under a scaling ladder, firelocks between my legs,* and the *Russians pelting stones from the parapet 6 or 8 yds from me*; I struggled from my temporary imprisonment, and scrambled up the side of the Ditch as well as I could, and then what a gauntlet there was to run; amid an almost worse fire than our advancing I made the best of my way to our works, numbers around me falling fast; when half way I was too exhausted to run, and walked; I then thought shall I ever reach the trenches alive, but so it was ordained, a kind & merciful Providence guarded me in this time of danger, and I reached a place of safety *unscathed,* save a bruise or two, prickings with Bayonets, & *loss of breath.*

Codrington had made preparations for the eventuality of a retreat.

I had long seen this must be the case: but was most anxious to keep a hold on the Redan if possible as the effect of the French occupation of the Malakoff would, I thought, send them [the Russians] away from the Redan soon: and I was unwilling to sound any retreat, which w[oul]d be a signal of confusion at once. But sure enough it came; and I prepared for it, in making the Regt. then in the 5th parallel, the 1st Royals, keep up their firelocks and bayonets so as to let them in: and I was most anxious just then; for in such cases the danger is a complete panic and giving up of anything. And sure enough, in some other parts of the parallel, the men were with difficulty kept in the trench – they were going back.

In the event, the British failure to take the Redan did not matter. The Malakhov was the key to the defences of Sevastopol. Now the French held it. In the course of that night loud explosions were heard in the town. Daybreak confirmed that the Russians had evacuated the south side of Sevastopol, retiring over their pontoon bridge across the harbour to the Severnaya. General Codrington was soon apprised of the news.

Even before I went down at daylight, the news had come to camp and been apparent that the enemy was off; and over hills and down ravines I saw as I rode down, seamen stragglers, soldiers – and any number of French, all streaming down. There was however no man, woman or child in the town – the plunder was all that of tables, chairs, boxes and some few valuables perhaps – and I question whether it would not have been just as well to have allowed our people to go in as the French did and get what they could out of unroofed, half burnt, and wholly deserted houses. The contrast was somewhat offensive as it was managed. Pelissier had promised that none of the French should be allowed to bring anything away: consequently orders were given to our sentries and parties to stop all things: it was vain with the French, either their orders were a deception, or they could not carry them out, and our men had the mortification of seeing French go by, either openly or dodging round with tables, chairs, boxes, anything, whilst all ours (unauthorised certainly) had to deposit theirs in a heap – the French almost laughing at them as they did so. The cavalry were posted also all along our front, and stopping French and English. I found a heap of trash collected near the Woronzow road with some angry and disappointed French, and several annoyed English. As the cavalry were to leave at sunset, a cart which they had brought this assembly of arms (useless) and furniture and odds and ends, up to my quarters. I had in the mean time sanctioned Sir G. Hampson in command, giving to the French what they saw them bring and deposit, for the irritation was not worth the old furniture and crockery.

Captain Scott of the 9th Regiment was meanwhile performing a different duty which he did not relish.

Spent the whole of yesterday from 5 AM to 8 PM in charge of the burying party of the Brigade. We first had to move off the wounded Russians; after that to collect and bury the dead of both parties. We put about 250 English and 150 Russians into the ditch at the angle of the Redan, and filled it on them from both sides. Besides those we buried several detached parties of Ruskies in different holes about the work. *Never* had to perform such a disgusting duty. The bodies were so mangled, and some of the Ruskies had been dead for days. Quite worn out when we at length got home.

The failure before the Redan was the subject of immediate inquest. Brigadier-General Ridley wrote to his cousin:

In the army here there is no use blinking the question (but I tell you now what you must keep to *yourself & George*, who as an old Guardsman & your husband I would trust) *there was* a sad *deficiency* of *pluck* & courage in the main bodies of the assaulting columns. *Nothing could exceed* the *gallantry* of the much abused *regimental officers*. Their self-devotion was most exemplary but far more than half their men failed them. I know Windham told Rokeby he never got up more than 400 men out of the 1st Column of 1000. The recruits joined this year have been accustomed to look for cover. It has all been *trench* fighting and night attacks. All the men learn to fight *cunning*. The old soldiers alone were to be depended on and alas we had lost so many of the right stuff. Whenever a regiment lost heavily in the 24 hrs in trenches some of the oldest & best soldiers were sure to be either killed or wounded. In my own Batt[alio]n I really lost some of my very best men. The men at the assault could not, as a general rule, be brought out in line across the works. At one time I hear they were ordered to *file* out, a sad mistake and one I thought had been found out on the 18th June. My late Sergeant Major Toseland joined the 33rd two days only before the assault as Adjutant & had the tip of his ear shot off. He told me they got three companies of their Regt into line and that the men followed them well, but the remainder could not be got out except by filing them. When the men got over the open which at the nearest point is close on *240* yards, up to the Redan Windham could not get them beyond the first traverses. There was no room to form in any large number & those who got in clung to the first cover and opened their fire. No doubt the thing was bungled. Windham I believe did all that man could do.

General Codrington too was reflective. Management of the assault had proved a poisoned chalice. One question troubled him. When it was widely known that Sevastopol was untenable without the Malakhov, why had the attack on the Redan been believed necessary? 'The chances of failure were not thought of so much as the chances of success', he concluded. 'The distance to go, the flank fire, the former failure of the same divisions under the same murderous fire were not considered.' Yet Codrington was enough of a realist to realize that blame for failure would redound to him. 'I suppose I shall see the verification of the fact that "Whenever an officer has to be roasted, there are brother officers always ready to turn the spit," ' he quipped.

Codrington's assessment was correct. The verdict upon him of Lieutenant-Colonel Anthony Sterling was damning:

> Codrington is universally reprobated. There he stood in the advanced trench, with all his Staff, about 250 yards from the angle of the Redan, with his men clustered on its rampart, neither advancing nor retiring for three quarters of an hour. If ever there was a time when a General should have played the part of a grenadier, that was the time. If he had rushed up, he might have failed in getting the men to move on; but he should have tried, and have died there. Could he have got fifty men to go over the parapet, the rest would have followed. England has suffered an indelible disgrace; and this young general, I should suppose, is extinguished.

Codrington tried to defend himself. He addressed the criticism directed towards him for not sending forward more supports to the Redan.

> The loss they had in their advance, showed me the utter impossibility of keeping formation over the open space of 280 yards! And without formation they only added to a helpless mass. Can't people see this, know this, understand this? It was palpable to me, that I should have thought it sending them to useless destruction. Even one's common personal courage I see in some letters (at home that is) is almost thought in question by my not going at once to the Redan. Why, who was to order and direct these very regiments that went out? If any one could have seen the crest of the Redan *empty*, bare of troops, whilst men were inside and falling for want of others, then indeed there would be some reason for fault – for my duty was to suffer no check, to bring on every thing possible *into* the Redan when the first troops had got in.

Sevastopol had fallen but it gave the British army little cause for satisfaction. Failure at the Redan. The courage of its troops impugned. The leadership of its generals questioned. Still, the war was surely won. Now it was only a question of making the Russians realize it.

10

PEACE

For many, the taking of Sevastopol had proved an anti-climax. Captain Maxwell Earle wrote to his father five days afterwards that 'I have seen more joy in the army after the taking of a rifle pit than after the fall of Sebastopol.' Moreover, the Russians had merely evacuated the south side of the town; on the northern side of the harbour the Severnaya district was being more strongly fortified than ever. While the Russians remained, the Allies were unable to use Sevastopol as a port through which to supply their armies. The failure to exploit victory at Sevastopol by inflicting a decisive defeat on the Russian field army, still ensconced upon the Mackenzie Heights, caused Lord Panmure intense irritation, and he was soon chiding General Simpson for his inactivity.

Meanwhile, the British Army in the Crimea, freed from the exertions of a siege, sought means to divert itself, as Captain Earle wrote on 21 September:

> Yesterday was the anniversary of the great Battle of the Alma and I can assure you it was a wet day in every sense of the word. It rained heavily in the afternoon and rather defeated the objects of some generals who had grand parades for the distribution of medals. On the other hand one could not walk 20 yards without finding some soldier who in commemorating the day had rather overshot the mark and had fallen down, not to rise again for many hours. One could only congratulate the survivors and wish them many happy returns.

As it emerged, the British soldier did not require an excuse to become inebriated. Earlier in the year, in an attempt to improve recruiting, the Government had offered the inducement of additional pay while on active service. The troops now had the wherewithal to drink to excess, as Lieutenant-Colonel Anthony Sterling, writing at the beginning of October 1855, confirmed: 'The result of the extra 6d a day given to our soldiers, with back pay to the amount of 45s per man, has been frightful

drunkenness. They are quite incurable, poor fools.' Lieutenant-Colonel
George Mundy of the 33rd Regiment agreed: 'Our privates are now
receiving on an average 2/6d per diem and the consequence is, *one third*
of the British Army are drunk and most of the others *not* sober. There
is no end of court martials, floggings &c &c.' By November Captain
Earle, who two months before had saluted the drunken indulgently, was
more censorious:

> Everything is being done to make the men comfortable, but the
> ridiculous amount of pay which they receive only induces them to
> commit excesses which are unprecedented. The extra 6d a day field
> allowance and 8d a day whenever they are on fatigue duty increases
> their pay to nearly 3/-, half a crown too much for any soldier. It only
> serves to fill the pockets of all the scoundrels who keep canteens in
> the Camp.

Attempts were made to try and persuade the soldiers to send money
home to their families, but to little avail. Nor was the threat of punishment sufficient to deter drunkenness, Earle lamenting the fact that in
the years before the outbreak of war the maximum number of blows
which could be inflicted in a flogging had been restricted to fifty: 'A man
cares nothing for 50 lashes, but 500 will certainly stop his drinking for
a month or two.'

For Captain Hopton Bassett Scott of the 9th Regiment, the situation
had begun to get out of hand when it interfered with his sporting
relaxation, as he wrote home on 8 October:

> We got up an eleven to play a cricket match at Karani today, but as
> usually happens here, on arriving at the ground we found the whole,
> or nearly so, of the Cavalry eleven, our opponents were [sitting] on
> various Courts Martial, the painful consequences of the new field
> allowance, an extra 6d per diem to the men. As it was to be in force
> from July 1st there were large arrears due, and most of them got
> about £2; and pretty scenes we have had ever since the beginning of
> this month . . . 'Put a beggar on horseback and see how he will ride'
> is a very old saying, and here there is ample proof the originator had
> truly studied human character. Nothing will suit our private now but
> *champagne*, fellows who before thought raw spirits the correct thing.

A few days later, Scott wrote home again:

We failed on Friday last in getting up the same match, and as it was late, Elmhirst, two others and I dined at a horribly dirty cafe at Kadakoi, lost our way on the road home, it being quite dark and raining hard, and after numerous adventures, we arrived at Camp at 1½ A.M. fearfully ducked. One of these said adventures on the road was when we passed a cafe which stands out in the wilderness by itself, and is kept by a well known old lady, Mrs Seacoal [r. Seacole], a nickname most probably, for she is as black as any coal. We dismounted, tied up our horses among a number which were standing there, and went in to get cigars. We found a number of French Officers having a wine party, and very uproarious. We looked on for a little very much amused, and then as they got up to leave we also proceeded to start again. When I got to where I left my pony I found him standing without a saddle to my great horror and discomfiture. The idea of a ride home on such a night on a bare-backed, cruelly sharp and rough paced animal, was startling. I called to Elmhirst to tell him of my perplexities and to beg he would wait, and having got a light searched the place in vain. Suddenly it struck me to examine the Frenchmen's horses before they went, and not finding it on any of them, was about giving up all hope, when I chanced to look at one a servant was on and recognised it. I collared the gentleman, who was quite taken aback, and could not understand how such an extraordinary thing could have occurred without his knowledge. We then went back to the room and stated what had occurred, but to our astonishment they all took the blackguard's part, said it was a mistake, that all the horses had been unsaddled, and their servants in a hurry had taken a wrong one, and so on. But as we knew it was not so, they failed lamentably in their arguments. One of them thought we wanted satisfaction, and told E. he should feel bound &c if Mons. required it. I told him the only satisfaction I could have was to see the man as severely punished as an English soldier would have been for robbing a French Officer. Finding they would not understand the justice of that we left them, and came to the conclusion on our road they were all in league, and intended to have given the saddle in part payment of the bill. I shall as soon think for the future of talking of French honesty as I should of telling them I suspected it.

Captain Maxwell Earle, the same month, was able to play his own small part in smoothing Anglo-French relations during the joint expedition to the Russian-held fortress of Kinburn. The plan to attack Kinburn was a French one, and had been suggested by them as a means of deflecting political pressure from the British for something to be done after the fall of Sevastopol. Situated on a spit, Kinburn guarded the entrance to the Bay of Kherson from the Black Sea, and commanded in turn the confluence of the rivers Bug and Dnieper; its capture, so the argument went, would disrupt Russian communications with Odessa and lay open to attack the naval base of Nicolaiev, sixty miles inland on the Bug estuary. The expedition, carrying 6,000 French and 4,000 British soldiers, anchored off Kinburn on 14 October. The following day, troops were landed three miles further down the spit, cutting off the fortress. On 16 October, the French overall commander of the expedition, General Bazaine, conferred with the commander of the British contingent, Brigadier-General the Hon. Augustus Spencer. Maxwell Earle was in attendance:

> He [Spencer] took me to the French General as his interpreter and we talked over several little matters important to them, but not worth relating here. The French general Bazaine, I must tell you, is a most agreeable, soldierlike, good natured little fellow and his chief idea is making himself of use to Spencer. It was determined at the conference that the cavalry should go out in the morning to reconnoitre and I was to go as the accompanying Staff Officer.... We went about 7 miles into the country and only saw 2 Cossacks. But we pillaged a village containing ducks, geese, chickens & in short poultry of every description. My share, which I killed with my own stick, was, 6 ducks & 2 fowls. But I must tell you that whilst I was tying my plunder to my saddle an enormous dog which had been barking harmlessly around me, suddenly caught me and gave me a very severe pinch. In fact had I not had buckskin trousers on it would have been an awkward affair. I therefore thought it advisable to draw my pistol and insert a Dean & Adams bullet in his head. This is the first shot I ever made with my revolver. The cavalry came home laden with provisions. On our return we heard the fleets bombarding the Fort. They commenced at 9 o'clock. At about 12 noon the liners [line-of-battle ships] went in and I must say the sight was grand. The wind blew the smoke quite clear of the ships and on either side broadsides were rattled in the miserable place. At 2 pm the firing ceased and we

saw the white flag at the fore of the Royal Albert. The General has asked for terms and the Admiral offered to permit his men to march out as prisoners without arms. But the officers might retain their swords. Ten minutes were given him to decide and he determined to surrender altho' his chief of engineers called him a coward for so doing. The place is actually shattered and I cannot imagine how they managed to remain inside so long. They lost about 60 men killed and wounded and I think all but 2 guns dismounted or hors de combat. About 60 guns (the lowest computation) have fallen into our hands and 1150 prisoners, 25 officers.

Yet success at Kinburn merely threw into sharp relief the strategic futility of the enterprise. Ten thousand troops accompanied by a combined fleet of seventy vessels was a sledgehammer to crack the Kinburn nut; but to attack Nicolaiev a force of 15,000 men was deemed necessary. The British were keen; the French were not. A garrison was left at Kinburn and the expedition returned. Captain Earle expressed despondence, writing to his mother on 5 November:

> It is really disheartening to find how much more we are daily being reduced to a contingent to the French army, Pelissier has it all his own way and poor old Simpson's want of activity makes us all more or less slaves to the will of the former. Can we not undertake an Expedition which only requires 15000 men? Are we for ever to be the tail end to every French undertaking? Because the French consider it too late for the Expedition are we to consider it so also? . . . If we are to be an 'English Contingent' don't send an old man to take charge of us, who is merely an obstacle in Pelissier's way. Simpson as Chief of the Staff was a valuable acquisition, Simpson Commander in Chief is a farce.

If the British were the tail end to a French expedition at Kinburn, it was even more the case at Eupatoria, on the west coast of the Crimea. Garrisoned by the Turks since shortly after the Allied landing at Calamita Bay the previous year, its defence had been the scene of a notable Turkish triumph over the Russians in January 1855, the unexpected news having been sufficient to hasten Tsar Nicholas I's death. It had long been contended that Eupatoria was the open right flank of the Russians outside Sevastopol, and at the end of September General d'Allonville sailed there with a French force. In October the 18,000 French and 17,000 Turks were joined by a British brigade of cavalry, 1,050 strong, accompanied by 'C' Troop Royal Horse Artillery, in which served Lieutenant William Stirling. The first sortie in which he took part, directed towards the village of Sak south of Eupatoria, comprised forty squadrons of cavalry (the British providing ten) and 5,000 infantry.

22nd [October]. We paraded at 4.30 A.M. very dark & cloudy. The Troop carried rations of oats for the horses, two days in their corn bags & the rest on the spare gun carriages & Flanders Wagon. Also one truss of hay per subdivision averaging about 450 lbs. The men took two days rations & the Commissariat carried the third. The Cavalry carried one days oats & the Commissariat the rest; they got no hay at all. The men of the troop carried their great coats & waterproof coats in front of their saddle &c, one change of clothing wrapped in a blanket & oildeck in rear without any sheep skin.

In the course of the sortie some ineffectual skirmishing took place but for Stirling the chief revelation was the difficulty of finding water.

On Monday the only water our horses got was salt water out of the lake & at 'Sak' it had all to be brought out of wells where it was stuff as black as ink, so of course many of them would not eat. Col. Lowe shot one of his horses wh[ich] fell down from exhaustion on the road & he expected he would have to shoot one or two more.

Nevertheless, on 27 October the exercise was repeated:

We went out on Saturday with much the same force as last time. Started about 10.30 A.M. & went along the spit. When we came to the other end and we came in sight of four squad[ron]s of the Enemies cavalry, the Turks were sent well to the front to tempt them to attack, but it was no use, they kept retiring as they advanced so the cavalry were ordered to the front to overtake them if possible but they had too long a start. The Turkish cavalry were in front then French Cavalry & last ours. We went at a good trot from the spit past 'Sak' till we came up within range of their old position near 'Chobotar', walking at intervals so as to keep distance from the leading squadrons. The Turkish & French Troops came into action on the right & d'Allonville ordered our Troop to come into action on the left in order to make them open a battery they had on their right to see what it was. But Lord George [Paget] never told Thomas that &

merely ordered him into action, so Thomas* took us much further
in advance than d'Allonville wished or than was necessary had he
known the object. However we were in a good place, all the shot
went over or ricocheted short of us.

There were 27 men killed or wounded & one French Officer
killed. We had a man of the reserve wounded & two horses of the
Troop so badly that we had to shoot them. This was about 4 P.M. &
after it we retired straight on 'Sak' where when we arrived it was just
getting dusk. I took the horses to water immediately; the wells are in
the valley leading down to the lake. There are a great many of them
& a French sentry was over each, five of them were told off to the
English & I occupied these. The water was very good & quite clear
but the supply must be small & could not have been used much
since we were last there, for the next morning all that was left was
as black as ink the same as before.

The skilful Russian tactics of not allowing themselves to be drawn
into a major combat, and the inability of the Allies, lacking an adequate
supply of water, to press them sufficiently to bring one about, stymied
operations at Eupatoria. In November the British brigade was withdrawn.

By then, at Sevastopol, changes had taken place in the British
command. General Simpson had taken the reproofs of his inactivity
badly and on 29 September tendered his resignation. It was accepted
but he nevertheless had to remain in post another six weeks, as the
Government had great difficulty in choosing a successor. Major-General
Sir William Codrington had for some months past been the intended
replacement should anything happen to Simpson. However, in the wake
of the failed attack on the Redan, doubts were raised whether Codrington
could now establish his authority were he to be elevated over the heads
of other more senior generals already serving in the Crimea. Most prob-
lematic was the position of Major-General Sir Colin Campbell, a vastly
experienced combat commander. Queen Victoria would have liked him
installed as Commander-in-Chief of the Army in the Crimea, but both
Lord Raglan before his death, and Lord Hardinge subsequently, deemed
him unsuitable. By 9 November, the day that the appointment was finally
announced, speculation about the identity of Simpson's successor had
intensified. Captain Earle considered the alternatives:

---

* Captain H. J. Thomas, 'C' Troop Royal Horse Artillery.

We are all Anxiously awaiting the news of who is to be our Com[-man]d[e]r in Chief. Codrington is thought the most likely and if you put Sir Colin aside I think the best (faute de mieux). Eyre's temper is greatly against him and la belle alliance would not be very secure in his hands. He is rash to a degree. We shall be overrun with Guardsmen if the former is selected and I forsee great discontent brewing amongst the line officers whose claims for promotion are far greater than those London fops. Rokeby, Barnard, Bentinck & Codrington were influential members of the Guards set in the Crimea and their influence built the nest which is now filled with their proteges. This nest, which is our Head Quarters, will not produce much to the credit of the British Army. Bentinck turned out an arrant imposter, Rokeby a weak minded vascillating old Beau and Barnard an excellent Chief of the Staff, and a good fellow, who likes the pomp and pageantry of war but is no soldier at heart. Codrington is a man of sense and high principle and made himself remarkable last winter by his care for the men. With him as C. in Chief, Windham Q[uarter] M[aster] General, Pakenham Adj[utan]t Genl and Barnard Chief of the Staff and no other Guardsman in the public offices, you will have an efficient army.

General Codrington had been unaware that he was the Government's original choice to succeed Simpson, should the need arise; and although he must have realized that he was a candidate, his correspondence with his wife does not betray the fact. It therefore came as something of a surprise when on 9 November, as he reported, 'About 10 o'clock, Steele came into my hut, "Well, you are Commander-in-Chief of this army." ' The man who had gone out with the Army of the East as a supernumerary major had risen to the supreme command. In the days which followed it helped Codrington that Sir Colin Campbell, perhaps anticipating the outcome, had already left the Crimea, and the willingness of Lord Rokeby to serve under a junior general earned the new commander-in-chief's gratitude. Nevertheless, as Captain Robert Hawley of the 89th Regiment averred, many remained unconvinced: 'The appointment of Codrington surely is unwise. It does not please the Army, for with it on the 8th he lost caste entirely.'

*

Among the business with which Codrington found himself occupied was the upshot of all the initiatives taken by the Government the previous winter and spring to rectify the army's logistical and manpower difficulties. A Land Transport Corps had been formed to convey supplies between Balaklava and Sevastopol. An Army Works Corps had been raised to improve the roads. A Foreign Enlistment Act had been passed by Parliament to allow the recruitment of German, Swiss and Italian mercenaries. A 20,000-strong contingent of Turkish troops had been taken into British pay. With Codrington's arrival there was also a wholesale change of personnel at Headquarters. Lieutenant-Colonel Robert Blane was his new Military Secretary; Ash Windham took over as Chief of Staff with enhanced powers over the Quartermaster- and Adjutant-Generals' Departments. Codrington wrote to his wife on 18 November:

> I am new, Chief of Staff new, Quarter Master Genl. new, Military Secy. new – and stronger than all, the System is new. So you may imagine that with Generals, Divisions, Brigades, Army Works Corps, Land transport Corps, Commissariat, Navy, Embarcations, Foreign Legions, Swiss Legions, Turkish contingents, Eupatoria, Kertch; huts, powder, clothing – and more painful than all, the representations of real grievances by officers who have done good service – you may imagine my head and hands are full.

Yet he had less time for the grievances of some than others. A week later he heard that moves were afoot to induce Sir Colin Campbell to return to the Crimea by dividing the army into two army corps and offering him the command of one of them. The death of General Frederick Markham left a vacancy for the other. 'Well it is wonderful', complained Codrington to his wife.

> But it is scarcely fair in its results to me, this system of making the two corps. And how it is made palatable to Sir C. Campbell, after [his] having gone away so decidedly, so positively – I know not! We shall see. It is supposed he is not very tractable and it is well known also that Eyre (who, now that Markham is dead, will I believe have the other Corps) is somewhat the same. I could not help saying to Blane, instead of the old idea of Lord Ellenborough's about putting the wild elephant between two tame ones, this seems like putting the tame one between two wild ones! It is as well when one can laugh at things, for there are plenty of serious things to think of.

Fortunately for Codrington's peace of mind, the scheme to create two army corps proved still-born.

The building of an all-weather road between Balaklava and Sevastopol was a priority to ensure that there was no repeat during the second Crimean winter of what had befallen the army during the first. At the same time, the capacity of the railway, which during the later stages of the siege of Sevastopol had been crucial in meeting the artillery's demands for ammunition, would be improved by sending steam loco-motives to operate out of Balaklava. However, the navvies of the Army Works Corps were both substandard and uncooperative, while the loco-motives lacked power. Codrington, in looking back to the experience of soldiers during the Peninsular War, lamented his lot:

> They had not locomotive engines which can't go up hill; and had no Army Works Corps who utterly declined to work under fire; and no Sanitary Commissioners to take care of them; and no Land transport Corps which had tails and a head without the middle viz. Non. Com[missioned] officers: and no road makers who were to make the road for us, but were found to require the assistance of 10,000 Army soldiers, poor dears, for six weeks.

Lieutenant-Colonel George Mundy of the 33rd expressed similar dis-satisfaction:

> There is nothing going on here but mismanagement and grumbling, our huts are infamous and our land transport, railway and working corps a perfect farce, the 1st useless by carelessness, the 2d not steam power enough & the 3d only building palaces for themselves.

The Land Transport Corps, a veritable Babel of Spaniards, Maltese, Croats, Tartars and Turks, had been criticized from the outset for poor care of its animals and a correspondingly high wastage rate. But the largely unskilled and under-motivated workforce was not always set a good example by its British overseers. George Howell of the Land Trans-port Corps had been sent to Kerch with elements of the British-paid Turkish Contingent, whence he wrote to his brother on 24 November 1855:

> I am on what they call Ease leave today but in plain English skulking, for I have been hard at work all this week so I have been making a

fuss riding to this place and that, seeming devilish busy but in fact doing nothing and striking off work at 12 o'clock midday 'For a change'. This is the way to get on here, do little work but make a show & fuss. Just seem to be doing a heap and its all right.

According to Howell, sickness and drunkenness were taking their toll at Kerch.

A funeral here is a very solemn, but a very common thing, no coffin, no mourners, a blanket is all you are conveyed in on a litter and the body rolls from one side to another as it is conveyed to its last resting place and no more thought of it. Please God keep me in health and out of the hospital. It is enough to kill a man to go into the hospital even if he is not ill himself, the groans of one and another with the rattles in his throat & the writhings of another & all in a foreign land without knowing what to ask for, its awful. I will not, as long as ever I can keep out, go near the Hospital but will take myself in time & doctor myself & so if possible prevent any illness of importance.

Although Howell was happy to shirk his duties, he was not prepared to see his charges do the same.

The Turk Fatigue Party or Building Corps who erect the huts, dig trenches &c &c are a very slow dilatory lot. In digging trenches the Beggars stop Devilish often & stick their spade or Axe before them, their arms across their breasts & say their prayers kneeling, this is whenever they feel tired which is very often but we have positive orders not to interfere with their religion so we let them do as they like in this respect, but one of my men the other day stopped 9 times in 2½ hours. Now though I did not dispute his devotions I thought this was too much of a good thing and as I knew Mahomet would not come to help him dig & do his work, I did not think Mahomet ought to have any more of his time so I layed my whip across his back which seemed to waken him up a bit.

Another British overseer with the Land Transport Corps was H. Clark, attached to the 4th Division at Sevastopol. He had a story to tell his uncle of a calamity which befell the Allied armies outside the town during November 1855.

I have had some very narrow escapes of my life since I have been
out here. I had a very providential one the other day on the 15th of
Nov. An Explosion . . . occurred from one of the French Batteries &
set fire to one of our Magazines of the Royal Artillery, called here
the right Siege Train or the right Attack. It was indeed an awfull
sight. Several lives where lost, & I myself had a very narrow escape.
[I] only left the spot an half an hour previous to the Explosion, [and]
when it was over I went to the spot where it occurred, & to my
astonishment I saw one who was in the bloom of life lay before me
a lifeless Corpse in a dreadfull shocking Manner almost burnt to a
cinder & another I saw the storekeeper he had shared the same fate.
I went a little farther on & there I saw an Officer who was in the act
of putting on his Gloves. He had one on & the other he was in the
act of pulling on. His head was burnt to a cinder. Several Horses
& Mules where [sic] killed & others seriously injured. Tents where
scattered about in all directions. Some of our Men & Mules where
hurt & they where at a distance of a quarter of a Mile. It shook the
whole earth for Miles & Miles around, one explosion after the other.
The sensation that it caused amongst us can better be imagined
than described. We thought at first the Russians where coming in
upon us & we began to scatter about. The Natives where running,
Yellowing & Hallowing all over the place. Horses & Mules got loose
& ran away. Some threw their riders.

A further series of – on this occasion – planned explosions during
January 1856 signalled the culmination of the Allied war effort directed
against Sevastopol. The dry docks, sophisticated and fabulously expensive
in construction, were the centre-piece of the Sevastopol naval base; their
elimination would sharply reduce the Russian naval threat in the Black
Sea. In order to demolish the docks, the Royal Sappers and Miners used
working parties taken from various infantry regiments. Three companies
of the 18th Regiment were among those employed, as Private Daniel
Bourke recalled many years later in his old age:

I was working with the miners drilling for the powder to blow up
the entrances to the great docks of Sebastipool. There were three
docks & they could flood each of them in ten minutes so as to allow
the largest battle ship to enter. As the Russian stores where we were
quartered were in range of their guns [on the north side of Sevas-

topol] it was a frequent occurrence for a shell or a shot to be sent screeming through our midst so you can imagine that things were lively here.

Major Nicholson of the Mechanics came down to my shaft where I was working & asked me how far I had bored the tunnel. I told him we were right under the steps (the steps were at each end of the dock & the ships used to enter through the flood gate at the side). He (Major Nicholson) went into my tunnel to see for himself & he became over powered with fowl air & became unconscious. I dragged him out as far as I could until my strength was exhausted & left him in sight of the entrance where I thought he was in a safe place. I told a sapper a man of my own Regiment Nick O' Neil to drag the Major out as I was exhausted. I was sitting down as I felt weak from the strain of dragging the Major so far. O'Neil brought him out & when the Major came to a few minutes afterwards he went to his own quarters. I heard no more of the incident for some time & then I was surprised to learn that Nick O'Neil had been presented with a good conduct medal for an act of bravery & a ten pound note for his gallant act in saving the Major's life. . . . My comrades wished me to bring the facts of the case before the chief but I did not care to do it. If O'Neil was unmanly enough to accept a medal for what he did not [do] I would not be one to try to take it from him. But I will swear that if the Major ever goes into a shaft where I am working & gets overcome that I for one will leave him there.

The destruction of the docks, and nearby Fort Nicholas by the French, moved General Codrington to write a dispatch worthy of the occasion. His egregious prose elicited from Lord Panmure a slightly ambiguous compliment: 'Your description of the explosion of Fort Nicholas is quite a composition and shall adorn the *Gazette*'. The newspapers however were not so charitable in their comments. A cutting in Codrington's papers entitled 'General Codrington and the Queen's English', taken from the *Scottish Press*, was scathing in its condemnation:

That General Sir William Codrington, K.C.B., cannot write a sentence in intelligible English is one of those unpleasant circumstances which the prominence of his position has made conspicuously evident to everybody. But a repeated perusal of those remarkable documents called 'despatches,' which Lord Panmure with wicked alacrity insists

on giving to the world '*pur et simple*,' has satisfied us that there is
much more wanting in the general than a knowledge of the ordinary
rules of grammatical construction, and that they disclose a shallow,
confused, peddling mind, the possessor of which is and must be
unequal to the high and onerous duties of commander-in-chief. Let
any one read the despatch of General Codrington giving an account
of the destruction of Fort Nicholas, and say if there be not reason to
fear that the estimate we have formed – harsh as it may seem – is
not without occasion. What a miserable maudlin bit of sentiment it
is from beginning to end, not unlike what might have been expected
from some boardingschool-miss, transformed into Ensign Clutterbuck's wife, who had gone a campaigning with her husband, and
was communicating her experiences to a dear friend and school-
companion tarrying at home in single blessedness. . . . 'The light of
the sun,' says General Codrington, 'played beautifully on the mass
of smoke, of which the lower part lay long and heavily on its victim.'
The lower part of what? The lower part of 'the light of the sun' or
of 'the mass of smoke?' We really never heard that granite walls could
become the 'victim' of either light or smoke. 'The state of the docks
has been given in detail in my letters. They are all destroyed.' What
are destroyed? His 'letters' or 'the state of the docks,' or the docks
themselves? But we may not pursue this vein farther. There seems to
us to be clear indications in these despatches of a want of manliness,
of nerve, of moral power, of greatness – of these qualities of mind
which, in a man placed in General Codrington's position, are indispensable.

Even Queen Victoria considered that a 'verbose' dispatch of a similar
date criticizing the press for betraying militarily sensitive information
was 'not altogether worded so as to be published with advantage'. Nor
did Codrington's literary style lack critics in the Crimea. Captain Maxwell
Earle was among those taken aback: 'Have you ever read any despatches
so atrociously badly written as Genl C's & the one on the drunkenness
of the army is no better than what a child could write. I certainly
expected better of him. I wonder he does not allow Windham to dictate
to him.' Lieutenant-Colonel Anthony Sterling too was unimpressed: 'I
have been struck by the extreme bad English written by Codrington,
with a good deal of ambitious attempt, too, at fine writing.'

Whereas the first Crimean winter had been a struggle for survival, during the second the army had the leisure time to seek diversions. Horse racing was popular. Theatricals was another favourite pastime. Maxwell Earle was a stalwart of the 4th Division's productions, appearing in performances of *Going to the Derby* and *John Dobbs*. He wrote to his father on 31 January 1856:

Our theatre, a handsome building is nearly completed and we hope to give another performance early next week. The 2nd Batt[alio]n of the Rifles performed two days ago, and gave great satisfaction especially to one person, a little more vulgar than the rest who stood up in the middle of the performance and declared that 'it was much better than the 4th Div[isio]n'. Comparisons are odious at any time, but on this occasion especially, for the person was surrounded by officers of the said 4th Div who had been invited to see the play. Fortunately we can bear comparison, for we have nearly 250 officers to select from and the others are confined to the officers & Non Com[missione]d officers of the 2nd Battn R[ifle] B[rigade]. I cannot see why men should be so jealous about which should make himself the greatest buffoon before an audience. We intend giving an evening over for the benefit of the Nightingale Fund, and we reckon on collecting nearly £150.

Other forms of relaxation were apt to cause concern. Earle wrote to his mother about a family friend, Lieutenant Christopher Musgrave of the 1st Battalion Rifle Brigade:

Kit I fear is fond of billiards and plays with Mundy of the 33rd whom my father will know as not only one of the best players in the world, but as one of the most accomplished gamblers about town. I only heard this last night. But I shall ask some good fellow of his corps to endeavour to prevent his betting.

A week later, Earle wrote again:

I am sorry that I cannot give so good an account of young Kit. I have ascertained that his propensities for gambling were alarmingly strong, but Lord Alex Russell his Com[man]ding officer has put a stop to it completely. At least as far as a Comding officer can do so by stopping all play in the Reg[imen]t. It is very fortunate for him that he is in the Rifles. There are many Regts in which he might go to the bad and no one would know or even care about it. Oxenden tells me 'Wait till we get him home.'

During the winter months, away from the Crimea, negotiations for a peace, which had proved so abortive at Vienna the previous spring, resumed. Although Russia had scored a significant success in Asia Minor on 25 November 1855 with its capture of the Turkish city of Kars, the military and diplomatic balance had otherwise tilted against St Petersburg. In December Austria presented the Russians with an ultimatum, threatening to enter the war on the Allied side unless its terms were met. The chief demands – the freedom of the Danubian principalities and the neutralization of the Black Sea – were essentially a restatement of the so-called Four Points, long under negotiation between the warring powers. On 16 January 1856, Tsar Alexander II accepted the Austrian ultimatum. A peace conference opened at Paris on 25 February, with the declaration of an armistice in the Crimea – to last until 31 March – following almost immediately. Soldiers from both sides, Allied and Russian, took the chance given them to fraternize, Corporal John Fisher of the 1st Battalion Rifle Brigade among them:

> Our men were soon wending their way towards the Tychernaia [Chernaya] anxious to get a nearer sight of the enemy they had been contending with and soon had the opportunity of seeing & bartering with them across the river, our men throwing halfpence across in return for crosses or any other little thing to take home as trophy.

The imminent prospect of peace did not altogether please the British Government. It had spent £130 million in the previous two years gearing itself for war. With its army strengthened by German, Swiss and Italian Legions, as well as by a Turkish Contingent, hopes had been entertained of switching the British forces in the Crimea to Asia Minor in order to reverse the verdict of Kars. A major naval expedition to the Baltic was also under preparation which, once it had reduced the fortress of Kronstadt (as it was thought fully capable of doing), would lay the Russian capital St Petersburg under the guns of the British fleet. But Napoleon III of France wanted peace for domestic reasons and his view prevailed. On 30 March 1856, the Treaty of Paris was signed. Its ratification on 27 April brought a formal end to hostilities. General Codrington, writing on 3 May, felt a weight lift from his shoulders: 'And so goodbye. All is checked now – no more completion of Land Transport, no more Sultan's cossacks, Turkish contingents, Swiss Legion, German Light Infantry – all will melt away.'

The subsequent Allied evacuation of the Crimea, considering the vast military build-up that had occurred during nearly two years of occupation, proceeded remarkably speedily. By 12 July, Codrington was ready to hand over possession of Balaklava to the Russians, as he told his wife:

> All was ready. I sent a company of [the] 50th out of town to meet the Russian Guard: marched in with them – and drew up opposite the 4 companies of 50th, there were about 30 cossacks of the Don mounted and about 50 infantry. But such a lot! I could not have conceived the Russians w[oul]d have sent such a dirty specimen of their troops. Never were [there] such figures in grey coats – so badly armed too – disreputable looking – we were all surprised and amused. I hope they intended to insult us, by such specimens: if so, it must have rather turned the tables if they heard the remarks. The Guard marched on board – the Russians posted their sentries – and the evacuation was completed. . . . [I] was made a present of a Cossack lance which will adorn E.S. as a mem[ento] that I was almost the last soldier in the Crimea as in duty bound.

During its second winter in the Crimea, the British army had been well supplied and coped with the rigours of the climate quite comfortably. The French army, in contrast, saw a progressive breakdown in its logistical and medical support and suffered terribly. That the British fared so much better was due to the measures – belated at the time – taken by the Government when catastrophe threatened to overwhelm the army in the winter of 1854–55. The Land Transport Corps and Army Works Corps, although undeniably profligate and derided by many, proved their worth. The Balaklava railway, offered to the Government at cost price by the consortium of Peto, Brassey & Betts and heralded at the time as a monument to private enterprise, contributed mightily to the maintenance of the fabric of the army. Measures of administrative reform, so long debated in the decades before the Crimean War, were finally implemented by a panic-stricken Aberdeen Ministry before it fell, and by the Palmerston Government which succeeded it. Control of the Commissariat was removed from the Treasury and given to the War

Department. The historic Board of Ordnance, whose role in the supply of matériel to the Army had long cut across that of the War Department, was swept away. Various commissions of inquiry were set up to investigate the failings of the departments tasked with the upkeep of the Army in the Crimea. The parliamentary Sevastopol or Roebuck Committee – upon which sat that perennial thorn in the flesh, A. H. Layard – proceeded despite the best efforts of the Palmerston Ministry to prevent it. The Committee's findings, printed in April 1855, were too polemical to be of much value. Altogether more substantial was the report of the commission, headed by Sir John McNeill and Colonel Alexander Tulloch, appointed to inquire into the Commissariat in the Crimea. While recognizing that the lack of a metalled road between Balaklava and the camp before Sevastopol had been a contributory factor in the breakdown of supply to the army, and that the home authorities had also been at fault for furnishing insufficient materials, it nevertheless criticized a number of army officers and other officials for the delay in distributing stores. In response, the former Commissary-General in the Crimea, William Filder, three generals – Lord Lucan, Lord Cardigan and Sir Richard Airey – and Colonel the Hon. Alexander Gordon, demanded an inquiry into the report. A Board of General Officers sat at Chelsea from 3 April until 4 July 1856. All five aggrieved men were as a result cleared by the so-called 'Whitewashing Board'.

By this stage of the process, the conclusions that might have driven a sustained process of change in military administration were in danger of being lost to sight. There had already been an inquiry into the report of an inquiry. This, however, was not enough. Finding that in its exoneration of Commissary-General Filder, the Board of General Officers criticized the Treasury for failing to meet his requests for supplies, the Government asked Sir Charles Trevelyan – the architect of the modern Civil Service – to furnish a report into the findings of the inquiry into the inquiry. It would have required Charles Dickens to do justice to the growing absurdity of it all. But by the time Trevelyan's report was published in 1857, public interest had waned. The process of reform had ground into the sand. It would only be resumed over a decade later, when Edward Cardwell became Secretary of State for War.

Another area in which there had been growing agitation for change was the social composition of the British army's officer corps. Allied to attacks on the aristocratic nature of the army's command, there had been calls for increased promotion from the ranks. Predictably, A. H. Layard was in the forefront of the movement. His campaign, however, did not find favour with his brother, Captain Arthur Layard, who was only a month away from his own death from cholera when he wrote the following on 7 July 1855:

> I often wish that I was near you when you are about to attack our Military System. I could put you often right and point out numerous abuses that are known only to military men, and which civilians cannot properly understand except they are explained to them fully. . . . With regard however to the promotion from the ranks, the Army I say the Army as I comprehend the majority of voices of those out here, do not think you have studied that subject enough. There is no parable case in the world of an army instituted like ours and until the filling of the ranks is drawn from a diffuse source, that extensive promotions from them is impossible. From my experience, and I am now in my 17th year, every man who is superior to his fellows, or even above average is sure to obtain a commission sooner or later. I can quote a case in the 38th, our late Adjutant. He never did a day's duty as private, he was found out to be a superior person even when at recruit's drill; he was made a corporal as soon as he was dismissed drill, and moved rapidly up until he became Sergeant Major, and then on the recommendation of Sir John Campbell obtained an Ensigncy in the regiment. In almost every regiment in the service you will find similar cases. Since the War broke out the raising from the ranks has become more frequent, but in many cases I doubt whether the promotion has benefited the individual. Promotion for men's acts of gallantry in the field is not advisable as a rule. There are many very gallant privates who would make very indifferent non commissioned officers, and many non commissioned officers very indifferent officers.

Captain Maxwell Earle agreed. As matters stood at present, the men had confidence in their officers.

> General Neil once remarked to the duke of Newcastle, how much superior our infantry was to the French. 'Because,' said the General, 'your officers are gentlemen, ours are only so in a few instances.' Have we not had proofs innumerable during the war of the superiority of

officers, gentlemen born, over those who have risen from the ranks. And especially so in action.

These were sentiments with which the majority of the ruling classes could sympathize. The army needed to be led by men with a stake in the country; a professional officer corps, dependent solely upon its pay, might seek to meddle in politics on its own behalf. The liberties of England would then be under threat. The system which allowed officers to purchase their commissions, ensuring that men of means would be promoted more rapidly, consequently remained in place until 1871, when it was abolished as part of the Cardwell reforms.

But other change was ineluctable. The introduction of first the Minié rifle, and then the Enfield, revolutionized the battlefield. The ordinary infantry soldier now possessed a weapon long-ranged and accurate enough to enable him to operate independently. He need no longer manoeuvre in line and fire in volleys to compensate for the inaccuracy of his musket. To that extent the thick skirmishing line into which the Light Division dissolved at the Battle of the Alma during its attack on the Great Redoubt, far from being an aberration, foreshadowed the tactics which, out of necessity, came to be adopted on the even more lethal battlefields of the Franco-Prussian War sixteen years later.

The British army, however, was shielded from the full effects of the battlefield revolution. For another sixty years it fought only colonial wars. Even the Anglo-Boer War of 1899–1902 gave it little more than an inkling of the scale of carnage possible on the modern battlefield. Yet the fact that the British army did not intervene again on the Continent of Europe until the outbreak of the First World War in 1914 was in itself a legacy of the Crimean War. A nation which had shown itself incapable on that occasion of fielding more than 30,000 of its own troops could exert no influence when, the following decade, Otto von Bismarck and Prussia set about reshaping Europe. Indeed, even before first Austria and then France were comprehensively defeated, in the wars of 1866 and 1870 respectively, Bismarck had – during the Schleswig-Holstein dispute of 1864 – made plain his view of Britain's military prowess. If Lord Palmerston intervened on the side of the Danes and the British army landed in Germany, Bismarck said, he would send the police force to arrest it! Fifty years later, as the War to end all Wars began, Bismarck's view was endorsed by Kaiser Wilhelm II in his blithe dismissal of Britain's 'contemptible little army'. Only in 1916, with the raising of Kitchener's volunteers, did Britain finally achieve a Continental-sized army, and only then could the troubled spectre of an underprepared British army's last foray into a war against a European opponent be laid to rest.

Bibliography

Adkin, M., *The charge: why the Light Brigade was lost*, London (1996)

Anderson, O., *A Liberal state at war: English politics and economics during the Crimean War*, London (1967)

Anglesey, Marquess of (ed.), *'Little Hodge' : being extracts from the diaries and letters of Colonel Edward Cooper Hodge, written during the Crimean War, 1854–1856*, London (1971)

Barthorp, M., *Crimean uniforms : British infantry*, London (1974)

——, *Heroes of the Crimea: the battles of Balaclava and Inkerman*, London (1991)

Bayley, C. C., *Mercenaries for the Crimea: the German, Swiss and Italian Legions in British service, 1854–1856*, Montreal (1977)

Bell, G., *Rough notes by an old soldier, during fifty years' service, from ensign G B to general C B*, London (1867)

Bentley, N. (ed.), *Russell's despatches from the Crimea 1854–56*, London (1966)

Boase, F., *Modern English biography*, London (1965 reprint)

Caldwell, G. and Cooper, R., *Rifle green in the Crimea*, Leicester (1994)

Calthorpe, S. J. G., *Letters from Head-Quarters; or, the realities of war in the Crimea*, London (1856)

Carver, M. (ed.), *Letters of a Victorian army officer: Edward Wellesley, Major, 73rd Regiment of Foot 1840–1854*, Stroud (1995)

Clifford, H. H., *Henry Clifford, VC: his letters and sketches from the Crimea*, London (1956)

Compton, P., *Colonel's lady and camp-follower: the story of women in the Crimean War*, London (1970)

Cooke, B., *The grand Crimean central railway*, Knutsford (1990)

Cope, W. H., *The history of the Rifle Brigade (The Prince Consort's Own)*, London (1877)

David, S., *The homicidal Earl: the life of Lord Cardigan*, London (1997)

Douglas, G. and Ramsay, G. D. (eds), *The Panmure papers*, London (1908)

Edgerton, R. B., *Death or glory: the legacy of the Crimean War*, Boulder, Colorado (1999)

Gernsheim, H. and Gernsheim, A., *Roger Fenton, photographer of the Crimean War: his photographs and his letters from the Crimea*, London (1954)

Gooch, B. D., *The new Bonapartist generals in the Crimean War: distrust and decision-making in the Anglo-French alliance*, The Hague (1959)

Hamley, E. B., *The story of the campaign of Sebastopol*, Edinburgh (1855)

Harris, S. M., *British military intelligence in the Crimean War, 1854–1856*, London (1999)

Hayward, J. B. (ed.), *Casualty roll for the Crimea*, London (1976)

Hibbert, C., *The destruction of Lord Raglan: a tragedy of the Crimean War, 1854–55*, London (1961)

Higginson, G., *Seventy-one years of a Guardsman's life*, London (1916)

James, L., *Crimea, 1854–56: the war with Russia from contemporary photographs*, Thame (1981)

Kelly, R. D., *An officer's letters to his wife during the Crimean War*, London (1902)

Kerr, P., et al., *The Crimean War*, London (1997)

Kinglake, A. W., *The invasion of the Crimea: its origin, and an account of its progress down to the death of Lord Raglan*, 6th edition, London (1885)

Kingsford, C. L., *The story of the Duke of Cambridge's Own (Middlesex Regiment)*, London (1916)

Lambert, A. D., *The Crimean War: British grand strategy against Russia, 1853–56*, Manchester (1990)

Lummis, W. M. and Wynn, K. G., *Honour the Light Brigade*, London (1973)

Lysons, D., *The Crimean War from first to last*, London (1895)

Mawson, M. H. (ed.), *Eyewitness in the Crimea: the Crimean War letters (1854–1856) of Lt. Col. George Frederick Dallas*, London (2001)

Maxwell, E. H., *With the Connaught Rangers in quarters, camp and on leave*, London (1883)

Mollo, J. and Mollo, B., *Into the Valley of Death: the British Cavalry Division at Balaclava 1854*, London (1991)

Nolan, E. H., *The history of the war against Russia*, London (1857)

Pack, R., *Sebastopol trenches and five months in them*, London (1878)

Paget, C. S. (ed.), *The Light Cavalry Brigade in the Crimea: extracts from* the letters and journal of the late Gen. Lord G. Paget . . . during the Crimean War, London (1881)

Pearse, H., *The Crimean diary and letters of Lieut.-General Sir Charles Ash Windham*, London (1897)

Rait, R. S., *Life of Field Marshal Sir Frederick Paul Haines*, London (1911)

Royle, T., *Crimea: the great Crimean War, 1854–1856*, London (1999)

Ryan, G., *The lives of our heroes of the Crimea*, London (1855)

Steevens, N., *The Crimean campaign with "the Connaught Rangers", 1854–55–56*, London (1878)

Sterling, A., *The story of the Highland Brigade in the Crimea*, London (1895)

Strachan, H., *Wellington's legacy: the reform of the British Army 1830–54*, Manchester (1984)

——, *From Waterloo to Balaclava: tactics, technology, and the British Army, 1815–1854*, Cambridge (1985)

Sweetman, J., *War and administration: the significance of the Crimean War for the British Army*, Edinburgh (1984)

——, *Raglan: from the Peninsula to the Crimea*, London (1993)

Taylor, A. J. P., *The struggle for mastery in Europe 1848–1918*, Oxford (1954)

Ward, S. G. P., *The Hawley letters: the letters of Captain R. B. Hawley, 89th, from the Crimea, December 1854 to August 1856*, London (1970)

Waterfield, G., *Layard of Nineveh*, London (1963)

Whinyates, F. A., *From Coruña to Sevastopol*, London (1884)

Wilkinson-Latham, R. J., *Uniforms and weapons of the Crimean War*, London (1977)

Woodham-Smith, C., *Florence Nightingale 1820–1910*, London (1950)

——, *The reason why*, London (1953)

Woodward, Sir L., *The age of reform*, 2nd edition, Oxford (1962)

Index of Contributors

Ranks are those held by the individuals concerned at the time of their last mention in the text. The figures in brackets are the Museum accession numbers of the papers from which extracts have been taken.

Elton VC, Captain Frederick Cockayne, 55th (The Westmoreland) Regiment of Foot (NAM. 1988–01–3)

Estcourt, Major-General James Bucknall Bucknall, Adjutant-General Army of the East (NAM. 1962–10–95)

Firkins, Private Edward John, 13th Regiment of (Light) Dragoons (NAM. 1986–02–75)

Fisher, Corporal John, 1st Battalion Rifle Brigade (NAM. 1976–06–38 & –39)

Forrest, Lieutenant-Colonel William Charles, 4th (Royal Irish) Regiment of Dragoon Guards (NAM. 1963–09–5)

Gage, Captain the Honourable Edward Thomas, Royal Artillery (NAM. 1968–07–484)

Goodenough, Lieutenant-Colonel Arthur Cyril, 34th (The Cumberland) Regiment of Foot (NAM. 1968–07–376–18)

Gordon, Lieutenant Charles George, Royal Engineers (NAM. 1968–07–449)

Gordon, Captain Samuel Enderby, Royal Artillery (NAM. 1961–12–406)

Griffiths, E. (NAM. 1975–01–50)

Grove, Captain Robert, 90th Regiment of Foot (Perthshire Volunteers) (Light Infantry) (NAM. 1968–07–376–18)

Hagger, Private Thomas, 23rd Regiment of Foot (Royal Welsh Fusiliers) (NAM. 1976–08–32)

Haines, Lieutenant-Colonel Frederick Paul, 21st Regiment of Foot (Royal North British Fusiliers) (NAM. 1968–07–146)

Harvey, Lieutenant Thomas Peter, 77th (The East Middlesex) Regiment of Foot (NAM. 1997–07–47)

Hawley, Captain Robert Beaufoy, 89th Regiment of Foot (NAM. 2003–01–38)

Higginson, Lieutenant and Captain George Wentworth Alexander Higginson, 1st (or Grenadier) Regiment of Foot Guards (NAM. 1962–10–97–16)

Hood, Private Alexander, 42nd (The Royal Highland) Regiment of Foot (NAM. 1978–05–47)

Horn, Lieutenant-Colonel Frederick, 20th (The East Devonshire) Regiment of Foot (NAM. 1968–07–288)

Howell, George, Land Transport Corps (NAM. 1972–08–51)

Hull, Private Robert, 50th (The Queen's Own) Regiment of Foot (NAM. 1978–04–39)

James, Henry Ridley, merchant navy (NAM. 1969–01–46)

General Index